DICTIONARY *of*
NATURE

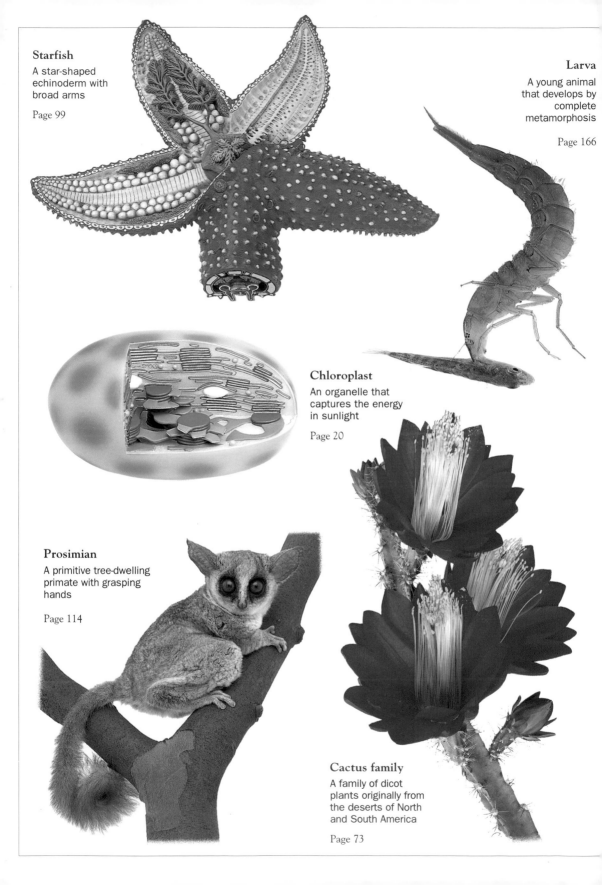

Starfish

A star-shaped echinoderm with broad arms

Page 99

Larva

A young animal that develops by complete metamorphosis

Page 166

Chloroplast

An organelle that captures the energy in sunlight

Page 20

Prosimian

A primitive tree-dwelling primate with grasping hands

Page 114

Cactus family

A family of dicot plants originally from the deserts of North and South America

Page 73

DICTIONARY of NATURE

Written by David Burnie

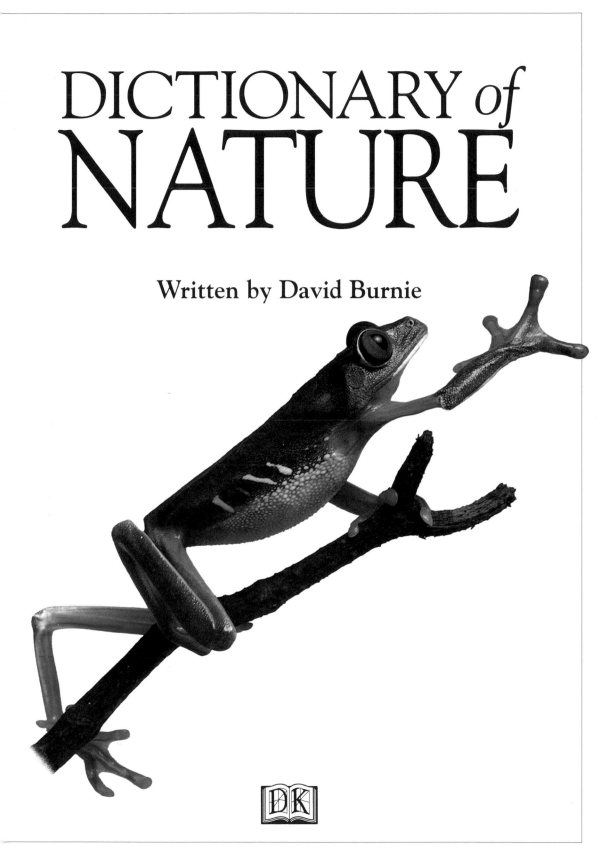

DK

A DK PUBLISHING BOOK

Project Editor Bridget Hopkinson

Art Editor Yaël Freudmann

Editor Fiona Robertson

Designer Nicola Webb

Production Samantha Larmour

Managing Editor Helen Parker

Managing Art Editor Peter Bailey

Picture Research Anna Lord

Educational Consultants Jackie Hardie,
B.Sc., M.Ed., C.Biol., F.I.Biol.,
The Latymer School, London
Kimi Hosoume B.A, Lawrence Hall of Science,
University of California at Berkeley

Editorial Consultant Dr. Philip Whitfield
Kings College, London

U.S. Editor Charles A. Wills

U.S. Consultant Harvey B. Loomis
Models supplied by Somso Modelle, Coberg, Germany

First American Edition, 1994
4 6 8 10 9 7 5 3
Published in the United States by
DK Publishing, Inc., 95 Madison Avenue
New York, New York 10016
Copyright © 1994 Dorling Kindersley Limited, London
Text copyright © 1994 David Burnie

Visit us on the World Wide Web at http://www.dk.com

Library of Congress Cataloging–in–Publication Data
Burnie, David.
    Dictionary of nature / David Burnie. – – 1st American ed.
      p.   cm.
    Includes index
    ISBN 1–56458–473–9
    1. Biology – – Encyclopedias, Juvenile.   [1. Biology – – Encyclopedias]   I. Title.
    QH302.5.B87   1994
    574' .03 – – dc20   93–30696
                                                                                              CIP
                                                                                              AC

Reproduced by Colourscan, Singapore
Printed and bound in Great Britain by Butler and Tanner

Safeguarding nature
This dictionary contains
photographs of many objects and
living things that can be seen in
the natural world. First-hand
observation is the key to finding
out about nature, but it should
not be allowed to cause harm to
living things, or to threaten their
survival. Wild animals and plants
should be studied where they live,
and not carried back to the home
or laboratory.

Scientific names
Throughout the explanatory text
in this book, common and
scientific names are used side by
side. In general, the main
reference to an individual species
consists of its common name in
bold type, followed by its two-part
scientific name, or binomial, in
italics. The main reference to a
group of closely related species,
or genus, consists of their
common name in **bold** followed
by a one-word generic name in
italics. Larger groups are identified
using the system of classification
explained on pages 56–57.

Numbers and measurements
Throughout this book, a billion
is used to mean one thousand
million. Two alternative systems
of measurement are used. In each
case, the first figure is the value
expressed in U.S. units . The
second figure, which is always in
parentheses ( ), is the same value
expressed in metric, or SI, units.
The metric system is generally
used for all scientific work.

Contents

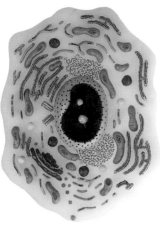

Cells

Living organisms can consist of just a single cell or many billions working together.
Find out more about cells on pages 18–23.

Replication

DNA carries the chemical instructions for life, and hands them on by copying itself, or replicating.
Find out more about DNA on pages 34–43.

Fossils

The fossil record shows how living things have changed during the Earth's existence.
Find out more about life's history on pages 44–55.

CLASSIFYING LIVING THINGS 56–59

The ways in which biologists identify and group living things

MICROORGANISMS 60–65

The world of life that can only be seen under a microscope

PLANTS 66–75

The diversity of plant life, from ground-hugging mosses to towering trees

FUNGI 76–79

Living things that feed by absorbing food from their surroundings

PLANT BIOLOGY 80–95

How plants live and grow, and how they use energy from sunlight

ANIMALS 96–115

The diversity of animal life, from simple life to animals with backbones

Microorganisms
Euglena is so small that it can swim around in a single drop of water. It is just one of many kinds of microscopic life. Find out more about microorganisms on pages 60–65.

Pollination
Flowers use their beautiful colors and scents to attract animal visitors. With the help of animals, pollen grains are transferred from one plant to another, so that seeds can be formed. Find out more about pollination on pages 92–93.

Spiders
Spiders help us by catching and eating huge numbers of insects. Find out more about spiders and their relatives on pages 100–101.

Skulls
An animal's skull protects
its brain from injury, and is
one of the toughest parts of the body.
The shape of the skull shows how its
owner lives, and also how it has evolved.
Find out more about your own skull, and
those of other animals, on page 140.

Behavior
The threat display of this lizard makes it look
more dangerous than it really is. Set patterns
of behavior – including displays like this
one – increase an animal's chances of
survival. Find out more about behavior
on page 158.

**Charles
Darwin**
More than any
other biologist,
Charles Darwin
helped to shape
the way we
understand
life on
Earth. He
showed that
living things evolve,
and explained what
makes these changes take place.
You will find a list of many other famous
biologists and naturalists on pages 178–181.

ANIMAL BIOLOGY 116–167
How animals live, and how they fuel their bodies

ECOLOGY 168–177
How living things fit into the world around them

PIONEERS OF BIOLOGY 178–181
More than 150 of the world's greatest biologists

INDEX 182–192
More than 2,000 key words, terms, and concepts used in science

ACKNOWLEDGMENTS 192

How to use this book

This dictionary explains the most important words and concepts in biology, and illustrates how they are used. It is a thematic dictionary, which means that the words are arranged into subject areas, such as "Photosynthesis," instead of being defined alphabetically. This enables you to find out about a whole subject, as well as about individual words. To look up a word, turn to the index at the back of the book. To look up a subject, you can either look in the index, or turn to the Contents on pages 5–7. This lists the different sections and subjects covered in this book.

Main illustration
A large photograph or artwork usually illustrates several related entries. It helps to explain the entries, or show how they are linked. This photograph of a leaf helps to explain the process of photosynthesis.

Cross reference
A small gray square (■) after a word shows that the word is an entry or occasionally, a subentry elsewhere in the dictionary. The "See also" box gives the page number of the entry.

Subentries
*A subentry is printed in **bold type**. It gives the meaning of a word that is related to a main entry. This subentry explains the meaning of the word "wavelength."*

Using the index
The index lists all the entries in alphabetical order and gives their page numbers. If you look up photosynthesis in the index, for example, you will find that the entry is on page 84. The word you want may be a main entry, or it may be a subentry, which is to be found in bold type within an entry. It may also be an entry in a table.

Main headings and introduction
A main heading introduces the subject. All the entries in this subject are concerned with photosynthesis. Each subject begins with an introduction that gives you a brief outline of what follows.

Photosynthesis

Plants can make their own food. They trap the Sun's energy with their leaves and use it to make food from simple substances. This process is called photosynthesis. Photosynthesis is vital to life on Earth because it provides food, either directly or indirectly, for almost every living thing.

Photosynthesis
A process that uses light energy to make food from simple chemicals

Photosynthesis means "putting together by light." It takes place in the chloroplasts inside plant cells. During photosynthesis, a plant uses the energy in sunlight to carry out a chain of chemical reactions. It makes the food substance glucose ■ from molecules ■ of carbon dioxide and water. Oxygen is formed as a by-product. Glucose is packed with energy and plants use it to fuel their growth. Plants also use glucose to make starch ■, which acts as an energy store, and to make cellulose ■, which builds cell walls.

Light
A visible form of electromagnetic radiation

Sunlight is energy that travels from the Sun in the form of waves. The distance between one wave and the next is called a **wavelength**. Different wavelengths give light its different colours. Sunlight is a mixture of wavelengths that range through the **visible spectrum** from violet to red. In photosynthesis, plants use the energy in some wavelengths more than others. Plants collect about one ten-thousandth of the light energy that reaches Earth.

Photosynthetic reaction
In photosynthesis, a single molecule of glucose is formed by combining six water molecules and six carbon dioxide molecules using energy from the Sun. Six oxygen molecules are also formed.

Sun

Water molecules

Carbon dioxide molecules

Photosynthetic pigment
A chemical that collects the energy of sunlight

A plant traps the light it needs for photosynthesis with special chemicals called photosynthetic pigments. When light strikes a pigment molecule, the molecule absorbs some of the light's energy. It passes on the energy to other chemicals so that photosynthesis can take place.

Chlorophyll
The main photosynthetic pigment in green plants

Chlorophyll is the main pigment involved in photosynthesis. It is found in the chloroplasts inside plant cells. Chlorophyll gives plants their green colour because it reflects green light, and absorbs red and blue light. There are several forms of chlorophyll. The most important form is called **chlorophyll a**. This is found in plants ■, green algae ■, and cyanobacteria ■.

Primary pigment
A pigment that fuels photosynthesis directly

Most plants contain several photosynthetic pigments. A primary pigment passes energy directly into photosynthetic reactions. In green plants, the primary pigment is chlorophyll a.

Leaf contains chlorophyll.

Accessory pigment
A pigment that collects extra energy

An accessory pigment collects extra energy in certain wavelengths, and passes it on to a primary pigment. Accessory pigments include **carotenes** and **xanthophylls**, which are a red or orange colour, and **phycobilins**, which are brown.

Annotation and captions
A headed caption explains what you can see in a picture. The caption to this picture explains how glucose is formed during a photosynthetic reaction. Details in a picture, such as the molecules used in photosynthesis, are pointed out by annotation.

Explanations

The explanation tells you more about the entry. It can help you to understand the definition, and to see how a term is used. It also shows how the entry is linked to others in the same subject. This explanation describes the role of thylakoids in photosynthesis.

Running heads

For quick reference, the running head shows you which section you are in. This section is Plant Biology.

Definitions

The definition is a short, precise description. This definition tells you what a thylakoid is.

Entry headings

This entry is Thylakoid.

Biographies

On page 85, you will find a biography of Jan Ingenhousz, who played a key part in finding out how photosynthesis works. This dictionary contains many biographies of famous scientists, linked to the subjects that they investigated. There is also a fuller alphabetical list of famous biologists on pages 178-181.

3 D Models

In some places, special models are used to show living structures. This model is of a chloroplast – an object in leaf cells that is far too small to be seen with the naked eye.

Plant Biology • 85

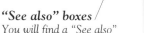

Colour (light wavelength)

Chlorophyll absorption spectrum
The pigment chlorophyll absorbs very little green light. This is why most plants look green.

Absorption spectrum

A graph that shows which wavelengths of light a pigment absorbs most

Every pigment has a characteristic absorption spectrum. Chlorophyll a absorbs red and blue light, but very little green light. Carotenes absorb more green light, but very little red.

Thylakoid

A membrane-bound sac that contains chlorophyll

Thylakoids are flat, disc-shaped sacs found inside chloroplasts. They are piled in stacks called **grana**, which are separated by a space, or **stroma**. Each thylakoid is packed with chlorophyll. When light shines onto a leaf, it travels into the chloroplasts and strikes the thylakoids. The chlorophyll in the thylakoids traps the light energy and photosynthesis begins.

Light reaction

A chemical reaction that can take place only in light

During the first part of photosynthesis, light energy splits up water molecules in a process called **photolysis**. This produces energy-carrying molecules such as ATP ▪. These reactions happen inside a thylakoid, and they can take place only in light.

Dark reaction

A chemical reaction that can take place in the dark

During the second part of photosynthesis, energy from ATP molecules and other energy carriers is used to remove oxygen atoms from carbon dioxide molecules. The carbon atoms are then combined to form glucose. These reactions take place in the stroma of a chloroplast, and they do not need light.

Jan Ingenhousz

Dutch physiologist
1730–99
Jan Ingenhousz was one of the first scientists to investigate photosynthesis. In 1771, **Joseph Priestley** (1733–1804) discovered that plants give off oxygen. Ingenhousz followed up this discovery. He showed that plants take in carbon dioxide and release oxygen when light shines on them. In the dark the opposite happens.

Carbon fixation

The conversion of carbon dioxide into organic compounds

All living things contain carbon ▪, but only some can "fix" carbon, or turn it directly into complex organic compounds ▪ such as glucose. Photosynthesis is the most important form of carbon fixation. Every year, plants fix about one hundred thousand million tonnes of carbon.

Photosynthetic bacteria

A group of bacteria that can carry out photosynthesis

Some forms of bacteria also make their food by photosynthesis. **Purple bacteria** and **green bacteria** carry out a kind of photosynthesis that does not produce oxygen. Cyanobacteria carry out photosynthesis in a similar way to plants.

See also

ATP 33 • Carbon 24 • Cell 18
Cellulose 27 • Chemical reaction 25
Chloroplast 84 • Cyanobacteria 61
Glucose 26 • Green algae 66
Light 25 • Organic compound 24
Plants 57 • Starch 27

Glucose molecule

Oxygen molecule

[Plant] cells

Unlike animals, plants are made of ... plant cells ... different from ... cells. These are enclosed by tough cell ... most contain chloroplasts – bright ... structures that trap the Sun's energy and ... plants to make their own food.

Cell

... plant

... is similar to an ... because it is ... by a flexible plasma ... However, outside ... rong wall which gives ... ape. Plant cells have ... organelles ▪ found ... ells, but most plant ... ntain vacuoles and ... Chloroplasts are ... in animals. ... s capture energy from ... is enables a plant ... its own food from ... arbon dioxide by a ... ed photosynthesis ▪.

Cell wall

The semi-rigid case that surrounds a cell

A plant cell wall is made up of layers of a tough carbohydrate called cellulose ▪, together with other substances. The wall is light and strong and it gives the cell its shape. The walls of neighbouring cells are fastened together, which enables the plant to hold itself upright. Fungi ▪ and bacteria ▪ also have cell walls, but these are not made of cellulose.

Vacuole

A large storage area inside a cell

Most plant cells contain a vacuole, which is a space filled with a watery fluid called **cell sap**. Some animal cells also have vacuoles, but they are much smaller than those in plant cells.

Turgor pressure

The pressure that keeps a plant cell rigid

The vacuole inside a plant cell takes in water by osmosis ▪. It pushes the cytoplasm against the cell wall, rather like air pressing outwards inside a balloon. This outward pressure enables the cell to keep its shape. When a cell is in this state it is **turgid**. If the vacuole is not full of water, it collapses and causes wilting.

Close-up of a plant cell
This photograph, taken by an electron microscope, shows a single plant cell. The large red area is the nucleus, and the round yellow areas are vacuoles.

Chloroplast

An organelle that captures the energy in sunlight

Chloroplasts contain chlorophyll ▪, a bright green pigment that traps the energy in sunlight. Chlorophyll is stored in disc-shaped sacs called thylakoids ▪. Chloroplasts are found in nearly all plant cells, except in roots or inside stems.

Granum (stack of thylakoids)

Thylakoid

Stroma (space between thylakoids)

Inside a chloroplast
A chloroplast is separated from the rest of the cell by a membrane. In this model, part of the membrane has been sliced away to reveal the thylakoids.

Cytoskeleton

A network of fine chemical threads throughout a cell

The clear part of a cell's cytoplasm ▪ contains a kind of scaffolding of chemical threads. These keep the cell's organelles in the correct position, and they move them during cell division.

See also

Animal cell 18 • Bacteria 60
Cell division 40 • Cellulose 27
Chlorophyll 84 • Cyanobacteria 61
Cytoplasm 18 • Fungus 76
Mitochondrion 18 • Nucleus 19
Osmosis 22
Photosynthesis 84
Plasma membrane 18 • Schwann 181
Thylakoid 85 • Wilting 87

Diagrams and other illustrations

A diagram shows the structure of an object, or a process that occurs in the living world. This diagram shows the structure of oxygen molecules, one of the products of photosynthesis.

"See also" boxes

You will find a "See also" box with each subject. This directs you to other entries or subentries that can help you understand the subject better. This "See also" box points to some of the chemicals that play a part in photosynthesis.

What is nature?

Imagine that you are trying to sleep. Just as you begin to doze off, something suddenly flies close to your ear. A high-pitched hum tells you that it is a mosquito, searching for a meal of blood. But how does the mosquito know you are there? How can it find you in complete darkness? Where has it come from, and how did it grow up? Why are there lots of mosquitoes in some parts of the world, but very few in others? These are the kinds of questions that scientists attempt to answer when they look at the natural world. They examine living things in detail and try to discover how each one works and how different living things fit together. By investigating all kinds of life, from mosses to mammals, they can discover features that are common to the whole of nature – including ourselves.

Microscope barrel

Water-filled sphere focuses light on specimen

Flame

Lens

Oil

The discovery of cells
In biology, as in all branches of science, one discovery often leads to another. In 1665, an Englishman named Robert Hooke (page 21) published drawings that he had made using an early microscope. Among these drawings were the first pictures of cells.

Cell nucleus

Cell wall

From cell to nucleus
In 1831, the British botanist Robert Brown studied plant cells, and noticed that each one seemed to contain a dark blob. He called this object a "nucleus," from a Latin word meaning "little nut." Other scientists soon noticed that all cells contain nuclei, but at the time no one knew what a cell nucleus did.

Looking at life

If you think of the Earth as an orange, life only exists in its outer peel. As far as we know, the Earth is the only place in the Universe in which living things are found. From the earliest days of history, people have been interested in living things. People who study the natural world are called naturalists. The first naturalists described many different plants and animals, but often confused first-hand observations with stories and legends. Today, scientists study nature by carefully gathering evidence and by drawing conclusions based on what they have found. With powerful microscopes and special chemical techniques, they can investigate even the tiniest parts of living things.

Living experiment
This scientist is watering plants grown in a specially controlled environment to test the effects of global warming. Global warming is caused by the buildup of gases such as carbon dioxide.

Heredity
In the late 19th century, Gregor Mendel (page 43) carried out breeding experiments with plants. He realized cells must have "elements," now called genes, which pass on characteristics between generations.

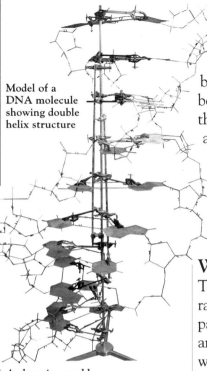

Recipe for life
During the first half of this century, genes were tracked down to DNA – a substance in cell nuclei. In 1953, James Watson and Francis Crick (page 35) discovered the structure of DNA. They showed how the DNA in a cell nucleus stores a chemical "recipe" for an entire living thing.

Model of a DNA molecule showing double helix structure

A changing world
The world's rain forests are home to an extraordinary variety of living things, from spectacular birds to unusual fungi. At the beginning of this century, rain forests covered a large part of the tropics. Now much of this has been cut down, either for timber or to make way for farms. Throughout the world, human activity threatens many wild places.

Breaking the rules

In biology, as in other sciences, our knowledge constantly increases as scientists discover more about the world around us. Occasionally, an important new discovery revolutionizes a whole branch of science. In 1826, for example, Friedrich Wöhler, a German chemist, heated some chemicals and, quite by accident, made a substance called urea. At that time, chemists thought that urea could only be made by an animal's body, but Wöhler managed to produce it on a laboratory bench. Wöhler's discovery helped to disprove the idea that the chemistry of living and nonliving things was different, and gradually made scientists realize that the two kinds of chemistry worked in the same way. This piece of history is important in illustrating how science works. In all kinds of science, explanations are constantly put to the test. If an experiment shows that a rule can be broken, the rule has to change.

Why study nature?

Today, many people live in cities. Truly wild places are rare, and the natural world often seems to play little or no part in our daily lives. So does nature really matter? The answer is that we cannot afford to ignore the natural world. Humans may dominate life on Earth, but we share the planet with many other living things, and are part of a huge web of life. By studying these forms of life, and the ways in which they interact, scientists can help us to live without harming nature, upon which we all depend.

Scientific method

Scientists carry out research in order to make precise observations about the natural world. When enough observations have been gathered and tested, they can be used as evidence to explain how or why things take place.

Leaf wrapped in porous black plastic to exclude the light

Observation

Information that is gathered in a scientific way

If you place a plant on a sunny windowsill, you might notice that its leaves slowly turn toward the light. This is a piece of accurate information based on first-hand experience, or an observation. Your observation might lead you to decide that leaves always face the light. This would be a hypothesis, and you could test it by carrying out experiments that involved moving the plant. If all the experiments confirmed your hypothesis, it could mean that the hypothesis was correct. In biology, as in all other sciences, accurate observations are extremely important, because they form the basis of scientific theories.

Experiment

A practical scientific test

An experiment tests an observation or a hypothesis under carefully arranged conditions. Most experiments are carried out indoors, in a **laboratory**, although in biology, some experiments are conducted outside. Experiments usually consist of a **test** and a **control**. For example, you could investigate the feeding behavior of bees by putting drops of sugar water in a colored dish. This would be the test. In the control, you would use identical drops and an identical dish, but the drops would contain only water. If the bees always gathered around the test dish but not the control dish, you would know the sugar was attracting them.

Leaf left in light

1 Starting the experiment
In this experiment, leaves are being tested to see if they produce starch in daylight. Some of the leaves are covered up, and others are left uncovered. The uncovered leaves are the control.

1 Growing upright
Seedlings usually grow with their leaves facing upward. This observation could be explained by a number of factors.

2 Reaching for light
Seedlings lit from one side face their leaves toward the light. This observation suggests that light affects the direction of the leaves.

Iodine solution

2 The leaf test
After several hours leaves are picked and treated with alcohol. Iodine is added to each leaf. The iodine turns dark blue if the leaf contains starch.

Leaf wrapped in porous black plastic

Variable

A factor that can change

A variable is something that changes, either in an experiment or in the natural world. Temperature is a variable, because it can go up or down. The rate of a chemical reaction is also a variable. These two examples are linked, because the rate of most chemical reactions depends on the temperature. The rate changes when the temperature does, and is said to be the **dependent variable**. The temperature is the **independent variable**, or **cause** because it alters the rate. In the living world, many different variables often act at the same time.

Constant

A factor that does not change

A constant is a quantity that always remains the same. For example, the weight of a glucose molecule ▦ is a constant, because it never changes.

Correlation

A mathematical link between two variables

A correlation suggests that two variables might be linked, but does not actually prove that they are connected. If two variables are said to be **positively correlated**, they increase or decrease together. If they are **negatively correlated**, one goes up while the other goes down.

Hypothesis

An explanation that can be tested by observation or experiment

A hypothesis is a possible explanation for something that has been observed. It is devised by taking all the available observations into account, and can be tested to see if it always holds true. Different hypotheses may explain the same set of observations in different ways.

See also

Cell 18 • Charles Darwin 45
Evolution 44 • Molecule 25
Principle of recapitulation 165

Theory

An explanation that seems to fit scientific observations

A theory is a generally accepted scientific explanation. It fits all the observations made about a subject, and seems to show how or why something happens. For example, Charles Darwin's ▦ theory of evolution ▦ seems to explain why living things slowly change as time goes by.

Law of science

A statement or explanation that always appears to be true

A scientific law or **principle** is a theory that has been thoroughly tested, and that has shown itself to be true. It explains things that have happened, and also makes predictions about events that have not yet taken place. Very occasionally, a law has to be altered or replaced when a new and unexpected observation is made. For example, the principle of recapitulation ▦ now no longer holds true.

Proof

A scientific demonstration that something must always be true

A proof shows that something is always true. Unlike a theory or a scientific law, it is not likely to be changed or replaced as more observations are made. Most proofs involve mathematics. For example, using math, you could prove how many cells ▦ would be produced when a single cell divides a set number of times.

Untreated leaf

Leaf kept in dark treated with iodine solution

Leaf left in light treated with iodine solution

3 The result
The experiment shows that only those leaves that are exposed to light make starch. The leaves that are kept in the dark do not make starch.

The study of life

What makes something alive, and how does it survive in the changing world around it? These are two of the most important questions that are tackled in the study of life, or biology.

Life

The condition of being alive

We all know what it feels like to be alive, but life itself is difficult to define. It is usually summed up by all the characteristics that living things share. These characteristics include respiration, which involves the release of energy by chemical processes, as well as nutrition ▪ and excretion ▪. Living things also show growth ▪ and development ▪, because they get bigger and become more complex as they get older; they also show sensitivity, which means they can respond to the world around them. Most importantly, living things can reproduce.

Organism

Any living thing

An organism is any single thing, from a bacterium ▪ to a whale, that shows all the characteristics of life. A **super-organism** is a group of closely related living things that work like a single organism. Honeybees in a hive, for example, make up a super-organism, because they share the tasks involved in staying alive.

See also

Life cycle

A predictable pattern of changes during the life of an organism

At the beginning of its life, a living thing grows and develops. When it reaches a particular age or size, it begins to reproduce, and then eventually, it dies. This sequence of events is called a life cycle. The life cycle of some flies lasts for just 15 days, but the life cycle of an elephant can last for 70 years.

Death

The state of being dead

Things stay alive through a kind of chemical balancing act, called homeostasis ▪. When an organism dies, homeostasis stops, and the organism's cells ▪ gradually break down. Although death spells the end for an individual organism, it is very important for life as a whole. Gradual change, or evolution ▪, is possible only because things die, and because one generation succeeds another.

Flora

The plant life of an area

The flora of an area consists of all the different kinds, or species ▪, of plant that can be found there. A bacterial flora is similar, but consists of a collection of bacteria rather than plants. Your skin, for example, has its own bacterial flora. The word flora can also be used to mean a book that describes all the plants in an area.

Aristotle

Greek philosopher and naturalist

384–322 BC

Aristotle spent much of his life in the Greek city of Athens. The son of a doctor, he developed a great interest in logic and the natural world. Aristotle was one of the first people to look at animals in a scientific way. He noticed, for example, that dolphins were more like mammals than fish, and he made a special study of marine life. After Aristotle died, his work found its way into the hands of Arab scientists, and only reappeared in Europe more than a thousand years later. Aristotle's writings were unique because they were largely based on first-hand observations.

Fauna

The animal life of an area

The fauna of an area consists of all the different kinds of animal found there.

Biology

The study of life

Biologists study life, and the way living things work. Biology covers a huge range of subjects, and includes many sciences that deal with particular aspects of life. For example, **cell biology** is the study of how cells work, while **microbiology** is the study of things that can only be seen with a microscope. Taxonomy ▪ is the science of classifying living things, and ecology ▪ is the study of how living things fit into the world around them. Genetics ▪ is the study of how characteristics are passed down generations.

Botany

The study of plants

Plants are very important as they help to maintain the balance of the atmosphere, and can also be used as a source of food and medicines. Botanists study the way that plants live. They examine the way plants grow in the wild, and investigate the processes that occur inside living plants.

Seed capsule

Zoology

The study of animals

A zoologist investigates the way that animals live. This involves looking at animals in the wild, and examining the structure of their bodies. A **zoo** is a place where animals are kept in captivity. It is an abbreviation of **zoological garden**, which was what the first zoos were called.

Bursting flower bud

Poppy seeds

Medicinal plants
The first botanists were people who collected plants for use in making medicines. The opium poppy has been used in medicine for centuries, because its milky sap contains the painkilling drug morphine.

Stalks containing milky sap

Purified morphine

Anatomy

The study of the structure of living things

Anatomy is one of the oldest branches of biology. An anatomist looks at the structure of living things and works out how their different parts are shaped and fit together. This has provided important evidence of how living things are linked through evolution.

Physiology

The study of living processes

A physiologist studies exactly how the different processes in living things work, and what happens if any of these processes goes wrong. Subjects studied can include photosynthesis ▦, respiration, thermoregulation ▦, and gas exchange ▦.

Biochemistry

The study of the chemistry of living things

Biochemists study the chemicals in living things, and find out how they react with one another. In modern biochemistry, chemicals are often tracked inside living things, by labeling them with atoms that give out mild radiation. These atoms can then be followed as they move through cells or through whole organisms.

Molecular biology

The study of complex chemicals in living things

All life contains complex chemicals. A molecular biologist uses modern technology to investigate complex chemical molecules, such as proteins and nucleic acids, and discover exactly how living things work. Molecular biology is one of the fastest-growing life sciences.

Biological signposts

Many everyday words describe how things relate to each other, but these words are often not very exact. Biologists use specific scientific terms, which act as signposts to the different parts of living things.

Axis

An imaginary line dividing two identical halves

Many living things are **symmetrical**, which means they can be divided into two matching halves on either side of an axis. In animals, internal organs often do not match, and are **asymmetrical**.

SIMPLE SIGNPOSTS

Anterior

Anterior means in front. A fish's head is an anterior part of its body.

Dorsal

Dorsal means near the back of the body. A fish's dorsal fins are those on its back.

Ventral

Ventral means on the front of the body. In most fish, the ventral surface is the one that faces away from the surface of the water.

Longitudinal

Longitudinal means running the length of the body. A fish's backbone is longitudinal.

Transverse

Transverse means running across the body. A fish's ribs are transverse, because they run from its dorsal surface to its ventral surface.

Dorsal surface

Posterior region of body

Anterior region of body

Posterior

Posterior means behind. A fish's tail is a posterior part of its body.

Ventral surface

Peripheral

Peripheral means at or near the edge. A fish's fins are a peripheral part of its body.

Apex of stem

Distal point of leaf

Apical

Apical means at the apex. The apical part of a plant's stem is its tip.

Distal

Distal means at or near the farthest point. The distal part of a leaf is the farthest point from its stalk.

Superior

Superior means above. In a flower, a superior ovary is one that is positioned above the point where the petals are attached.

Proximal

Proximal means close to. The proximal part of a leaf is the part closest to the leaf stalk.

Proximal point of leaf

Inferior

Inferior means below or underneath. In a flower, an inferior ovary is one that is positioned below the point where the petals are attached.

Lateral branch

Lateral

Lateral means on the side. A plant's lateral branches grow from the side of the main stem.

Language of biology

Many of the words used by biologists are made up of parts or "roots" that come from Latin or Greek. If you get to know just a few of these word roots, you will find that biological terms become easier to understand.

Word root

A Latin or Greek word that forms part of a biological term

A single term may have several word roots. For example, arthropod comes from "arthro," meaning "jointed" and "pod" meaning "foot." An arthropod therefore has jointed feet.

LATIN AND GREEK WORD ROOTS

Root	Meaning	Example	Page reference
anti	against or opposed to	antibody	130
arthro	jointed	arthropod	100
auto	self	autotroph	33
bio	life	biology	14
carn	meat or flesh	carnivore	113
chloro	green	chloroplast	20
cyano	blue	cyanobacteria	61
cyt	a cell	leucocyte	128
derm	skin	epidermis	141
di	two or twice	disaccharide	26
ecto	outside	ectoderm	164
endo	inside	endoderm	164
epi	upon, all over	epidermis	82, 141
exo	outside	exoskeleton	136
gastro	stomach	gastropod	98
gen	a cause of something	antigen	130
genesis	formation	morphogenesis	164
hemo	blood	hemoglobin	129
herb	plant	herbivorous	116
hetero	different	heterozygous	43
homeo	similar	homeostasis	132
homo	same, identical	homologous	59
karyo	cell	karyotype	39
macro	large	macromolecule	25
meso	in the middle	mesoderm	164
micro	small	microorganism	60
mono	one, single	monosaccharide	26
morpho	shape	morphogenesis	164
myco	mold, fungus	mycologist	77
omni	all	omnivorous	116
peri	near, around	peripheral	148
photo	light	photosynthesis	84
phyll	a leaf	mesophyll	82
phyto	a plant	phytochrome	89
plasm	living matter	cytoplasm	18
pod	a foot	arthropod	100
poly	many	polysaccharide	26
troph	something that feeds	autotroph	33
vor	to eat	carnivore	113
zoo	animal	zoology	15

Animal cells

Cells are the tiny units from which all living things are made. Some organisms consist of just a single cell, while others, such as humans, are made up of trillions. A cell is a self-contained unit of living matter. It takes in energy and uses it to build itself up and to reproduce.

Cell

A tiny unit of living matter

Cells are the basic building blocks of all living things. Most of a cell is made up of a jellylike fluid called cytoplasm. This is surrounded by a thin layer, or membrane, that lets substances pass in and out. The cell is controlled by a nucleus, which contains the information needed to make it work. Cells reproduce by dividing ■ in two. Plant cells are different from animal cells. They have a rigid cell wall ■ and often contain vacuoles ■.

Animal cell

A cell from the body of an animal

An animal cell is like a tiny jelly-filled bag. It is enclosed by a flexible plasma membrane, and therefore does not have a rigid shape like a plant cell. An animal cell must take in food to obtain energy to survive. Most animal cells are microscopic, but some egg cells can measure 4 inches (about 10 centimeters) across, and nerve cells can be 3 feet (about 1 meter) long.

A blood cell
This color-enhanced electron micrograph shows a cross section of a white blood cell. The large yellow and blue circle is the cell nucleus.

Plasma membrane

A thin barrier that separates a cell from its surroundings

A **membrane** is a thin barrier. The plasma membrane that surrounds a cell is made up of a double layer of phospholipid ■ molecules. Although a plasma membrane is extremely thin, it is very strong, and will seal itself if it is broken. A plasma membrane is differentially permeable ■. This means that it blocks the path of some substances but lets others pass into and out of the cell. Similar membranes form parts of organelles inside the cell.

Cytoplasm

The contents of a cell, excluding the plasma membrane and nucleus

Cytoplasm is the jellylike fluid inside a cell that contains the organelles. The cytoplasm often circulates around the cell. Together with the nucleus, cytoplasm makes up the living material, or **protoplasm**, of a cell.

Organelle

A tiny structure inside a cell that has a particular function

Organelles are controlled by the nucleus. Each one carries out a particular task involved in maintaining the life of a cell. For example, lysosomes are organelles that digest food, and mitochondria release energy.

Mitochondrion

An organelle that releases energy

A mitochondrion (plural **mitochondria**) carries out aerobic respiration ■. This process breaks down food to release energy. A mitochondrion is a sausage-shaped structure that has two membranes. The outer membrane separates the mitochondrion from the rest of the cell. The inner membrane is folded into flaps, called **cristae**, on which food substances are broken down.

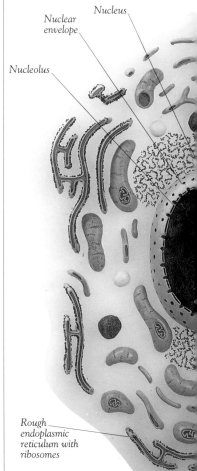

Nucleus
Nuclear envelope
Nucleolus
Rough endoplasmic reticulum with ribosomes

Animal cell
This model of an animal cell shows the many different organelles that are scattered in the jellylike cytoplasm. Most animal cells measure about 0.0004 inches (0.01 millimeters) across.

Nucleus

The control center of a cell

The nucleus (plural **nuclei**) is the largest structure in most animal cells. It directs a cell's activities and contains the cell's chemical instructions, which are stored in DNA . The nucleus is separated from the cytoplasm around it by a **nuclear envelope** or **nuclear membrane**. The nucleus often has a small dense area, called a **nucleolus**, which helps produce ribosomes.

Sacs from Golgi body

Golgi body

Plasma membrane

Mitochondrion

Smooth endoplasmic reticulum

Cytoplasm

Endoplasmic reticulum

A system of membranes that makes and stores a range of substances

The endoplasmic reticulum, or **ER**, is a complicated network of folded membranes. These membranes surround spaces that are separated from the rest of the cell. The membranes of **rough endoplasmic reticulum** are studded with ribosomes and they make proteins ■. Membranes of **smooth endoplasmic reticulum** do not have ribosomes. They make lipids ■ and hormones ■.

Golgi body

A packaging and transport system for substances made by a cell

A cell's Golgi body is a collection of membranes that gathers and packages different substances, such as enzymes ■ and hormones. The membranes form flattened sacs that are arranged like a pile of plates. Parts of the sacs often break away and travel to the plasma membrane. Once they have joined up with the membrane, they eject their contents from the cell.

Ribosome

A cluster of chemicals that assembles proteins

Ribosomes are tiny chemical granules found throughout the cytoplasm, and on the surface of the endoplasmic reticulum. Ribosomes play an important part in making proteins. They help "read" parts of the genetic code ■ stored in the cell's DNA. They then use the code to assemble protein molecules, which carry out many different tasks. Rapidly growing cells need to make lots of proteins, and they often contain thousands of ribosomes.

Lysosome

A reservoir of digestive chemicals

A lysosome contains powerful enzymes that can digest living matter. Normally, a cell uses its lysosomes to digest the food it takes in. However, a cell sometimes uses lysosomes to destroy itself. This happens during metamorphosis ■, when an animal needs to change its shape in order to develop.

Cilium

A short, hairlike projection that can beat backward and forward

An animal cell uses a cilium (plural **cilia**) to move things that are nearby, or to move itself. Not all cells have cilia, but those that do often have hundreds.

Beating cilia
The cells lining your trachea have cilia that move dust away from your lungs. This is a color-enhanced electron micrograph.

Flagellum

A long hairlike projection that is mainly used in movement

A flagellum (plural **flagella**) is longer than a cilium. It whips from side to side to move a cell along. Sperm ■ cells use flagella to move.

See also

Aerobic respiration 33

Cell division 40 • Cell wall 20

Differentially permeable membrane 22

DNA 34 • Enzyme 31 • Genetic code 36

Hormone 134 • Lipid 28

Metamorphosis 166 • Phospholipid 28

Protein 30 • Sperm 160 • Vacuole 20

Plant cells

Like animals, plants are made up of cells. However, plant cells are quite different from animal cells. They are enclosed by tough cell walls and most contain chloroplasts – bright green structures that trap the Sun's energy and enable plants to make their own food.

Plant cell

A cell from a plant

A plant cell is similar to an animal cell ■ because it is surrounded by a flexible plasma membrane ■. However, outside the plasma membrane, a plant cell has a strong wall that gives it a fixed shape. Plant cells have many of the organelles ■ found in animal cells, but most plant cells also contain vacuoles and chloroplasts. Chloroplasts are never found in animals. Chloroplasts capture energy from the Sun. This enables a plant cell to make its own food from water and carbon dioxide by a process called photosynthesis ■.

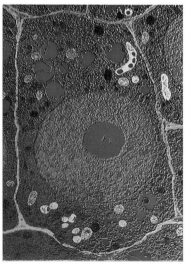

Close-up of a plant cell
This photograph, taken by an electron microscope, shows a single plant cell. The large red area is the nucleus, and the round yellow areas are vacuoles.

Cell wall

The semi-rigid case that surrounds a cell

A plant cell wall is made up of layers of a tough carbohydrate called cellulose ■, together with other substances. The wall is light and strong, and it gives the cell its shape. The walls of neighboring cells are fastened together, so the plant can hold itself upright. Fungi ■ and bacteria ■ also have cell walls, but these are not made of cellulose.

Vacuole

A large storage area inside a cell

Most plant cells contain a vacuole – a space filled with a watery fluid called **cell sap**. Some animal cells also have vacuoles, but they are much smaller than those in plant cells.

Turgor pressure

The pressure that keeps a plant cell rigid

The vacuole inside a plant cell takes in water by osmosis ■. It pushes the cytoplasm against the cell wall, rather like air pressing outward inside a balloon. This outward pressure enables the cell to keep its shape. When a cell is in this state it is **turgid**. If the vacuole is not full of water, it collapses and causes wilting ■.

Chloroplast

An organelle that captures the energy in sunlight

Chloroplasts contain chlorophyll ■, a bright green pigment that traps the energy in sunlight. Chlorophyll is stored in disk-shaped sacs called thylakoids ■. Chloroplasts are found in nearly all plant cells, except in roots or inside stems.

Granum (stack of thylakoids)

Thylakoid

Stroma (space between thylakoids)

Inside a chloroplast
A chloroplast is separated from the rest of the cell by a membrane. In this model, part of the membrane has been sliced away to reveal the thylakoids.

Cytoskeleton

A network of fine chemical threads throughout a cell

The clear part of a cell's cytoplasm ■ contains a kind of scaffolding of chemical threads. These keep the cell's organelles in the correct position, and they move them during cell division ■.

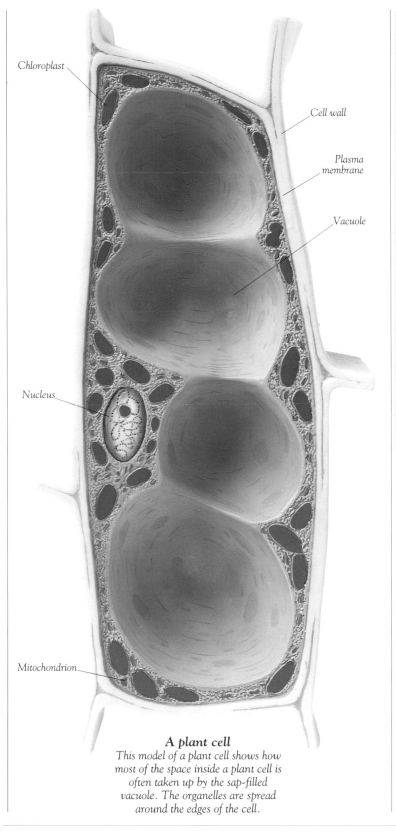

Chloroplast

Cell wall

Plasma
membrane

Vacuole

Nucleus

Mitochondrion

A plant cell
*This model of a plant cell shows how
most of the space inside a plant cell is
often taken up by the sap-filled
vacuole. The organelles are spread
around the edges of the cell.*

Jakob Schleiden

German
botanist
1804–81

Plant cells were
first observed by the English
physicist **Robert Hooke**
(1635–1703) in 1665. But it
was not until the 19th century
that scientists realized the true
importance of cells. Jakob
Schleiden was responsible for
this breakthrough. He used a
microscope to examine plants,
and discovered that all their
parts are made up of tiny
units, or cells. Together with
Theodor Schwann ▨, he
established the idea of **cell
theory**. This states that all
forms of life are made up of
cells, and that living things
grow and reproduce because
their cells can divide. It also
states that new cells can be
made only from existing ones.

Eukaryotic cell

A cell that contains a nucleus
bounded by a membrane

Living things can be split into
two main groups, according to
the kind of cells that they have.
Plants, together with animals,
fungi, and some forms of single-
celled life, make up a group
called the **eukaryotes**. A
eukaryotic cell has a nucleus ▨
and many kinds of organelle.

Prokaryotic cell

A cell that does not have a nucleus

The simplest living things on
Earth are the **prokaryotes**. These
include bacteria and
cyanobacteria ▨. Their cells do
not have nuclei. They also lack
many organelles, such as
mitochondria ▨ and chloroplasts.

Molecular movement

Cells are living units that constantly absorb food and expel waste products and other chemicals. Molecules of these substances pass in and out of cells through their outer membranes, which contain tiny openings.

Differentially permeable membrane

A porous barrier

The plasma membrane ■ around a cell ■ is differentially permeable. This means that the membrane contains tiny holes, or **pores**, that let only small molecules ■ pass through.

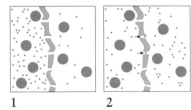

1   **2**

Osmotic movement
When a differentially permeable membrane separates a weak and strong solution (1), water molecules move through it until both solutions are equally diluted (2). The larger solute molecules cannot pass through.

Osmosis

The flow of water through a differentially permeable membrane from a weak to a strong solution

A **solution** is a liquid with a substance dissolved in it. The dissolved substance is called a **solute**. The liquid, or **solvent**, is often water. Osmosis occurs when two solutions of different strengths are separated by a differentially permeable membrane. The membrane blocks the path of the large solute molecules, but allows the smaller water molecules to pass through until the two solutions are of equal strength.

Osmotic pressure

The pressure needed to stop a solvent moving through a differentially permeable membrane

Osmotic pressure is high if there is a large difference in strength, or **concentration**, between the solutions on either side of a differentially permeable membrane.

Water potential

The tendency of water to move through a differentially permeable membrane during osmosis

The water potential of a cell depends on the concentration of the solution inside it. If the concentration is high, its water potential is low. The higher water potential outside the cell drives water into the cell. Plants take up water in this way. The concentrated sap in their cells is stronger than soil water, so water molecules flow into plant cells.

Osmoregulation

The control of the concentration of cell fluid

Many living things keep the fluid inside their cells at the same concentration, regardless of the conditions around them. They do this by pumping water or ions ■ into or out of their cells.

See also
Cell 18 • Ion 24 • Molecule 25
Plasma membrane 18

Diffusion

The spreading out of a substance from an area of high concentration

During diffusion, molecules spread out more evenly. Diffusion takes place in both living and nonliving things. Like osmosis, diffusion does not need energy. Substances such as oxygen, carbon dioxide, and salts move in and out of cells in this way.

Bowl of water   *Ink*

Ink diffusion
If you drop ink into water, it sinks at first, then diffuses throughout the water.

Active transport

A form of transport that uses energy to make a substance more concentrated

Cells often need to concentrate substances, rather than letting them spread out. They do this by active transport. This process probably involves carrier protein molecules. These use energy to carry the substance from one side of a cell membrane to the other.

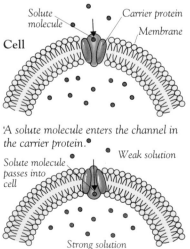

Solute molecule   *Carrier protein*
          Membrane
Cell

'A solute molecule enters the channel in the carrier protein.

Solute molecule   *Weak solution*
passes into cell

Strong solution

The carrier uses energy to change shape, pushing the solute molecule into the stronger solution inside the cell.

Tissues & organs

Animals and plants are made up of many different kinds of cell. Their cells are arranged in groups, called tissues, each of which carries out a particular function. In some living things, groups of tissues form organs.

Tissue

A group of similar cells that work together

Most animal and plant cells ■ exist in groups, called tissues. The cells in a tissue look similar, and they all carry out the same work. Vertebrates ■, including humans, have four main groups of tissue. These are epithelial tissue, connective tissue, muscle tissue, and nervous tissue.

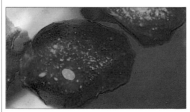

Onion tissue
This light micrograph of a layer of onion tissue shows large, rectangular cells arranged in bands. The dark spot at the center of each cell is the cell nucleus.

Organ

A structure made of two or more tissues that carries out a particular set of tasks

A vertebrate's body contains many different organs, such as the heart ■, lungs ■, and stomach ■. Each organ plays a different part in keeping the body alive. Organs form several **organ systems**. The digestive system ■ and the circulatory system ■ are both major organ systems in the human body.

Differentiation

The specialization of cells as a plant or animal develops

Every human starts life as a single cell. This cell multiplies by dividing many times. As the divisions succeed each other, groups of cells become differentiated, which means that they develop to perform a particular task.

Muscle tissue

A tissue that produces movement

Muscle tissue contains special cells that can contract. Muscles ■ contract and relax to move all the parts of an animal's body, from eyelids to limbs.

Epithelial tissue

A tissue that forms a lining on or in an animal's body

Epithelial tissue covers all the surfaces of an animal's body, both inside and outside. Skin is an epithelial tissue.

Mouth tissue
This cell, which is stained blue, comes from epithelial tissue lining the mouth.

Bichat made a great contribution to our understanding of how cells work together. He showed that organs are made up of different groups of cells, and that the same kinds of cell sometimes occur in different organs. Bichat called these groups of cells "tissues," because they were often thin and flat, like a piece of fabric. His work laid the foundations of **histology**, which is the study of tissues and organs.

Connective tissue

A tissue that supports an animal's body and holds it together

Connective tissue is the most common tissue in an animal's body. Bone ■ and cartilage ■ are both kinds of connective tissue. Blood ■ is a liquid connective tissue that circulates throughout an animal's body.

Nervous tissue

A tissue that carries electrical signals

Nervous tissue contains nerve ■ cells that carry electrical signals from one part of an animal's body to another. This enables the animal's body to work as a single unit.

See also
Blood 128 • Bone 137 • Cartilage 137
Cell 18 • Circulatory system 126
Digestive system 120 • Heart 125
Lung 124 • Muscle 142 • Nerve 147
Stomach 120 • Vertebrate 104

The chemistry of life

Chemicals are not just found in laboratories. They also form the many different substances that make up living things. Without chemical reactions, plants and animals would not be able to live.

Hydrogen / *Carbon*

Atom

The smallest particle of an element

An atom is made up of particles called **protons**, **neutrons**, and **electrons**. An atom can be split into these particles, but it is the smallest part of an element that can exist on its own. Atoms make up all substances. At one time, scientists believed that the atoms in living things were different from those in nonliving things. But today we know that they are exactly the same.

Carbon atom
This atom of carbon has six electrons (blue) surrounding the central nucleus, which is made up of six protons (red) and six neutrons (gray).

Element

A pure substance that contains only one kind of atom

Only a small number of the millions of substances that exist are made of just one kind of atom. These are the elements. Just over 90 elements occur naturally on Earth. About 25 of these are essential for life. The most common elements in living things are hydrogen, carbon, nitrogen, and oxygen.

Chemical bonds in methane

Carbon atoms form four chemical bonds. You can see this in a methane molecule, which has one carbon atom bonded with four atoms of hydrogen.

Ion

An atom or group of atoms that has lost or gained electrons

The electrons in an atom carry a negative electrical charge. This charge is balanced by an atom's nucleus, which is positively charged. If an atom gains or loses electrons, it becomes **ionized**. This means that instead of being electrically balanced, or neutral, it now has an electric charge that attracts or repels other ions.

Chemical compound

A substance formed when two or more elements combine

Compounds often have properties different from the elements that make them up. The atoms in a compound are combined in exact proportions, and they are held together by chemical bonds.

Carbon

An element found in all living things

Life on Earth is based on the element carbon. In living things, carbon atoms combine with the atoms of other elements to form a vast range of compounds.

Chemical bond

A link between atoms or ions

There are two main types of chemical bond. In a **covalent bond**, neighboring atoms share electrons. Most organic compounds are held together in this way. In an **ionic bond**, ions are held together by electrical forces. Ionic bonds hold together substances such as salts.

Organic compound

A chemical compound that contains carbon

In living things, there are four main kinds of organic compound – carbohydrates ■, lipids ■, proteins ■, and nucleic acids ■. All of these are based on the element carbon. Organic compounds, such as plastics, can also be made artificially.

Inorganic compound

A compound that does not contain carbon

Most of the inorganic compounds found in living things are simple substances. They include water, oxygen, and minerals ■. Carbon dioxide is usually classed as an inorganic compound, even though it contains carbon. During photosynthesis ■, plants use carbon dioxide to form organic compounds.

Molecule

A chemical unit made of two or more atoms linked together

A molecule is made up of atoms that are linked together by chemical bonds. Molecules can consist of just a few atoms or of many thousands. In a pure chemical compound, the molecules are all similar.

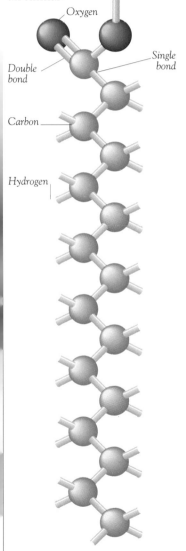

Oxygen

Double bond

Single bond

Carbon

Hydrogen

A molecule containing carbon
This molecule of palmitic acid shows how carbon atoms can link together to form long chains. Palmitic acid is found in vegetable oils.

Macromolecule

A giant molecule

Many of the organic compounds found in living things have very large molecules called macromolecules. They are made up of chains of carbon atoms. Some protein molecules have over a million atoms, and a human DNA ▧ molecule has hundreds of millions of atoms.

Polymer

A chemical compound made up of repeated units

Polymers are compounds formed by lots of smaller units called **monomers**. Polymers have many uses in living things. They can store information and energy, and build cell walls ▧. Polysaccharides ▧ are natural polymers made of glucose ▧ units. Nucleic acids such as DNA are polymers of nucleotide ▧ units.

Chemical reaction

A chemical change

In a chemical reaction, new compounds are formed from existing ones. In living things, proteins called enzymes ▧ help to speed up chemical reactions.

Oxidation

A chemical reaction in which a substance is combined with oxygen

When wood burns, oxidation takes place. Oxygen is used to form new compounds. Living things use oxidation to break down food substances. This occurs in aerobic respiration ▧ when cells ▧ combine glucose with oxygen in order to release energy.

Reduction

A chemical reaction that removes oxygen from a substance

In living things, reduction reactions usually require energy. The energy is used to remove oxygen atoms from a substance, and to make large molecules from smaller ones. Plants use reduction in photosynthesis to make food from inorganic molecules.

Water

A liquid that is essential to life

All living things contain water. Water is a chemical compound of hydrogen and oxygen. It is a good solvent, which means that it can dissolve many different substances. Nearly all the chemical reactions that take place in living things occur in a watery solution.

Animals drink to replace lost water

Carbohydrates

Carbohydrates are packed with vital energy. Animals use energy from carbohydrates such as sugars and starch to fuel their cells. Plants make their own carbohydrates, which they use for energy and to build their cell walls.

Oxygen

Carbon

Hydrogen

Carbohydrate

An organic compound that contains carbon, hydrogen, and oxygen

Carbohydrates are organic compounds ∎ that are essential sources of energy in living things. A carbohydrate molecule ∎ is usually made up of an equal number of carbon ∎ and oxygen atoms ∎, with twice as many hydrogen atoms. Simple carbohydrates, such as sugars, often have molecules containing less than 20 atoms. The molecules of complex carbohydrates, such as starch, contain many thousands of atoms.

Monosaccharide

The simplest kind of carbohydrate

Monosaccharides are the building blocks from which all other carbohydrates are made. They usually have six carbon atoms or fewer, and their atoms are often arranged in a ring. These simple molecules dissolve easily in water. Glucose is an important monosaccharide.

Disaccharide

A carbohydrate made of two monosaccharides

A disaccharide is a carbohydrate made up of two monosaccharides linked together. The monosaccharides may be the same or they may be different. Disaccharides include substances such as maltose and sucrose.

Polysaccharide

A carbohydrate made of many monosaccharides

When simple carbohydrates link together, they form long chains called polysaccharides. Cellulose and glycogen are both polysaccharides made up of glucose units. Because polysaccharides have long molecules, they do not dissolve easily in water.

Sugar

A simple carbohydrate that has a sweet taste

Most sugars are monosaccharides or disaccharides. They dissolve easily and can be broken down quickly to release energy.

Fructose

A sugar common in plants

Fructose is a monosaccharide found in fruit and honey. It tastes much sweeter than sucrose, of which it forms a part.

Energy store
Honey is an energy reserve containing fructose. Bees store honey in their hives.

Glucose molecule
The simple sugar glucose is a major energy source in living things. A glucose molecule is made up of six carbon atoms (black), six oxygen atoms (red), and 12 hydrogen atoms (white). Five carbon atoms and one oxygen atom join together to form a six-sided ring.

Glucose

The most common sugar in living things

Glucose is a monosaccharide with molecules that contain six carbon atoms. Glucose is a vital energy source in living things. It is found in most plant and animal cells ∎ and is broken down during respiration ∎ to release energy. Plants make glucose by photosynthesis ∎ and often store it as starch. Animals obtain glucose by breaking down food, such as starch, in the digestive system ∎. Glucose is carried around an animal's body by the blood ∎ and is constantly replaced as it is used up.

Amylose molecule
Plants build up long starch molecules by linking together units of glucose. The amylose molecule above shows only the carbon and oxygen atoms that form the rings of glucose.

Oxygen   Carbon

Maltose

A sugar made of two glucose units

Maltose is a disaccharide. It is made by plants and also by animals when they digest starch. Sprouting, or germinating 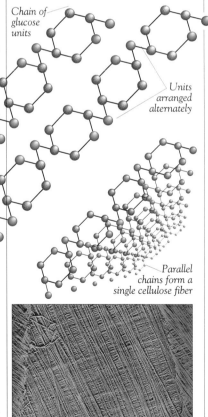, seeds contain large amounts of maltose. The malt used to make beer and whisky comes from barley seeds that have been germinated in a malting house.

Lactose

A sugar that is found in milk

Lactose is a disaccharide made from glucose and another sugar called **galactose**. Mammals make lactose as a nourishing food substance for their young.

Sucrose

A sugar that is found in plant sap

Sucrose is the sugar that we eat. It is a disaccharide made up of one unit of glucose and one unit of fructose. White **refined sugar** is almost pure sucrose. It is made by evaporating the sap from **sugarcane** or **sugar beet** plants, and removing any impurities.

See also

Amylopectin molecule
Some starch molecules link together to form branching chains. This kind of starch is called amylopectin.

Starch

A carbohydrate that plants use to store energy

Wheat, rice, and potatoes are all packed with starch. Starch is a compound made of two polysaccharides, and plants make it by adding together glucose units in two different ways. Part of starch is made up of **amylose**, which has molecules that are straight chains. The rest is made up of **amylopectin**, which has branching molecules.

Oxygen

Carbon dioxide

Glycogen

A carbohydrate that animals use to store energy

Animals use glycogen in the same way that plants use starch. Glycogen is made from glucose. When an animal needs energy, it can convert glycogen back into glucose very quickly. In the human body, glycogen is stored mainly in the liver 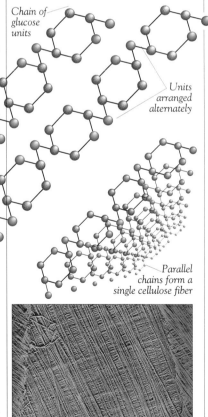.

Cellulose

An insoluble carbohydrate that plants use as a building material

Cellulose is made by plants, and it is the most abundant organic compound on Earth. Cellulose molecules consist of thousands of glucose units linked end to end. Plants use these long molecules to build their cell walls 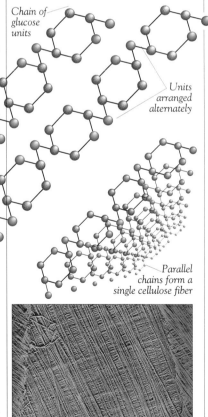.

Cellulose chains
Chains of glucose units make up the cellulose fibers that form a plant cell wall. The units are arranged alternately in each chain. Many parallel chains form a single fiber of cellulose.

Chain of glucose units

Units arranged alternately

Parallel chains form a single cellulose fiber

Fibers of cellulose
Cellulose is very strong because its fibers form a criss-cross mesh that resists tearing in both directions.

Lipids

Animals and plants use lipids for many different jobs. Fats and oils are lipids that store energy and provide insulation, waxes create waterproof coatings, and phospholipids form a vital part of cell membranes.

Lipid

An insoluble organic compound

Lipids are a group of organic compounds ■ that include fats, oils, and waxes. Lipids repel water and can therefore be used to separate substances from their watery surroundings. Fats and oils form concentrated energy reserves that can be stored inside cells ■. A lipid molecule ■ is made up of chains of carbon and hydrogen atoms ■, with a small number of oxygen atoms.

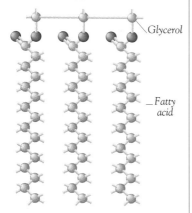

Glycerol

Fatty acid

Energy-storing molecule
Fats and oils contain complex molecules called triglycerides that store energy. A triglyceride molecule is made up of three fatty acids combined with glycerol.

See also

Artery 126 • Atom 24 • Cell 18
Chemical bond 24 • Hormone 134
Molecule 25 • Organic compound 24
Plasma membrane 18 • Vitamin 29

Butter

Polyunsaturated margarine

Saturated and unsaturated fats
Butter contains saturated animal fat and margarine contains vegetable oil.

Fat

A lipid that is normally solid at room temperature

Fats are found mainly in animals. Animals store fats in their cells to use as an energy reserve. Some animals have a layer of fat under their skin to keep them warm. Animal fats are rich in **saturated fatty acids**. These have molecules in which the carbon atoms are linked to other atoms by single chemical bonds ■. This makes fats solid at room temperature.

Oil

A lipid that is normally liquid at room temperature

Oil globules repel water

Oils are more common in plants than in animals. Plants use oils to store energy. Seeds are often stocked with oil to fuel their early growth. Oils are rich in **unsaturated fatty acids**. The chains of carbon atoms in these molecules contain at least one double chemical bond that links to two neighboring carbon atoms. **Polyunsaturated fatty acids** are those with more than one double bond. Oils are liquid at room temperature.

Wax

A lipid that is often used as a protective coating

Waxes are soft, slippery substances that resist attack by other chemicals. Animals and plants produce waxes to protect structures such as skin, hair, leaves, and fruit. Wool is protected by a soft wax called **lanolin**, which is often used in shampoo and skin creams. Bees make honeycombs from **beeswax**.

Beeswax candle

Phospholipid

A form of lipid that makes up membranes

Phospholipids form the plasma membrane ■ around cells. A phospholipid molecule has two "tails" that are **hydrophobic**, which means they repel water. The "head" of the molecule is **hydrophilic**, and attracts water. In water, phospholipid molecules line up to form a double layer with their heads facing in opposite directions.

Steroid

A complex lipid in which the carbon atoms are arranged in rings

A steroid is a lipid found in animal tissues. Steroids have molecules that often contain four connected rings of carbon atoms. Steroids include some vitamins ■ and hormones ■, but the most common steroid is **cholesterol**. This forms a vital part of cell membranes, and many other substances. However, too much cholesterol can be bad for you. If you eat a lot of fatty food, cholesterol can build up in your arteries ■ and cause heart disease.

Vitamins & minerals

Living things need vitamins and minerals to carry out chemical reactions. Animals need to take in vitamins in their food because they cannot make them for themselves.

Vitamin

An organic compound that animals need in small amounts

An animal's body needs vitamins to work properly. Vitamins help chemical reactions ▪ take place in the metabolism ▪. If an animal's diet lacks an important vitamin, the animal may develop a **vitamin deficiency disease**.

Mineral

An inorganic compound that living things need

All living things need minerals. Animals take in minerals with food, and plants obtain minerals from the soil. Humans need some minerals in large amounts, and others, called **trace minerals**, only in tiny quantities.

Healthy eating
Fruit and vegetables are rich sources of vitamins and minerals. Citrus fruits and potatoes contain lots of vitamin C.

See also

Chemical reaction 25
Inorganic compound 24
Metabolism 32 • Organic compound 24

VITAMINS

Vitamin	Function in body	Source
A	Helps growth, vision, body's defenses	Green vegetables, fish oil, egg yolk, dairy food
D	Regulates calcium in bone growth	Sunlight, fish oil, egg yolk
E	May prevent fatty acid breakdown in cells	Green vegetables, plant oils
K	Helps build chemicals that make blood clot	Green vegetables
C	Helps build the protein collagen	Citrus fruits, tomatoes, potatoes, leafy vegetables
B_1 (thiamin)	Helps break down carbohydrates	Whole grains, liver, peas & beans, yeast
B_2 (riboflavin)	Helps control oxidation & reduction	Milk, leafy vegetables, eggs
Niacin	Helps control oxidation & reduction	Lean meat, fish, wheat germ, yeast
B_6	Helps break down fatty acids & amino acids	Whole grains, liver, egg yolk
B_{12}	Helps make proteins	Liver, kidney, fish, eggs
Pantothenic acid	Enables energy production in respiration	Meat, milk, eggs, vegetables, yeast
Folic acid (folate)	Helps make nucleic acids	Green leafy vegetables, liver, wheat germ, fruit
Biotin	Helps make & break down fats & carbohydrates	Whole grains, liver, eggs, milk

KEY MINERALS

Mineral	Function in body	Source
Calcium	Helps build bones & teeth, helps nerves function	Milk, eggs, grains
Chlorine	Maintains balance of ions in tissues, forms acid in stomach	Table salt
Iron	Forms a vital part of hemoglobin in blood	Meat, eggs, nuts, green vegetables
Magnesium	Helps build bones & teeth	Green vegetables, meat, milk
Phosphorus	Helps build bones, helps form phospholipids	Dairy food, meat, grain
Potassium	Maintains balance of ions in tissues, helps nerves function	Meat, fruit, vegetables
Sodium	Maintains balance of ions in tissues, helps nerves function	Table salt, meat, vegetables
Sulfur	Forms a vital part of many proteins	Meat, eggs, dairy food
Copper	Helps form bones, helps produce hemoglobin	Liver, fish, nuts
Iodine	Forms a vital part of thyroid hormone	Fish
Manganese	Activates many different enzymes	Meat, grains
Zinc	Forms vital part of some enzymes	Fish, liver, other foods

Proteins

Some of the largest and most complicated substances in living things are proteins. Each one is made of a chemical chain, which is folded up in a special way. The precise shape of this chain is the key to the way each protein works.

Protein

An organic compound made up of amino acid units

Proteins are organic compounds ▦. They perform many functions in living things, from controlling chemical reactions ▦ to building structures such as hair. Some also act as hormones ▦. A protein molecule ▦ is made up of amino acid units joined together in an exact sequence. This sequence gives the protein its shape and enables it to do its particular job.

Amino acid

An organic acid that contains nitrogen

Amino acids are the building blocks of proteins. Living things produce thousands of proteins from only 20 different kinds of amino acid. The amino acids can be arranged in a vast number of different sequences, just as the letters of the alphabet can form thousands of different words. Every amino acid molecule has an atom ▦ of carbon ▦ linked to an **amino group**. This group has one nitrogen atom and two hydrogen atoms.

Silken protein
A spiderweb is made from a protein. The protein is liquid inside the spider's body, but turns solid as the web is spun.

Essential amino acid

An amino acid that the body cannot make

The human body can make 10 of the 20 amino acids needed to manufacture proteins. The other 10 amino acids must come from food. These are called essential amino acids.

Peptide linkage

A chemical bond between amino acids

A peptide linkage is a chemical bond ▦ that holds amino acids together in a chain. The linkage is formed when two amino acids react and lose a water molecule. It is also called a **peptide bond**.

Polypeptide

A short chain of amino acids

A polypeptide molecule contains fewer than 40 or 50 amino acid units. A protein begins as a small polypeptide, and then gains more and more amino acid units until it becomes a long protein chain.

Protein structure

The chemical and physical makeup of a protein

Proteins have complex and varied structures. A protein molecule's **primary structure** is its sequence of amino acid units. Neighboring amino acid units often attract each other. This makes parts of the protein molecule fold up to give it a distinctive **secondary structure**. The **tertiary structure** is the shape of the whole molecule.

Quill

Feather-light protein
Birds' feathers are made from the structural protein keratin. This versatile protein is light, strong, and flexible.

Structural protein

A protein that is used as a building material

Structural proteins support and protect parts of living things. Hair, nails, and feathers are all protective materials made from the structural protein **keratin**, which forms strong, flexible fibers. Inside an animal's body, the tendons that link muscles to bones are made from another structural protein called **collagen**. Collagen forms strong, elastic fibers.

Transport protein

A protein that is used to carry other substances

Transport proteins get substances from one place and release them in another. Hemoglobin  is one of the most important transport proteins in animals. It carries oxygen and carbon dioxide in the blood.

Macaw flight feather

Parallel barbs on feather lock together to form a smooth surface

Enzyme

A protein catalyst that speeds up chemical reactions in living things

Many of the chemical reactions that take place in living things, such as digestion, would happen very slowly without enzymes. Enzymes are proteins that act as **catalysts**, which are substances that speed up chemical reactions. An enzyme works by attracting **substrates**, the molecules involved in the reaction. These fit into a part of the enzyme called the **active site**. The substrates react with each other to form **products**, which then move away from the enzyme. The enzyme is not affected by the reaction, and is immediately ready to attract more substrate molecules.

Denatured protein

A protein in which the structure has been changed

During **denaturation**, the position of a protein's amino acid units is altered by heat or by chemical changes. For example, when an egg is boiled, the protein in the egg white changes from a cloudy fluid to a white solid. This cannot be reversed.

Anselme Payen

French chemist 1795–1871

Payen discovered the first enzyme known to science. He worked in a factory that made sugar from sugar beet roots. There he became interested in the chemical reactions carried out by plants. In 1833, Payen discovered that germinating grain makes a substance that turns starch into glucose. He called it diastase. Payen showed that diastase worked even after it was taken out of the plants that made it.

Immunological protein

A protein that is used to deactivate foreign substances

If an animal's body is invaded by microorganisms, special proteins bind to the surface of the attackers to make them harmless. These proteins are called antibodies. The human body makes a vast number of different antibodies that tackle a wide range of invaders.

Storage protein

A protein that is used for storage

Plants and animals use proteins for storing nutrients. **Gluten** is a storage protein in wheat grains.

Enzyme-controlled reaction

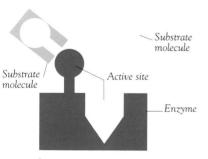

Substrate molecule

Substrate molecule

Active site

Enzyme

An enzyme attracts two substrates, which fit into the active site like a key in a lock.

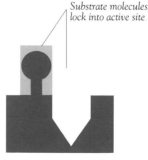

Substrate molecules lock into active site

The substrates are held close together by the enzyme. They react and form products.

Products move away from enzyme

The enzyme can now attract more substrate molecules. It is not affected by the reaction.

Energy & respiration

All living things use energy. They need it for growing, moving, and responding to the world around them. Most forms of life obtain energy by combining food with oxygen during respiration.

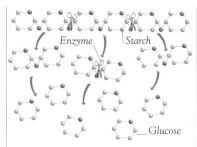

Enzyme *Starch*

Glucose

Energy

The capacity to do work

In living things, energy exists in several forms. **Chemical energy** is stored in chemical compounds ■. These are broken down to release the energy of movement, or **kinetic energy**, and **heat energy**.

Metabolism

All the chemical processes that take place in a living thing

Living things need to break down and build up substances all the time. This two-way process is called metabolism. Any chemical that is involved in a metabolic reaction is called a **metabolite**. Many metabolites come from the digestion of food. **Catabolism** is the part of metabolism in which organic compounds ■ are broken down into simple molecules ■ to release energy. In **anabolism**, simple molecules combine to form more complex ones. This process requires energy.

Metabolic rate

The rate at which a living thing releases energy

An animal's metabolic rate depends on its level of activity. The metabolic rate is high when an animal is active and using up a lot of energy, and low when it is inactive and using less energy. Some animals pass the winter in a deep sleep, called hibernation. During this sleep, their metabolic rate falls to a low level, and they use up their stored energy slowly.

Breaking down starch
Complex molecules, such as starch, are important energy sources. Enzymes "cut up" starch molecules to make glucose. Glucose is then broken down during respiration to release energy.

Respiration

A chemical process in which food is broken down to release energy

Respiration, or **cellular respiration**, is a series of chemical reactions ■ that takes place inside cells ■. During respiration, organic compounds such as glucose ■ are broken down to release energy. The term respiration can also refer to the physical process that supplies oxygen to an animal's body. In humans and many other vertebrates ■, this involves breathing ■.

Anabolism (building up)

Catabolism (breaking down)

Carbohydrates, Lipids, Proteins, Nucleic acids

Energy usually needed

Metabolism
There are two sides to metabolism – building up substances in anabolism, and breaking them down in catabolism.

Energy usually released

Simple molecules

Energy equation
During aerobic respiration, glucose molecules combine with oxygen. This produces carbon dioxide and water, and releases a large amount of energy.

Aerobic respiration

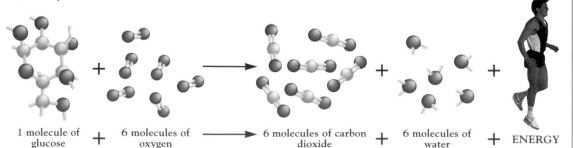

| 1 molecule of glucose | + | 6 molecules of oxygen | → | 6 molecules of carbon dioxide | + | 6 molecules of water | + | ENERGY |

Aerobic respiration

A kind of respiration that requires oxygen

During aerobic respiration, cells break down glucose (an organic compound) by combining it with oxygen. This is called oxidation ▪. It produces carbon dioxide and water, which are inorganic compounds ▪, as waste products. Aerobic respiration releases a large amount of energy, but it can only work if oxygen is available.

Anaerobic respiration

A kind of respiration that does not involve oxygen

Not all living things need oxygen to obtain energy. Many organisms can break down glucose anaerobically, which means "without air." Glucose is only partly broken down during anaerobic respiration and it forms new organic compounds. This process does not release very much energy.

Alcoholic fermentation

A kind of anaerobic respiration that occurs in fungi and plants

Alcoholic fermentation is carried out by fungi such as yeast ▪, and also by some kinds of plant. During this process, cells break down glucose anaerobically and turn it into alcohol and carbon dioxide. Alcoholic fermentation is used to make alcoholic drinks such as beer and wine. It is also used in baking to make bread rise.

Lactic acid fermentation

A kind of anaerobic respiration that occurs in animals

During vigorous exercise, muscles use up oxygen faster than the blood can supply it. Without oxygen, muscle cells cannot carry out aerobic respiration. Instead, the cells break down glucose anaerobically to release the energy needed by the muscles. This also produces **lactic acid**, which acts as a poison, or **toxin**. Lactic acid builds up in the muscles and eventually keeps them from working properly. It also makes them ache.

Lactic acid builds up in muscles during hard exercise

Panting helps take in oxygen

Leg muscles ache

Oxygen debt

The amount of oxygen needed to break down lactic acid

After hard exercise, lactic acid that has built up in the muscles must be broken down by aerobic respiration. The amount of oxygen required for this job is called the oxygen debt. Panting helps the body take in extra oxygen.

ATP

An energy carrier in all living things

When cells respire, they release heat and chemical energy. This energy is used to make **adenosine triphosphate**, or ATP. This substance carries the energy to where it is needed in the body.

Hans Krebs

German biochemist 1900–81

Krebs carried out research into how cells release energy during aerobic respiration. He discovered that glucose is broken down in a chain of reactions. This is now called the **citric acid cycle** or **Krebs cycle**. At each step in the cycle, a little of the original energy is released.

Autotroph

A living thing that makes its own food

An autotroph can make its own food. All green plants and some bacteria ▪ are **autotrophic**. They turn water and carbon dioxide into organic compounds by photosynthesis ▪. Autotrophs are vital to life on Earth, because they alone produce the organic compounds that all other living things depend upon for food.

Heterotroph

A living thing that eats food made by other living things

All animals, including humans, are **heterotrophic**, which means that they cannot make their own food. Animals have to take in the organic compounds they need for food by eating plants or other animals.

Nucleic acids

Nucleic acids form sets of instructions for living things. They store the information needed to assemble the proteins that build cells and make them work. With the help of enzymes, one kind of nucleic acid, DNA, can copy and pass on its instructions to every new cell in a living thing.

DNA molecule
Most of the cells in the human body contain about 6.5 feet (2 meters) of DNA. A DNA molecule has a spiral shape, called a double helix, and its two strands are linked by huge numbers of base pairs.

Nucleic acid

A complex organic compound that carries information

Nucleic acids are organic compounds ▪ made up of small molecules ▪ called nucleotides. There are two kinds of nucleic acid – DNA and RNA. DNA carries genetic ▪ information. In most cells ▪, it is stored inside the nucleus ▪. RNA acts as a "shuttle" service, copying the DNA's information and carrying it away to be put into action.

DNA

A substance that stores information in all living things

A molecule of DNA, or **deoxyribonucleic acid**, can contain millions of atoms ▪. It is made up of two strands, which twist around each other to form a shape called a **double helix**. The strands are held together by chemicals called bases. The exact sequence of these bases forms genetic information that varies from one living thing to another.

Nucleotide

One of the molecules that add together to make a nucleic acid

Nucleic acids are polymers ▪ of nucleotides. A nucleotide molecule is made up of a sugar, a base, and a phosphate group. The sugars link up to form a nucleic acid's "backbone," and the bases make up its genetic information.

Base

A substance that forms a store of information in a nucleic acid

Bases work like the letters of an alphabet. They spell out a long set of instructions that tells a cell how to make the proteins ▪ it needs. Each kind of nucleic acid has just four bases or "letters." In DNA, the bases are **cytosine, guanine, adenine,** and **thymine**. RNA has the same bases, but uses **uracil** instead of thymine.

Base pair

Two bases linked chemically

In a DNA molecule, every base is chemically linked to its partner on the opposite strand of the double helix. Bases do not pair up at random. Instead, adenine always pairs with thymine, and cytosine always pairs with guanine. This precise pairing is like a negative and a positive in photography – each DNA strand carries the same information, but in a different form. Therefore, one strand is a **complementary copy** of the other. Base pairs also form in some RNA molecules.

Replication

The process by which a nucleic acid molecule copies itself

When a cell divides ▪, its DNA molecules copy themselves, or replicate, in order to pass on a set of instructions to each new cell. During replication, each DNA molecule "unzips" itself, so that its strands separate. The two strands then form complementary copies of themselves with the help of an enzyme ▪ called **DNA polymerase**. Two new DNA molecules are produced, each with one old strand, and one new one.

Replicating DNA
DNA replicates with the help of an enzyme. As the DNA strands unwind, the enzyme assembles the parts needed to make two new molecules. The new molecules are normally identical.

Double helix unzips

New DNA molecule

New strand, or complementary copy

RNA

A group of nucleic acids that handle the information used to make proteins

Unlike DNA, a molecule of RNA, or **ribonucleic acid**, has only a single strand. RNA carries out several important tasks in the making, or synthesis ▦, of proteins. Messenger RNA copies parts of the DNA's code, and transfer RNA uses this information to link up the molecules that form proteins.

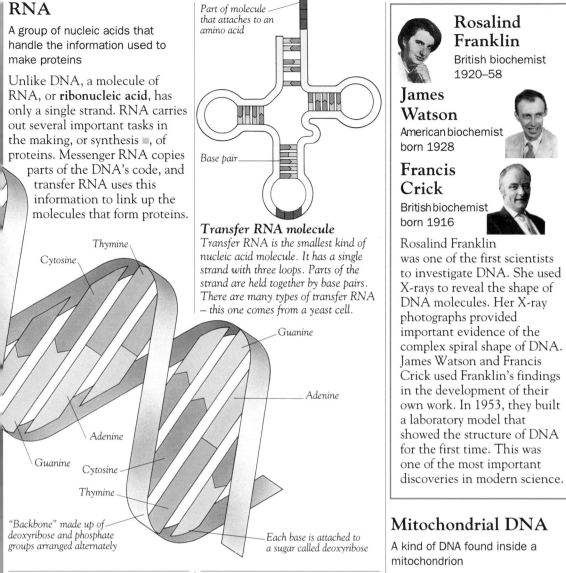

Part of molecule that attaches to an amino acid

Base pair

Transfer RNA molecule

Transfer RNA is the smallest kind of nucleic acid molecule. It has a single strand with three loops. Parts of the strand are held together by base pairs. There are many types of transfer RNA – this one comes from a yeast cell.

Thymine
Cytosine
Guanine
Adenine
Adenine
Guanine
Cytosine
Thymine
"Backbone" made up of deoxyribose and phosphate groups arranged alternately
Each base is attached to a sugar called deoxyribose

Rosalind Franklin

British biochemist
1920–58

James Watson

American biochemist
born 1928

Francis Crick

British biochemist
born 1916

Rosalind Franklin was one of the first scientists to investigate DNA. She used X-rays to reveal the shape of DNA molecules. Her X-ray photographs provided important evidence of the complex spiral shape of DNA. James Watson and Francis Crick used Franklin's findings in the development of their own work. In 1953, they built a laboratory model that showed the structure of DNA for the first time. This was one of the most important discoveries in modern science.

Mitochondrial DNA

A kind of DNA found inside a mitochondrion

Many cells also have small, circular molecules of DNA in their mitochondria ▦. The DNA molecules in bacteria ▦ are similar to mitochondrial DNA.

Messenger RNA

A kind of RNA that forms a copy of the information stored in DNA

A strand of messenger RNA, or **mRNA**, is a copy of part of a DNA strand. It is made by enzymes using a strand of DNA as a model. This takes place during a process called transcription ▦. Once it has been constructed, messenger RNA moves away so that the information it has copied can be used by transfer RNA and other chemicals to make proteins.

Transfer RNA

A kind of RNA that collects the amino acids that form proteins

To make a protein, amino acids ▦ have to be collected and assembled in the right sequence. This job is carried out by transfer RNA, or **tRNA**. During translation ▦, transfer RNA receives instructions from messenger RNA. They tell it how to link amino acids in the right order. There is a different transfer RNA for each of the 20 amino acids that make proteins.

The genetic code

Your body cells use the genetic code to interpret the information stored inside DNA. This information instructs cells how to make the proteins that build and control cells. Without the code, the genetic information you inherit from your parents would be meaningless.

Genetic code

The chemical code used by DNA and RNA

A molecule ▪ of DNA ▪ contains a huge sequence of chemicals, called bases ▪, arranged in a particular order. The genetic code tells a cell ▪ how to convert the DNA's sequence of bases into a sequence of amino acids ▪. Amino acids form the protein ▪ molecules that build cells and make them work.

Codon

A three-base group used in the genetic code

The "words" used by the genetic code are called codons. Each codon is three bases long and has an exact meaning. There are four kinds of base altogether, so they can be arranged in 64 different groups of three. A codon specifies a particular amino acid or shows where a chain of amino acids should start or stop.

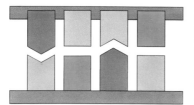

Making a codon
This diagram shows the four possible base pairs in a DNA molecule. A codon is made up of three base pairs, arranged in any order.

Gene

A basic unit of heredity that carries the instructions needed to make a particular protein

The DNA in human cells stores between 50,000 and 100,000 genes. Each gene contains codons that instruct cells how to make certain proteins. Proteins build and control cells. By making different proteins at different times, genes can act as switches to alter the way cells work. Genes are the basic units of heredity ▪; they are passed on to the next generation without being divided into smaller units. However, a gene can exist in different forms called alleles ▪. Every living thing produced by sexual reproduction ▪ has a unique collection of alleles.

Protein synthesis

The manufacture of a protein

Cells can make proteins only by following instructions from a gene. This process is called protein synthesis. It happens when a gene is **expressed**, or put into action.

Controlling gene

A gene that affects the expression of other genes

Some genes are expressed almost all the time. Others are only expressed once during a lifetime. Controlling genes make proteins that turn other genes on or off.

Transcription

The process of copying the DNA's genetic code

Transcription is the first stage of making a protein. During transcription, the two strands of a DNA molecule pull apart. An enzyme ▪ called **RNA polymerase** then assembles a strand of messenger RNA ▪, using one of the DNA strands as a template. When the RNA strand is complete, the DNA molecule closes up again, and the messenger RNA moves away.

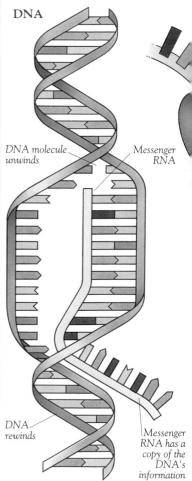

DNA

DNA molecule unwinds

Messenger RNA

DNA rewinds

Messenger RNA has a copy of the DNA's information

Transcription
The process of transcription starts when part of a DNA molecule unwinds. A single-stranded molecule of messenger RNA is then built up piece by piece.

Translation

The process of "reading" a strand of messenger RNA

Translation is the second stage of making a protein. Chemical clusters called ribosomes ■ move along the strand of messenger RNA. The ribosomes "read," or translate, the strand's instructions one codon at a time. With the help of transfer RNA ■ molecules, the ribosomes convert the sequence of codons into a sequence of amino acids. This forms a protein molecule.

Genotype

The genetic makeup of a cell or a living thing

A living thing's genotype is the genetic information it inherits from its parents. It includes genes or alleles that affect shape, size, color, and how a living thing works. The genotype also includes alleles that are not put into action, or expressed. These may be expressed in the next generation. The genotype interacts with the environment to produce the phenotype.

Har Gobind Khorana

Indian-American biochemist born 1922

Khorana was one of the biochemists who helped crack the genetic code. When he started investigating the genetic code, scientists knew that it worked by using groups of three bases, called codons. There were only four bases, so there were 64 possible combinations of three-base groups. Khorana made molecules containing all of the 64 possible codons, to see which amino acid each one specified. Through his work, a complete picture of the genetic code was built up.

Phenotype

The visible characteristics produced by a genotype

A living thing's phenotype is the physical shape produced by its genotype. Two living things can have the same genotype, but different phenotypes, because the environment influences the effect of genes or alleles. For example, if two plants with the same genotype grow up in different conditions, they may grow into different shapes.

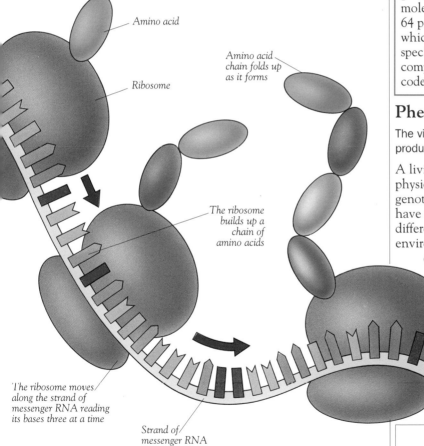

Amino acid

Ribosome

Amino acid chain folds up as it forms

The ribosome builds up a chain of amino acids

The ribosome moves along the strand of messenger RNA reading its bases three at a time

Strand of messenger RNA

Translation

During translation, a ribosome attaches itself to a strand of messenger RNA and reads the bases. With the help of transfer RNA (not shown here) it collects the amino acids coded by the bases. Eventually, the ribosome reaches a part of the code that tells it to stop, and the completed protein molecule is released.

Chromosomes

Almost every cell in your body has a set of chromosomes. These structures store the DNA that contains the instructions needed to make cells work. Chromosomes pass on genetic material from one generation to another.

Chromosome

A structure that contains all or part of a cell's DNA

DNA ▪ molecules are packaged into threadlike structures called chromosomes. In most cells ▪, chromosomes are found in the cell nucleus ▪. However, in bacteria ▪ the DNA is loosely spread out in their cells. Chromosomes contain all the information needed to make a cell work. They are therefore vital to a cell and its offspring, and they are handed on when a cell divides.

Chromatids

Centromere

Human chromosome
This chromosome is made of two strands called chromatids. They are joined by a centromere.

Chromosomes
This color-enhanced electron micrograph shows chromosomes (pink) gathering at the center of a cell before it divides.

Chromatid

One of two strands that are linked in a replicated chromosome

Before a cell divides, a chromosome makes a copy of itself, or replicates ▪. This creates a chromosome that now has two strands called chromatids. It forms an X-shaped structure that is held together by a **centromere**. When a cell divides by mitosis ▪, the two chromatids are pulled apart.

Chromatin

The substance that makes up a chromosome

Every chromosome contains a long molecule ▪ of DNA. This is wrapped around protein ▪ molecules called **histones**. Together, the DNA and proteins make up a substance called chromatin. Chromatin is named after the Greek word for "color," because it easily absorbs the chemical stains used by biochemists to make cell parts visible.

Chromatin strand

Histones

Chromosome

Chromosome structure
DNA is packaged into a chromosome in a complicated series of loops. The DNA coils around bundles of histones to make a "string of beads" structure. This coils again into a chromatin strand. The chromatin then folds into loops that coil up to form a chromosome.

DNA molecule

Condensed chromosome

A tightly coiled chromosome

If you look at cells under a microscope, you will probably not be able to see any chromosomes. This is because chromosomes are normally unwound and are so fine that they are invisible. Chromosomes only become visible when they wind up, or condense, just before a cell divides.

Haploid cell

A cell that has a single set of chromosomes

The cells used in sexual reproduction ■ normally contain just one set of chromosomes. These are haploid cells. They are produced by the kind of cell division ■ called meiosis ■. When a male and a female haploid cell combine during fertilization ■, they form a new diploid cell.

Diploid cell

A cell that has a double set of chromosomes

Almost every human cell contains a double set of chromosomes. These originally came from each parent – one set from the father, and one set from the mother. Cells like this are called diploid.

Homologous chromosome

One of a matching pair of chromosomes in a diploid cell

A diploid cell contains two sets of chromosomes. The chromosomes in each matching pair are called homologous chromosomes or **homologues**. During the kind of cell division called meiosis, homologous chromosomes pair up and swap pieces.

Karyotype

The complete set of chromosomes inside a cell

The chromosomes inside a cell are usually jumbled up, which makes them hard to study. Biochemists use a simple technique to solve this problem. They stain the chromosomes with dye so that they can be photographed. They then cut up the photograph, and arrange the pictures of the individual chromosomes in homologous pairs. These are ordered according to size. In humans, there are 23 pairs. Both the technique and the chromosome set are called karyotypes.

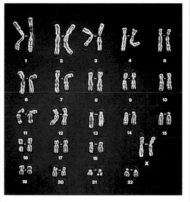

Female karyotype
This karyotype shows a full set of human female chromosomes. They are arranged in homologous pairs, which are identical in size and staining pattern. The female sex chromosomes, labeled "X," are on the fourth row, far right.

Chromosome number

The number of chromosomes in a cell

Every species ■ of living thing has a precise number of chromosomes in its cells. A diploid human cell contains 46 chromosomes, a dog has 78, and a pea plant has 14 chromosomes. Fruit flies, which are often used to investigate heredity ■, have eight chromosomes.

Sex chromosome

A chromosome that determines sex

A close look at human chromosomes shows an important difference between women and men. Women have a pair of matching X chromosomes. Men have just one X chromosome paired with a smaller Y chromosome. The combination of X and Y chromosomes determines a person's sex.

Male sex chromosomes
This picture shows the two sex chromosomes in a human male. They are different sizes.

Autosome

Any chromosome that is not involved in determining sex

Autosomes make up 44 of your 46 chromosomes. They determine most of the characteristics of your body, but not your sex.

Genome

A complete set of chromosomes

A genome is the total collection of genes ■ in a single set of chromosomes. So far, scientists have identified and located about 2,000 of the 100,000 genes carried by human chromosomes. In the **Human Genome Project**, scientists aim to map the entire human genome.

Cell division

Every day, your body makes billions of new cells. It does this by cell division. When a cell divides, its chromosomes separate in an intricate series of movements. This process makes sure each new cell receives the correct genetic material.

Cell division

The process by which cells reproduce

As living things mature, they grow bigger. However, their cells ■ stay almost exactly the same size. Living things grow because their cells divide and increase in number. Cells divide in two different ways – mitosis and meiosis.

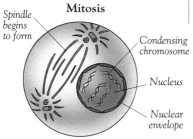

Mitosis

Spindle begins to form

Condensing chromosome

Nucleus

Nuclear envelope

Early prophase of mitosis
At the beginning of mitosis, the chromosomes tighten up, or condense. A network of tiny tubes, called a spindle, begins to develop.

Cell cycle

The life cycle of a cell

Every cell in your body has its own life cycle. During one part of the cycle, the DNA ■ in the cell nucleus ■ copies itself. In other parts of the cycle, the cell either divides or rests. Some cells, such as skin cells, complete one cycle every 24 hours. Other cells, such as those in the brain, complete several cycles before birth, then stop forever.

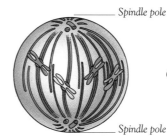

Spindle pole

Spindle pole

Late prophase
The nuclear envelope disintegrates. The spindle begins to move the chromosomes.

Mitosis

The division of a cell nucleus to produce two identical cells

Mitosis produces two new cells with exactly the same genetic material as the original cell. Just before mitosis begins, each chromosome ■ copies itself and forms two chromatids ■. During mitosis, the chromatids pull apart to form two separate nuclei. Then the cytoplasm ■ divides to form two identical new cells.

Somatic cell

A cell that is not involved in sexual reproduction

Somatic cells make up almost all of your body cells. They divide only by mitosis. Every new somatic cell therefore has a double set of chromosomes like the cell that produced it. This kind of cell is called diploid ■. Somatic cells are not involved in reproduction, so cannot pass on genes ■ to the next generation.

Chromosome

Metaphase
The chromosomes line up across the center of the spindle.

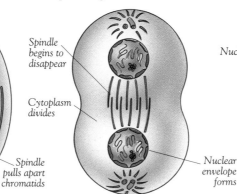

Chromatid

Spindle begins to disappear

Cytoplasm divides

Spindle pulls apart chromatids

Nuclear envelope forms

Anaphase
The chromatids that make up each chromosome move apart and travel to opposite ends of the spindle.

Telophase
An envelope surrounds each set of chromatids, forming a new nucleus. The cytoplasm begins to divide.

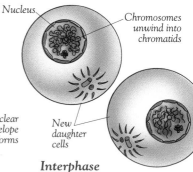

Nucleus

Chromosomes unwind into chromatids

New daughter cells

Interphase
Once cell division is complete, the chromatids unwind. The two new cells have identical genetic material.

Meiosis

A form of cell division that produces differing cells

Meiosis is a form of cell division that makes sex cells. Sex cells are all genetically different from each other. Meiosis consists of two divisions, one after the other. During these divisions, genes or alleles ■ are mixed up. Four new cells are produced, each with a unique mixture of alleles. Each new cell has half the genetic content of the original cell.

First prophase of meiosis
When meiosis begins, the cell has two sets of chromosomes (1). Each chromosome has two chromatids. Homologous chromosomes line up in tetrads and swap pieces (2).

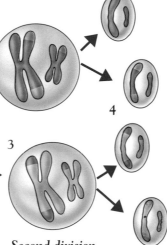

1

2

First division
Homologous chromosomes separate in the first division. Two new cells are formed, each with a single pair of chromosomes (3).

Sex cell

A cell that is involved in sexual reproduction

Sex cells, or **gametes**, are formed by meiosis, and they are used in sexual reproduction ■. In humans, the sex cells consist of sperm ■ in men, and ova ■ in women. Sex cells are unlike the rest of the body's cells, because they are haploid ■, or have only a single set of chromosomes. During sexual reproduction, they pass on their genes to the next generation.

Spindle

A network of tiny tubes that separates chromatids when a cell divides

During cell division, chromatids separate, so that they end up in different cells. A spindle is a structure inside a cell that pulls apart the chromatids. It has two poles that line up on opposite sides of the nucleus. The poles are connected by tiny tubes, which drag the chromatids toward them.

Meiosis

4

3

Second division
In the second division, the two chromatids in each chromosome are pulled apart. Four new cells are formed, each with a pair of single-stranded chromosomes (4).

Crossing over

The swapping of genes between homologous chromosomes

When meiosis begins, pairs of homologous chromosomes ■ line up side by side and form **tetrads**. Each chromosome has two chromatids, so a tetrad is a single unit of four. The chromatids in each tetrad form bridges, called **chiasmata**, and swap pieces with each other. Afterward, the chromosomes pull apart. Crossing over gives each chromosome a new combination of genes.

Pairing up
Before a cell divides by meiosis, it has one set of chromosomes from each parent. The matching chromosomes line up to form tetrads.

Crossing over
The chromatids that make up the matching chromosomes overlap each other and swap pieces.

Recombination
The chromosomes then separate. Each one now has a new combination of genes or alleles from both parents.

Recombination

The mixing of genes to produce new combinations

During meiosis, genes are mixed in two different ways. They are mixed by crossing over, and also by **random assortment**. This occurs because the original cell has two sets of chromosomes, each from a different parent. During meiosis, these two sets do not stay together. They divide up at random, so that every new cell usually receives chromosomes from both sets.

See also

Allele 42 • Cell 18 • Chromatid 38
Chromosome 38 • Cytoplasm 18
Diploid cell 39 • DNA 34
Gene 36 • Haploid cell 39
Homologous chromosome 39
Nucleus 19 • Ovum 160
Sexual reproduction 160 • Sperm 160

Heredity

A living thing produced by sexual reproduction inherits a unique set of genes. This means that each member of a species has its own distinct characteristics. Color, shape, and size are all affected by the way in which genes are handed down from one generation to another.

Heredity

The link between successive generations of living things

All living things produce offspring that are similar to themselves. They do this by passing on genes ■. A feature that can be passed on in this way is called an **inherited characteristic**.

Variation

The natural differences between living things

Many living things seem to look the same. For example, one sparrow looks very much like another. However, animals and plants that are produced by sexual reproduction ■ always vary from their relatives. This is because each one has its own unique collection of genes. Variation is important, because it enables a species ■ to change slowly through evolution ■.

Allele

One of two or more forms of the same gene

In most human cells ■ there are two sets of matching or homologous chromosomes ■. These contain genes that exist in corresponding pairs, called alleles. Alleles are alternative versions of the same gene. They are always in the same position, or **locus**, on homologous chromosomes.

Dominant allele

An allele that usually shows itself in a living thing's phenotype

Genes exist in more than one form. Each form, or allele, can have different effects on the visible characteristics, or phenotype ■, of a living thing. For example, in the locus that controls eye color, one allele may produce blue eyes, and one may produce brown. In most cases, only one of the two alleles is put into action, or expressed. This called a dominant allele.

Recessive allele

An allele that is masked by a dominant allele

If a recessive allele is partnered by a dominant allele, it will not be expressed. However, it is still part of the genetic information, or genotype ■. This means it can be passed on to the next generation. It will only be expressed if it is later partnered by an identical recessive allele.

Mendelian ratio

The ratio of different phenotypes produced when living things breed

Research into genetics shows that characteristics are not inherited in a random way. Instead, they follow predictable mathematical patterns. These patterns are known as Mendelian ratios after Gregor Johann Mendel, who discovered them. They can be used to show how characteristics are passed on from one generation to another.

Mendel's peas

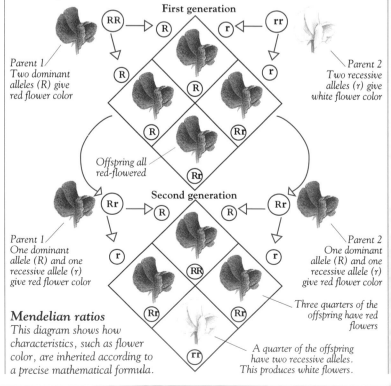

First generation

Parent 1 / Two dominant alleles (R) give red flower color

Parent 2 / Two recessive alleles (r) give white flower color

Offspring all red-flowered

Second generation

Parent 1 / One dominant allele (R) and one recessive allele (r) give red flower color

Parent 2 / One dominant allele (R) and one recessive allele (r) give red flower color

Three quarters of the offspring have red flowers

Mendelian ratios
This diagram shows how characteristics, such as flower color, are inherited according to a precise mathematical formula.

A quarter of the offspring have two recessive alleles. This produces white flowers.

Homozygous cell

A cell with identical alleles

A cell that is homozygous has identical alleles that control particular features. The alleles can be either both dominant or both recessive. They are situated in the same position, or locus, on homologous chromosomes.

Heterozygous cell

A cell with different alleles

A heterozygous cell has two different alleles, one dominant and one recessive, in the same locus on homologous chromosomes.

Natural variation
Puppies in a litter often look different because each one inherits a unique set of genes from its parents.

Linked alleles

Alleles that tend to be inherited together

During sexual reproduction, alleles are reshuffled like cards in a pack. But the shuffling is not always very thorough. Alleles that are close to each other on the same chromosome often stay together, so they are passed on as a group. These are linked alleles.

Sex-linked allele

An allele that is carried by a sex chromosome

Sex chromosomes ■ contain many alleles, as well as the ones that determine sex. This means some characteristics are common in one sex but rare or absent in the other. For example, red-green color blindness is more common in men than in women.

Mutation

A change in a cell's genetic material

Genes or alleles are reshuffled by meiosis ■, but they can also be altered. This occurs accidentally, either by a chance rearrangement in a DNA ■ molecule or by a change in the shape or number of chromosomes. Changes like this are called mutations. If a mutation occurs in a sex cell ■, it can be passed on from one generation to another. Mutations are a source of variation in living things, and they allow evolution to take place.

Genetics

The study of heredity

Genetics is the study of how inherited characteristics are passed on. Scientists often carry out experiments that involve breeding many generations of bacteria ■, plants, or animals. Bacteria and fruit flies are useful in genetic experiments because they breed quickly and are easy to keep.

Gregor Johann Mendel

Austrian botanist 1822–84

Mendel was an Austrian monk who founded the science of genetics. He carried out experiments to see how characteristics are inherited by pea plants. By carefully selecting which plants bred with which, he discovered that characteristics are inherited in pairs. He also found that usually only one characteristic in each pair is shown in the phenotype. Mendel's work was a major breakthrough, but it went unnoticed for many years.

Genetic engineering

The artificial alteration of a living thing's genotype

In genetic engineering, scientists deliberately change genotypes by moving genes from one organism to another. By doing this, genetic engineers can give an organism characteristics that it does not normally have. Genetically engineered bacteria can be used to make substances such as human hormones ■. Doctors use the manufactured hormone insulin ■ to treat the disease diabetes.

See also

Theory of evolution

The Earth is populated by millions of different kinds of plants and animals. Where did they come from? People have been trying to answer this question for hundreds of years. Today, by looking at fossils, we can see that living things have slowly evolved from a few simple organisms.

A living fossil
This fish is a coelacanth. Scientists thought it had become extinct millions of years ago, until a living coelacanth was caught off Africa in 1938.

Evolution

A gradual genetic change in a group of living things

Evolution is the process by which living things change as one generation succeeds another. Evolution is extremely slow, so many generations have to pass before any change is noticeable.

Creationism

The belief that living things were all specially created

Some people do not believe that living things evolve. Instead, they think that they were specially created in the forms we see today. This idea is called creationism, or **creation science**.

Lamarckism

A theory of evolution put forward by Jean Baptiste de Lamarck

Lamarck ■ believed that living things evolved by developing characteristics during their lives, and then passing on these characteristics to their offspring. Scientists now know that these **acquired characteristics** cannot be inherited.

Darwinism

A theory of evolution put forward by Charles Darwin

Darwin's theory of evolution is based on three observations – that all living things vary, that they can pass on their characteristics, and that they are involved in a struggle for survival. In this struggle, some living things do better than others, and so survive to produce more offspring. As a result, their characteristics become more common in later generations. This process is called natural selection. Over many generations, natural selection produces change, or evolution.

Neo-Darwinism

The modern version of Darwin's theory of evolution

When Darwin devised his theory of evolution, scientists did not know about genetics ■. Since then, geneticists have made many discoveries that support Darwin's ideas. They have shown how variations ■ can appear in living things through mutations ■ in genes ■, and also how these variations can be passed on from one generation to another. Biochemists have discovered that evolution takes place in the molecules ■ that make up living things. These discoveries form the basis of neo-Darwinism.

Fossil

The remains of a living thing that have been preserved

Fossils are the remains of living things that have been turned into rock, or **mineralized**. They are usually made of the hard parts of organisms – for example, shells, bones, teeth, and wood. Fossils provide a **fossil record** that gives evidence of evolution.

Prehistoric fly
This fly has been preserved in copal, a fossilized tree sap, for millions of years.

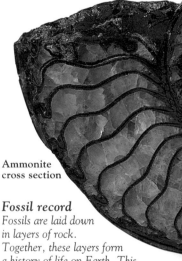

Ammonite cross section

Fossil record
Fossils are laid down in layers of rock. Together, these layers form a history of life on Earth. This ammonite became fossilized after it sank into sediment on the seabed long ago. By comparing ammonites from layers of rock of different ages, scientists can see how they evolved.

See also

Allele 42 • Gene 36 • Genetics 43
Lamarck 179 • Molecule 25
Mutation 43 • Species 48
Variation 42

Dodo
The dodo was hunted to extinction in the 18th century

Extinction

The permanent disappearance of a species

As living things evolve, some species ■ grow in numbers, while others decline. Eventually, a species may die out altogether, or become extinct. Species such as the **dodo** (*Raphus cucullatus*), a flightless bird, have become extinct during human history. The fossil record shows that many other species, such as ammonites, became extinct further back in time.

Natural selection

A weeding out process that favors the fittest forms of living things

According to Darwinian theory, natural selection is the main driving force behind evolution. In natural selection, living things that are badly suited or "fitted" to their environment are slowly "weeded out" because they fail to survive. The fittest survive better, and produce more offspring, thus passing on their genes to future generations.

Artificial selection

A deliberate form of selection used in breeding plants and animals

Crops, farm animals, and domestic pets have not evolved in the same way as living things in the wild. They have been produced by artificial selection. In this kind of selection, humans choose plants or animals that have particular characteristics. These individuals are then selected and bred to emphasize their desirable characteristics.

Gene pool

All the genes in a group or species

Evolution is hard to see, because visible changes build up very slowly. But evolution is happening all the time. Natural selection gradually alters the complete collection of genes, or gene pool, present in a species. Some alleles ■ become more common, while others dwindle and eventually disappear.

Struggle for survival

The competition for resources among living things

All living things have the potential to reproduce in vast numbers. For example, a single poppy can produce thousands of seeds, and some fish lay millions of eggs. But usually their numbers stay the same. This is because their offspring depend on limited resources, and have to struggle to survive. Many die from lack of food and space, or are eaten by predators, before they can reproduce. This struggle, or **competition**, allows natural selection to occur.

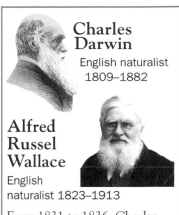

Charles Darwin

English naturalist 1809–1882

Alfred Russel Wallace

English naturalist 1823–1913

From 1831 to 1836, Charles Darwin sailed around the world on a survey ship called the *Beagle*. He filled many notebooks describing the hundreds of different plants and animals that he saw. On his return to England, Darwin became convinced that living things evolved, and he spent years developing a theory to explain how it had occurred. In 1858, Darwin was amazed to hear from Alfred Russel Wallace, who had come up with the same theory – natural selection. Darwin and Wallace became allies, and published their ideas at the same time. In 1859, Darwin put forward his theory of evolution in his famous book, *On The Origin of Species*.

Struggling to survive
This fossilized starfish is over 65 million years old, but looks similar to starfish today. Starfish have evolved very slowly during the struggle to survive.

Evolution in action

Through the process of evolution, living things become more suited to the world around them. They adapt to their environments by developing special features such as scented flowers, streamlined shapes, or bright warning colors.

Evolutionary partners
Flowers and insects often coevolve. A toadflax has evolved specially shaped flowers that dust bees with pollen as they crawl in to reach the nectar.

Honeybee

Toadflax

Adaptation

A process that makes living things better suited to their way of life

Through natural selection ▦, living things tend to become better suited, or adapted, to the world around them. Adaptation does not affect only shape, size, and color, it can also affect behavior ▦ or internal processes. The word "adaptation" can also refer to any feature that helps a living thing survive.

Adaptive radiation

The evolution of many different species from a single species

During adaptive radiation, a single species ▦ gives rise to a variety of new species that have different ways of life. Adaptive radiation is often triggered when a species moves to a new area, or when its competitors decline in numbers. Darwin's finches ▦ evolved through a burst of adaptive radiation.

Coevolution

A form of evolution in which living things affect each other's adaptations

Many plants have come to depend on particular species of animals for pollination ▦. Their flowers are shaped so that only certain kinds of animal can pollinate them. In turn, the animals depend on the plants for food, and often have special mouthparts to enable them to feed in this way. This is an example of coevolution, because the plants and animals have evolved together.

Convergent evolution

The evolution of similar characteristics in unrelated living things

A **humpback whale** (*Megaptera novaeanglia*) and a **whale shark** (*Rhincodon typus*) look almost the same, but inside they are different – a whale is a mammal, and a shark is a fish. They look alike because natural selection produces similar characteristics to suit similar ways of life.

Preadaptation

An adaptation for one way of life that is also useful for another

Evolutionary adaptations often have unexpected uses. For example, **purple martins** (*Delichon urbica*) once nested on cliffs, but when humans built houses, the martins used their cliff-nesting skills to make homes under the eaves of roofs. Their behavior is the result of preadaptation.

Baby gorilla

Polymorphic

Existing in more than one form

Many species have several forms that exist alongside each other. For example, the **banded snail** (*Cepaea nemoralis*) has several different shell patterns, in the same way humans have several different blood groups ▪. These are examples of polymorphism, which means "many forms." In a polymorphic species, natural selection maintains a balance between the different forms.

Polymorphic plant
The crown anemone is an example of a polymorphic species. Its flowers can be red, purple, or white.

Human baby

Mimic

A living thing that imitates another

Many harmless animals have evolved so they look or behave like ones that are dangerous. This is an example of **mimicry**. Predators cannot distinguish between a mimic and the animal that it copies, so they avoid both.

Parallel evolution

Similar evolutionary changes in related living things

In parallel evolution, related species evolve in similar ways to accommodate similar lifestyles. Bees and wasps ▪ both demonstrate parallel evolution, because they have both evolved group, or social ▪, ways of life.

Molecular evolution

Evolutionary changes in individual molecules

Living things evolve because their DNA ▪ slowly changes. DNA controls the making of proteins ▪, therefore proteins also change as one generation follows another. Biochemists can tell how closely different species are related by looking at the structure of their DNA, or of the protein molecules ▪ that they have in common.

Monarch

Viceroy

Natural mimic
The harmless viceroy butterfly mimics the colors of the poisonous monarch.

Warning coloration

Colors that warn of danger

Wasps have evolved yellow and black markings as a signal to other animals. The colors show predators that the wasp has a dangerous sting and should not be attacked. Many other animals have similar warning coloration. It shows potential enemies that they are dangerous, or that they taste unpleasant.

Industrial melanism

An evolutionary adaptation triggered by smoky air

Industrial melanism is an example of evolution in action. In places with smoky air, dark forms of the **peppered moth** (*Biston betularia*) become more common than light gray ones. The dark moths are better camouflaged against their sooty background, so they are less likely to be spotted and eaten by birds. This means the dark moths reproduce in greater numbers.

Molecular evidence
Biochemical evidence shows that of all the animals in the Animal Kingdom, the great apes are most closely related to humans.

The origin of species

Biologists have classified over 2 million species of living things, and there are many more still waiting to be discovered. This variety of different species is the result of evolution. As time goes by, the evolutionary process causes some species to disappear, and new ones to develop.

Plant hybrid
Wheat is a plant hybrid that arose naturally, but was then improved by humans to produce high-yielding crops.

Species

A group of living things that can breed together in the wild

A species is a group of living things in the natural world. In the wild, the members of a species breed only with other members of the same species. In classification ▪, every species has a scientific name ▪. **African elephants** (*Loxodonta africana*), **bristlecone pines** (*Pinus longaeva*), and **swallows** (*Hirundo rustica*), are examples of species. The term species can be singular or plural.

Speciation

The evolution of new species

Species slowly change through the process of evolution ▪. Speciation occurs when a group within a species becomes reproductively isolated. This means that its members no longer interbreed freely with all the other members of the species. As time goes by, the members of the new group become more and more different. Eventually, they are unable to breed with their relatives, and so a new species is formed.

Reproductive isolation

A geographical or biological barrier that prevents interbreeding

Different species, or groups within a species, can be kept apart in a variety of ways. Often they are **geographically isolated**, which means that they live in different places and do not meet. Even if they can meet, they may be **biologically isolated**. This means they may have different numbers of chromosomes ▪, or different ways of breeding.

Isolated tortoises
In the Galápagos Islands, giant tortoises living on different islands have developed very different shell shapes.

Subspecies

A group within a species that has recognizable characteristics

In any one species, there is variation ▪ between individuals. Sometimes, similar variations are shown by a whole **population**, or members of a species that share the same area. If the variations are distinct, the population is called a subspecies. A subspecies is often the first step in the evolution of a new species.

Hybrid

The offspring of parents from two different species

Occasionally, parents from different species crossbreed to produce offspring. The result is called a hybrid. Hybrids can occur in nature, but often they are sterile or unable to reproduce. Different species of plant or animal are often crossbred by humans to produce a combination of particular features. Farmers have developed varieties of wheat that can resist certain diseases and also produce good bread.

Microevolution

Small-scale evolutionary changes

Microevolution is the underlying process of evolution. It makes small changes in a species as one generation succeeds another.

Macroevolution

Major evolutionary changes that create new species

Macroevolution happens very slowly. It involves changes that are important enough to allow new species to develop.

Darwin's finches

A group of finch species found on the Galápagos Islands

The 13 species of finches found on the Galápagos Islands played an important part in the development of Darwin's ■ theory of evolution. Darwin observed the finches when he visited the islands in 1832. He later realized that they must all have evolved from a common ancestor that came to the islands from South America. The original finch probably ate seeds, but its descendants have evolved a variety of ways of life. Some are insect eaters, while others feed on seeds. The way in which the finches have evolved is an example of adaptive radiation ■.

South America

Galápagos Islands

The first finches
At some point in the past, a flock of finches managed to reach the Galápagos Islands from the South American mainland, more than 546 miles (880 kilometers) away.

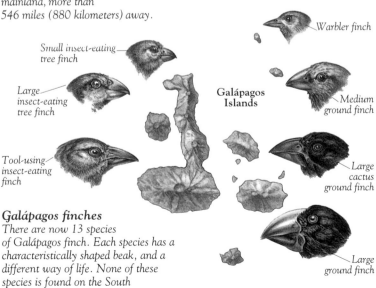

Small insect-eating tree finch

Large insect-eating tree finch

Tool-using insect-eating finch

Warbler finch

Galápagos Islands

Medium ground finch

Large cactus ground finch

Large ground finch

Galápagos finches
There are now 13 species of Galápagos finch. Each species has a characteristically shaped beak, and a different way of life. None of these species is found on the South American mainland.

Missing link

A species that links two groups of living things

Fossils ■ form a sort of history book of evolution. However, it is a book with many missing pages. Occasionally, an important fossil is unearthed, showing how a new group of living things developed from a species that already existed. The fossil provides the "missing link" in our knowledge of the evolutionary process. *Archaeopteryx* is an example of this. It is the fossil of a dinosaur ■ that links reptiles to birds.

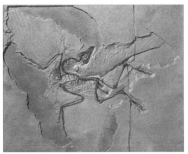

Missing evidence
Archaeopteryx is the fossilized skeleton of a reptilelike bird, which may have been a relative or the ancestor of modern-day birds. It is evidence that birds may have evolved from reptiles.

Stephen Jay Gould

American paleontologist born 1942

Stephen Jay Gould has spent much of his career studying fossils to see what they tell us about evolution. He is one of the leading supporters of the theory of punctuated equilibrium. This is the idea that a large number of new species appear in sudden bursts. Darwin also suggested this possibility and, since Darwin's time, new fossils have been discovered that seem to support this theory. Gould has written many books on evolution. They explain how this process of change affects everything in the natural world, including ourselves.

Gradualism

The theory that evolution occurs slowly and smoothly

Since Darwinism ■ became widely accepted, biologists have wondered how fast evolution takes place. Some believe that it happens at an even rate, with new species appearing gradually as time goes by. This theory is called gradualism.

Punctuated equilibrium

The theory that evolution can happen in sudden bursts

Parts of the fossil record seem to show that species change suddenly, rather than gradually. Some biologists believe this is the normal way in which evolution works. This idea is called punctuated equilibrium, because each species experiences a period of stability, broken by a sudden evolutionary change.

The history of life

The Earth has existed for about 4.5 billion years. The first living things probably appeared about 3.8 billion years ago. Since that time, many life forms have flourished and disappeared, leaving fossils as evidence.

Geological time scale

A timetable of the Earth's history

Geologists divide the Earth's history into four different time spans called **eons**, **eras**, **periods**, and **epochs**. Eons are the longest, and epochs the shortest. Each interval marks a particular stage in our planet's history.

Stratum

A distinct band of rock

A stratum (plural **strata**) is like a layer in a sandwich. It is formed by a process called **sedimentation**. During sedimentation, particles of sand and mud sink to the bottom of a river, lake, or seabed. As the sediment builds up, the deepest layers are squashed together to make rock. Rock strata provide a calendar of the Earth's history. Scientists can date a rock stratum by the fossils ■ embedded within it.

The fossil record

Fossils show that life underwent an explosion of diversity about 500 million years ago. Although living things first appeared long before this time, they were soft-bodied and left few traces of their existence.

bya = billions of years ago
mya = millions of years ago

Fossil of a bryozoan colony from the Ordovician Period.

Fossil of Sagenocrinites, a sea lily from the Silurian Period.

Fossilized bark of Lepidodendron, a giant club moss from the Carboniferous Period.

Fossil of Procynosuchus, a mammal-like reptile from the late Permian Period.

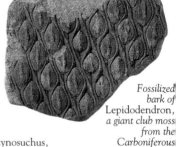

Fossil of Archaeopteryx, the earliest known bird, from the Jurassic Period.

Fossilized shell of an ammonite. Ammonites first appeared over 500 mya, but died out at the end of the Cretaceous Period.

Jaw bone of Phiomia, an elephant-like mammal from the Tertiary Period.

Skull of Glyptodon, a giant armadillo from the Quaternary Period.

Fossilized colony of Collenia, a Precambrian alga.

PRECAMBRIAN EON

Archaean Era 4.5–2.5 bya
The first forms of life appeared about 3.8 billion years ago. These had single cells.

• Protozoic Era 2.5 bya–570 mya
Simple plants and animals appear.

Fossil of Xystridura, a trilobite from the Cambrian Period.

PALEOZOIC ERA

Cambrian Period 570–505 mya
Invertebrates are common in the seas. Trilobites appear.

Ordovician Period 505–438 mya
Mollusks and crustaceans appear, along with early fish-like vertebrates without jaws.

Silurian Period 438–408 mya
Land plants evolve. Fish with jaws appear. Coral reefs flourish in the seas.

Devonian Period 408–360 mya
The first insects and amphibians appear on land. Vascular plants form forests.

Fossil of Pteraspis, a fish from the Devonian Period.

Carboniferous Period 360–286 mya
Vast forests flourish that will form coal. The first reptiles evolve from amphibians.

Permian Period 286–245 mya
Reptiles diversify. Ferns and conifers become widespread. Period ends with the greatest mass extinction ever known.

Skull and backbone of Diplocaulus, an amphibian from the Permian Period.

MESOZOIC ERA The Age of Reptiles

Triassic Period 245–208 mya
Dinosaurs and mammals appear. Conifers and ferns form forests.

Jurassic Period 208–144 mya
Dinosaurs flourish. Archaeopteryx, the earliest known bird, evolves from reptiles.

Cretaceous Period 144–65 mya
Flowering plants appear. Dinosaurs continue to flourish. Period ends with a catastrophic mass extinction.

Skull of Triceratops, a dinosaur from the Cretaceous Period.

Ice age

A period of time in which polar ice becomes extensive

In the past, the Earth's climate has often become so cold that ice from the poles and mountains has spread over large areas of land. This is called an ice age, and it can last for over a million years. Ice ages are made up of several **glaciations**, in which the ice advances and then retreats. The last glaciation reached its peak about 18,000 years ago.

Mass extinction

The sudden disappearance of a wide variety of species

During the Earth's history, large numbers of species have become extinct in relatively short spaces of time. The greatest mass extinction was the **Permo-Triassic Crisis**, which occurred about 245 million years ago. About 65 million years ago, the dinosaurs died out in the **Cretaceous Extinction**. No one knows what caused these events, but some scientists think the Cretaceous Extinction followed a climate change created by the impact of a meteorite.

See also

Dinosaur 109 • Extinction 45
Fossil 44 • Species 48

CENOZOIC ERA The Age of Mammals

Tertiary Period 65–1.8 mya
Mammals diversify. Primates evolve. The first hominid appears.

Quaternary Period 1.8 mya–present
Many mammals, such as the mammoth and sabre-toothed tiger, die out during repeated ice ages. Homo sapiens appears, and the human population starts to expand.

Skull of Homo erectus from the Quaternary Period.

The origin of life

How did life on Earth begin? Many scientists believe that living things originally came from nonliving chemicals. Over millions of years, random chemical reactions created compounds that could copy themselves. Once this had happened, a form of evolution began that eventually led to the first real life.

The first sign of life?
This glass apparatus contains a mixture of gases that simulate the atmosphere of the early Earth. Sparks of electricity, simulating lightning, make the gases combine to form the complex molecules typical of all living things.

Spontaneous generation

The theory that living things can be generated from nonliving things

In the past, people thought that complete living things appeared from nonliving substances. For example, they thought that meat somehow created, or generated, the maggots that appeared in it when it was left alone. In 1668, this idea received a serious setback. Francesco Redi ■ showed that maggots would not appear in meat if flies could not lay their eggs on it. Later, Lazzaro Spallanzani and Louis Pasteur ■ both carried out experiments that provided more evidence against the theory of spontaneous generation.

Biogenesis

The theory that all life now comes from existing life

Today, every living thing on Earth is the offspring of another living thing. But where did the first life form come from? If you could wind back the clock of life, you would see living things gradually becoming simpler. Many scientists now believe that the first life form was simple enough to have evolved ■ from nonliving chemicals.

Abiotic synthesis

A process that makes organic compounds without the help of living things

All living things are made up of organic compounds ■, which are compounds that contain carbon ■. Experiments show that organic compounds may originally have appeared through abiotic synthesis. This is a process of random chemical reactions ■. Abiotic synthesis requires special conditions before it can work. It needs a large supply of energy, such as lightning, and a reducing atmosphere. These conditions probably existed on Earth billions of years ago.

Reducing atmosphere

An atmosphere that contains hydrogen, but no oxygen

For its first billion years, the Earth's atmosphere contained no oxygen. In chemical terms, it was a "reducing" mixture. This means that it could react with substances by adding hydrogen atoms ■ to them. Reactions like this may have formed the first organic compounds from simple chemicals such as carbon. The presence of oxygen in the air today means that these reactions can no longer happen.

Harold Urey
American chemist 1893–1981

Stanley Miller
American chemist born 1930

Harold Urey was interested in how the Earth formed, and which gases were present in its early atmosphere. In 1952, he suggested that substances in the atmosphere may have reacted randomly to form the chemical building blocks of life. His pupil, Stanley Miller, tested this idea using sealed apparatus. He made a mixture of gases to imitate the early atmosphere. He then flashed an electric spark through the gases, to simulate lightning, over water, to simulate the early sea. After a week, he

discovered that amino acids ■ had been formed. Miller's work is an example of abiotic synthesis.

Stanley Miller

Primeval soup

The watery mixture of chemicals in the seas of the early Earth

In the Earth's early history, many chemicals were released by volcanic eruptions. Some of these chemicals became part of the atmosphere, while others were washed into the seas. The chemical-rich seawater formed a mixture that is often called "primeval soup." This watery mixture could have become more concentrated in some places, such as rock pools along the shore. Another source of chemicals would have been volcanic vents, deep on the seabed. Life may have originated in environments such as these.

Chemical evolution

A gradual change in chemical compounds

A vital step in the origin of life would have been the chance appearance of chemical compounds that could copy themselves, or replicate ■. Once these compounds existed, scientists believe that they would have evolved, much like living things do now. As raw materials were used up, there would have been a struggle for survival ■. The most successful chemical compounds would have become more common, paving the way toward living things.

See also

Microfossils

Microscopic fossils

The first forms of life were tiny prokaryotic cells ■. Although they did not have any hard parts, they have left traces in rocks. Microscopic fossils ■ have been found in rocks that are over 3 billion years old.

Early fossils
Stromatolite fossils like this provide evidence of the earliest forms of life on Earth – microorganisms.

Modern stromatolites
Stromatolites still exist today. They are formed by millions of microorganisms. These stromatolites are in Australia.

Stromatolite

A rocklike structure produced by microorganisms

Stromatolites are dome-shaped layers of sediment that are built up very slowly by cyanobacteria ■. They form hard deposits that fossilize easily. Fossil stromatolites are the earliest evidence of life on Earth. Some, from Western Australia, are 3.5 billion years old.

Abbé Lazzaro Spallanzani

Italian biologist
1729–99

Spallanzani helped show that living things are always produced by other living things. He knew about the existence of microorganisms ■, and he carried out a number of experiments to see how they developed in soup, or broth. He sealed the broth in a container, then heated it, so that any microorganisms were killed. Spallanzani found that no microorganisms appeared unless the container was opened to the air. This showed that the theory of spontaneous generation was incorrect.

Exobiology

The study of possible life beyond Earth

If life arose on Earth by chance, it may well have done so in other places in the Universe. Scientists who study planets that may support life are **exobiologists**.

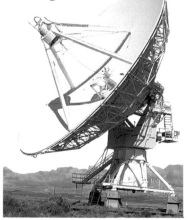

Looking for extraterrestrial life
Exobiologists use radiotelescopes to search for signs of life elsewhere in our galaxy, or even beyond it.

Human evolution

Humans have existed for over a million years, but in the history of living things, our species is relatively new. Before we evolved, several humanlike species existed. Scientists are still trying to piece together where and how they lived, and which ones were our ancestors.

Sloping skull

Australopithecine
Although the australopithecines walked upright like modern humans, the brains of these apelike early hominids were only a quarter the size of ours.

Human evolution

The process by which the human species has developed

Like all living things, humans have been shaped by evolution ■. **Paleoanthropology** is the study of the fossils ■ of our extinct ■ ancestors. **Paleoanthropologists** are scientists who try to piece together fossil clues to discover how humans evolved.

Hominid

A family of primates that includes humans and the immediate ancestors of humans

Humans belong to a family ■ of primates ■ called hominids. Unlike other primates, such as the apes ■, hominids have large brains and walk on two legs. Within the hominid family, humans form part of a smaller group, or genus ■, called *Homo*. The genus *Homo* includes humans and our extinct ancestors. The first hominids appeared on Earth about 3 to 4 million years ago.

Chimpanzee
The chimpanzees and other apes have sloping skulls and protruding jaws.

Bipedal locomotion

Walking on two legs

An important step in the evolution of hominids took place when they began to stand upright and walk on two legs. It left their hands free to become specially adapted for gripping things, which eventually enabled them to make simple tools.

The first steps
These fossilized footprints were left in damp volcanic ash by three hominids, nearly 4 million years ago. Mary Leakey's team unearthed them in Africa in 1977.

Hominoid

A superfamily of primates that includes the hominids and apes

The hominoids make up a large superfamily of primates. This classification group ■ includes the hominids and also animals that are like hominids, but are not directly related, such as the great apes ■. Unlike most other primates, hominoids have large heads and no tails. They also have **opposable thumbs**, which are mobile thumbs that can be pressed against the fingers to grip tools and objects. Fossil evidence shows that hominoids have existed for over 15 million years.

Large, protruding jaws

Australopithecines

A genus of early hominids known from fossils found in Africa

Australopithecines belong to the genus *Australopithecus*, and are the oldest hominids discovered by paleoanthropologists. Their name means "southern ape," because the first fossil was found in South Africa, in 1924. Australopithecines lived between at least 4 million and 1 million years ago. They walked on two legs, but had small brains. Paleoanthropologists have now found several kinds of australopithecine, but they are unsure which of them, if any, are the direct ancestors of humans.

Lucy

A fossilized australopithecine found in Africa in 1974

"Lucy" is the fossilized skeleton of a female australopithecine. She died over 3 million years ago in what is now part of Africa. When paleoanthropologists discovered parts of her fossilized skeleton, they were very excited. The skeleton was about 40 percent complete, which is very unusual for a fossil of this great age. It showed that Lucy had walked on two legs, even though she had a small brain. Before this, paleoanthropologists thought that hominids developed large brains before they walked upright.

Homo

The genus that includes the human species and the immediate ancestors of humans

The first members of the genus *Homo* probably appeared about 2 million years ago. Unlike the australopithecines, they had large brains. The genus includes several species ▮, but all except humans have become extinct. Some paleoanthropologists believe that the earliest species was **Homo habilis**, or "handy man." They have found fossils and stone tools belonging to *Homo habilis* in East Africa. **Homo erectus**, or "upright man," lived more recently, between 1.5 and 0.5 million years ago. Fossils of *Homo erectus* have been found in Southeast Asia as well as Africa.

Homo sapiens

The current form of the human species

The modern human race belongs to the species *Homo sapiens*, which means "wise man." This species appeared about 300,000 years ago, and eventually replaced *Homo erectus*. Originally, there were two forms of *Homo sapiens*, but one of them, Neanderthal Man, died out.

Domed skull

Homo sapiens
This skull is from a modern human. Compared with other hominoids, modern humans have fairly flat faces and high domed skulls.

Flint hand axe

Making tools
Early humans learned how to make tools by chipping away at stones. In some parts of East Africa, the ground is littered with hand axes like this one, which is about 200,000 years old.

Neanderthal Man

A form of *Homo sapiens* that died out about 30,000 years ago

Neanderthal Man first appeared about 200,000 years ago. Their brains were about the same size as ours, or even a little bigger, but they had differently shaped heads with heavy ridges over the eyes. "Neanderthalers" may have interbred with our ancestors, or they may have just died out.

Sloping skull

Bony crest above eyes

Neanderthal Man
Neanderthal remains have been found in Africa, Europe, and Asia. This extinct form of Homo sapiens *looked similar to modern humans. They made many tools, and sometimes buried their dead in special graves.*

Louis Leakey

British paleoanthropologist 1903–1972

Mary Leakey

British paleoanthropologist born 1913

Richard Leakey

Kenyan paleoanthropologist born 1944

In the 1920s and 1930s, Louis Leakey discovered a range of hominid fossils and stone tools in East Africa. He and his wife Mary went on to make many more important discoveries, including the fossils of several australopithecines and *Homo* species. In 1977, Mary Leakey made a sensational discovery – a set of preserved footprints, which were created nearly 4 million years ago. Their son, Richard Leakey, has also made major fossil discoveries.

Eve hypothesis

The proposal that all modern humans are the descendants of a single woman

Studies of mitochondrial DNA ▮ in modern humans suggest that hominids originated in Africa, and then spread from there to many parts of the world. According to the Eve hypothesis, modern humans are descendants of one woman who lived in Africa about 200,000 years ago.

See also

Classification

The natural world contains a huge variety of living things, from giant whales to microscopic bacteria. Biologists use a system of classification to make sense of this variety. Classification identifies different species and shows how they are related to one another through evolution.

Classification

A way of identifying and grouping living things

Biologists classify living things by looking at their similarities and differences. They can then arrange them in groups according to their characteristics. When a form of life is classified, biologists give it a two-part scientific name. This name identifies it and shows which group it belongs to in the living world.

Classification scheme for the serval

Kingdom *Animalia*
Phylum *Chordata*
Class *Mammalia*
Order *Carnivora*
Family *Felidae*
Genus *Felis*
Species *serval*

Classifying a wild cat
The serval, Felis serval, is classified into the groups shown above.

Classification group

A category used in classification

In classification, living things are sorted into groups. The groups are called **taxons** and are ranged in order of size. The smallest complete group is a species ■. A **genus** (plural **genera**) contains one or more closely related species, and a **family** contains one or more genera. Families are grouped into **orders**, and orders into **classes**. A **phylum** (plural **phyla**) contains one or more classes, and the biggest group of all, a **kingdom**, contains several phyla. In the plant kingdom, a phylum is called a **division**. Extra groups, such as **superfamily** or **subphylum**, are also used. Of all these groups, only a species actually exists in nature. The rest have been devised to show how different species are related.

Scientific name

A name that identifies a species

A scientific name identifies one species from the many millions on Earth. It is sometimes called a **binomial**, because it has two parts. For example, the scientific name for the **house sparrow** is *Passer domesticus*. The first part is the **generic name**, which identifies the genus, or group of species, to which the sparrow belongs. The second part is the **specific name**, which identifies one particular species of sparrow. Such scientific names, from Latin or Greek, are used by scientists whatever language they speak.

Common name

An everyday name for a species

A common name, such as "house sparrow" or "sunflower," is an everyday name for a living thing. A common name usually differs from one language to another.

Seabird relatives
The four seabirds, below, belong to the same genus, Sula, but each one belongs to a different species. They all feed by diving for fish, but they have different sizes and markings, and most live in different parts of the world.

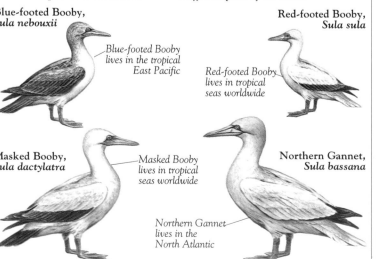

Blue-footed Booby, *Sula nebouxii*
— *Blue-footed Booby lives in the tropical East Pacific*

Red-footed Booby, *Sula sula*
Red-footed Booby lives in tropical seas worldwide

Masked Booby, *Sula dactylatra*
— *Masked Booby lives in tropical seas worldwide*

Northern Gannet, *Sula bassana*
Northern Gannet lives in the North Atlantic

Five Kingdoms System

A commonly accepted system of classification

When biologists first developed the system of classification, they used just two kingdoms – plants and animals. Later on, they had to add more kingdoms to make room for other forms of life that did not really belong in either the plant or the animal kingdom. Today, most systems of classification are based on five kingdoms – monerans, protists, fungi, plants, and animals.

Plants

A group of multi-celled organisms that make their own food by photosynthesis

Plants, which make up the **Kingdom Plantae**, live by photosynthesis ▪. During this process, they harness the energy in sunlight and use it to convert simple substances into food. The plant kingdom contains species that grow flowers and form seeds, as well as simpler species that do not. The plant kingdom contains over 400,000 species.

Animals

A group of multi-celled organisms that live by taking in food

Animals form the **Kingdom Animalia**. They live by eating food. Every animal can move at least part of its body, although some animals spend their whole life in one place. The largest animals are the vertebrates ▪, which have backbones. However, 97 percent of animals are invertebrates ▪, with no backbone. The animal kingdom contains over two million species.

FUNGI

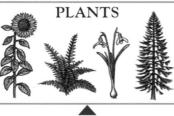

PLANTS

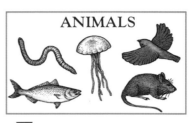

ANIMALS

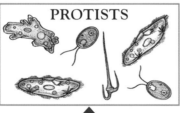

PROTISTS

Divided kingdoms
The five kingdoms can be divided into two groups. The first group contains the monerans, which have simple cells. The other four kingdoms make up the second group, which contains living things that have complex cells.

The evolution of the kingdoms
The single-celled monerans are the oldest forms of life. The more complex living things that make up the other four kingdoms probably evolved from the monerans, but scientists are not sure exactly how this happened.

Fungi

A group of organisms, mostly multi-celled, that live by absorbing food

Fungi make up the **Kingdom Fungi**. They sometimes look like plants, but they live in a very different way. A fungus has no leaves. Instead of using sunlight to make food, it absorbs simple food substances from living or dead matter. The kingdom contains about 100,000 species.

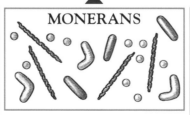

MONERANS

Monerans

A group of single-celled organisms that do not have a nucleus

Monerans make up the **Kingdom Monera**. They are microscopic life forms made of simple, or prokaryotic cells ▪, which do not contain a nucleus. This kingdom includes bacteria ▪, and also cyanobacteria ▪. Monerans were the first forms of life to evolve on Earth. The kingdom contains about 4,000 species.

Protists

A group of single-celled plantlike or animal-like organisms

Protists make up the **Kingdom Protista**. They have complex, or eukaryotic cells ▪. Protists include animal-like forms, often called protozoa ▪, as well as plantlike organisms. Although protists usually consist of a single cell ▪, there is often no clear division between single-celled and multi-celled life forms. For example, many algae ▪ live as single cells, but have close relatives that live together and look like plants. Many biologists include all algae in this kingdom, but others include only single-celled species. The kingdom contains at least 50,000 species.

Taxonomy

Classifying living things is an exact science. Before deciding which species a plant or animal belongs to, biologists have to identify certain key characteristics. Once they have done this, they can see how the plant or animal fits into the natural world, and also trace its evolution.

Quick classification
Key characteristics allow a taxonomist to classify each of these insects quickly.

Taxonomy

The science of classifying living things

Taxonomists are scientists who specialize in classification ■. They identify and name the vast array of organisms in the living world by looking carefully at their characteristics. They also show how species ■ are thought to be linked through evolution ■.

Systematics

The study of the relationships between living things

In systematics, biologists try to chart the path of evolution to discover how different forms of life have come about. They do this by examining living things, as well as the remains of organisms that have been preserved as fossils ■.

Phylogeny

The evolutionary history of a particular group of living things

A phylogeny shows how the different species in a group, such as reptiles ■, are thought to be linked through evolution. It can be shown in a diagram called an **evolutionary tree**. The branches of the tree link each species with its ancestors, and also with its descendants, if it has any.

A phylogeny of dinosaurs
This diagram shows how dinosaurs are thought to be linked through evolution. The two main branches, or clades, are based on the shape of the hip bones, an important ancestral characteristic in dinosaur classification. Paradoxically, birds are descended from lizard-hipped dinosaurs.

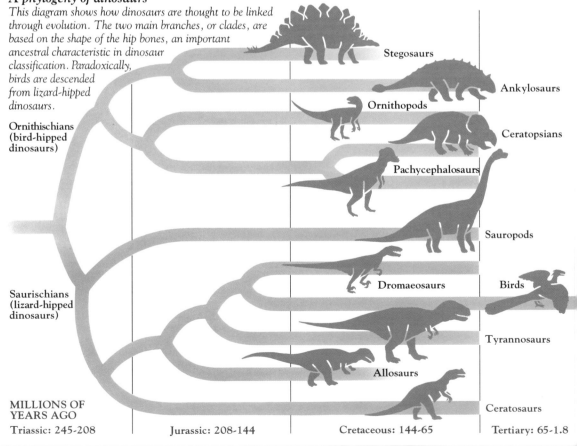

Stegosaurs

Ankylosaurs

Ornithopods

Ceratopsians

Pachycephalosaurs

Ornithischians (bird-hipped dinosaurs)

Sauropods

Dromaeosaurs

Birds

Saurischians (lizard-hipped dinosaurs)

Tyrannosaurs

Allosaurs

MILLIONS OF YEARS AGO

Ceratosaurs

Triassic: 245-208 | Jurassic: 208-144 | Cretaceous: 144-65 | Tertiary: 65-1.8

Clade

A group of living things that includes a single shared ancestor

During the process of evolution, a single species sometimes gives rise to a whole new collection of species. In taxonomy, the original species and its descendants make up a clade. Darwin's finches ■ and their shared ancestor make up a typical clade.

Grade

A level of development in evolution

Many groups of living things contain species that are related, but do not share a single ancestor. This kind of group is called a grade. The species in a grade have the same level of development, but they have reached it by slightly different routes. Reptiles are an example of a grade. Although they are similar, they have evolved from more than one ancestor.

Ancestral characteristic

A characteristic handed on by an ancestral species

An ancestral characteristic is a characteristic that has been handed on to a group of species by their shared ancestor. For example, feathers ■ are an ancestral characteristic of birds ■. Ancestral characteristics work like signposts. Because they are shared by all the members of a group, they help biologists to classify different species.

See also

Derived characteristic

A recently developed characteristic

Every living thing has a mixture of ancestral characteristics and more recent characteristics that are derived from them. For example, a flying fish has a backbone ■, gills ■, and fins like all other fish ■. These are ancestral characteristics. But it also has an important derived characteristic. Some of its fins have become enlarged and act as wings, which enable the fish to glide over the water.

Homologous structure

A structure found in different species that has the same evolutionary origin

Homologous structures are structures that have evolved from the same starting point. They may look different, but they have the same underlying plan. Homologous structures provide evidence that two species have evolved from a shared ancestor. For example, bats' wings and human arms are homologous structures that evolved from the limbs of a shared ancestor.

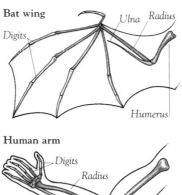

Bat wing — Ulna, Radius, Digits, Humerus

Human arm — Digits, Radius, Ulna, Humerus

Matching bones
A bat's wing and a human arm are homologous structures. Although they appear different on the outside, they are both built from the same set of bones.

Carolus Linnaeus

Swedish botanist
1707–78

Carolus Linnaeus trained as a doctor, but he spent much of his life studying plants. He traveled throughout Europe and compiled several books listing the plants and animals he came across. In order to classify them, Linnaeus devised a system of two-part, or binomial, scientific names ■. He made up these names to save time, because the scientific names of his day could be over 10 words long. Linnaeus's system of classification is still used by biologists today.

Analogous structure

A structure found in different species with the same function, but a different evolutionary origin

A tortoise and a snail both have hard shells that protect them from predators. Yet, although their shells do the same job, they are built quite differently. They are examples of analogous structures. They seem similar, but they have evolved in different ways.

Key

A way of identifying living things by examining their characteristics

A key is a series of questions designed to help identify a plant or animal. Each question asks about one important characteristic of the species, and each answer narrows down the range of species to which it may belong. At the end of the questionnaire, if all the questions have been answered correctly, the species will be identified.

Bacteria & viruses

Bacteria live everywhere, but they are so small that you can only see them with a microscope. Your body contains about 100,000 billion of these tiny life forms. It is also home to viruses – strange bundles of chemicals that can only reproduce with the help of living cells.

Bacteria

A group of microscopic, single-celled organisms

Bacteria (singular **bacterium**) are the most abundant living things on Earth. They belong to the moneran ▪ kingdom. Each bacterium consists of a single cell ▪, which is strengthened by a tough cell wall ▪. The cell is prokaryotic ▪, which means that it has no nucleus ▪ or complex cell organelles ▪. Bacteria live in many different ways. Some species ▪ feed on dead matter and play an important part in the recycling of nutrients. Others feed on living things. These bacteria are often called **germs**, and sometimes cause diseases ▪. Many species of bacteria live in groups called colonies ▪, and can often be identified by the shape and color of the colony.

Microorganism

Any form of life too small to be seen without a microscope

Bacteria are just some of the many forms of life that are too small for us to see. Other kinds include protozoa ▪, single-celled algae ▪, and some fungi ▪. These microscopic organisms are known as microorganisms or **microbes**. Viruses are often called microorganisms, even though they are not usually classified as living things.

Infection

A growth of microorganisms in something living or dead

If a microorganism settles where there is warmth and a good supply of food, it can grow and reproduce very quickly. The result is an infection. In the human body, this can produce infectious diseases such as tuberculosis, cholera, and typhoid. However, infections are not always harmful. Cheese and yogurt are made by infecting milk with bacteria.

Infectious sneezes
Many diseases are spread by sneezing. Infectious microorganisms are present in saliva, and sneezing propels tiny droplets of saliva into the air, where they may be breathed in by another person.

Bacillus

A rod-shaped bacterium

Bacilli

Bacteria have characteristic shapes that help scientists to identify them. A bacillus (plural **bacilli**) is a straight, rod-shaped bacterium that is about three or four times longer than it is wide. One species of bacillus, *Bacillus anthracis*, causes the cattle disease **anthrax**.

Coccus

A round bacterium

Cocci

A bacterium with a round shape is called a coccus (plural **cocci**). In some species of coccus, the cells are scattered a short distance apart. In others, such as **diplococcus**, they are arranged in pairs. **Streptococcus** is a kind of bacteria that forms chains. There are many species of coccus on and in the human body. *Streptococcus mutans* lives in the mouth and is one of the bacteria that cause tooth decay.

Bacillus

Plasma membrane
Cell wall
Nucleoid region
Ribosome
Pili

Spiral bacterium

A coiled bacterium

There are several kinds of spiral bacteria. **Spirochaete** bacteria have twisted cells that look like corkscrews. They spin around to move through liquids. Others, called **vibrioids**, have cells shaped like commas.

Spiral bacteria

Cyanobacteria

A group of bacteria that make their own food by photosynthesis

Cyanobacteria, or **blue-green algae**, live by photosynthesis ■. They use energy from the Sun to change simple substances into food. Most cyanobacteria live in water, and some species have floats that keep them near the surface. Cyanobacteria play an important part in nitrogen fixation ■. They collect nitrogen from the air and turn it into a form that plants can use.

Capsule

Flagellum

Folded plasma membrane

Bacterial cell
This rod-shaped bacterium, or bacillus, is surrounded by a cell wall, and also by a tough outer layer called a capsule. Tiny hairlike threads, called pili, help glue it to the surface of its food, or to other cells.

Binary fission

A kind of reproduction that involves splitting in two

Bacteria usually reproduce by splitting in two, to make a pair of identical cells. In the right conditions, they can do this about once every 20 minutes. In theory, a single bacterium could produce nearly 5,000 billion billion offspring in 24 hours. In reality, a shortage of food usually prevents this from happening.

Endospore

A resting stage formed by some bacteria against difficult conditions

An endospore is a tough cell that can withstand harsh conditions. Some can survive in boiling water for several hours. An endospore may remain sleeping, or **dormant**, for thousands of years until conditions become favorable again. Then it will begin to grow, or germinate ■.

Virus

A package of chemicals that infects a living cell

A virus consists of a length of nucleic acid ■ surrounded by a protein coat, called a **capsid**. In some viruses, the capsid is enclosed by a covering called an **envelope**. Viruses are far smaller than cells. They are not usually classified as living organisms because they cannot grow and reproduce on their own. Instead, a virus relies on a living host ■ cell to help it make copies of itself.

Cold virus
Viruses cause many diseases in plants and animals. The virus shown above causes the common cold in humans.

Viral replication

A form of viral reproduction

When a virus infects a cell, its nucleic acid takes over the cell's chemical reactions, or metabolism ■. The virus's genes ■ instruct the cell to produce all the parts needed to form new viruses. When the replica viruses have been assembled, they usually break out of the cell.

Robert Koch

German bacteriologist 1843–1910

Robert Koch was the first scientist to prove that bacteria cause diseases. In 1876, he isolated the bacteria that produce the cattle disease anthrax, and then grew them in a laboratory. He found that when he infected healthy cattle with the laboratory bacteria, the cattle developed the disease. In 1882, Koch discovered the bacillus that causes tuberculosis, which is sometimes called **Koch's bacillus**. In 1905, Koch won the Nobel prize for his work.

HIV

The virus that causes AIDS

HIV, which is short for Human Immunodeficiency Virus, is a virus that infects cells in the human immune system ■. It weakens the body's defenses against infection, so that other microorganisms can attack. AIDS, short for Acquired Immunodeficiency Syndrome, is the disease that results from an HIV infection. Like many viruses, HIV can remain hidden, or latent, in the body for long periods without producing any signs of disease.

See also

Protozoa

A single spoonful of pond water or a handful of soil can contain thousands of protozoa. These tiny single-celled organisms include species that have no fixed shape, and others with intricate shells that are hundreds of times smaller than a pinhead.

Protozoa

A group of single-celled organisms that live by taking in food

Protozoa (singular **protozoon**) are members of the protist ▧ kingdom. Each protozoon is made of a single cell ▧. Protozoa are heterotrophic ▧, which means that they have to take in food, rather than make it by photosynthesis ▧.

Amoeba

A protozoon with a cell that has no fixed shape

An amoeba (plural **amoebas**) looks like a tiny bag of jelly. Its single cell is surrounded by a plasma membrane ▧, and it moves by changing shape. An amoeba feeds by surrounding its food and engulfing it. There are many species ▧ of amoeba. Some live in water and soil, while others are parasites ▧ that live inside plants or animals. One species, *Entamoeba histolytica*, feeds on other living cells and causes the disease **dysentery**.

Nucleus *Cytoplasm*

Food vacuole

Amoeboid movement

A kind of movement produced by changing shape

An amoeba moves by changing the state of its cytoplasm ▧. It makes parts of this jellylike substance turn solid to form temporary outgrowths. These are called **pseudopods**, which means "false feet." The rest of the amoeba flows into the pseudopods, and then forms new pseudopods. By this process, the amoeba slowly moves along.

Contractile vacuole

A structure that pumps water out of a cell

Protozoa that live in fresh water contain a higher concentration of dissolved substances in their cells than the water around them. As a result, water moves into their cells by osmosis ▧. Many protozoa, including amoebas, collect this water in a reservoir, or vacuole ▧. Every few minutes, the vacuole contracts and squirts out the unwanted water.

Pseudopod reaches out to engulf food

Food

Contractile vacuole

Amoeba
An amoeba constantly changes its shape. It sends out pseudopods in order to move, and to engulf food. It contains vacuoles that digest food, and a contractile vacuole to pump out water.

Shelled amoeba

An amoeba that is partly covered by a case

In some species of amoeba, the cell is protected by a shell. The shell is made of minerals secreted by the amoeba or built up from tiny particles that it collects.

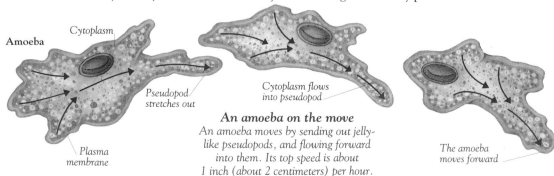

Amoeba

Cytoplasm

Pseudopod stretches out

Cytoplasm flows into pseudopod

Plasma membrane

The amoeba moves forward

An amoeba on the move
An amoeba moves by sending out jelly-like pseudopods, and flowing forward into them. Its top speed is about 1 inch (about 2 centimeters) per hour.

Slime mold

A kind of amoeba that reproduces by gathering together in groups

Slime mold amoebas behave in a very unusual way. For part of their life cycle, the amoebas live and feed on their own. But when food is in short supply, they gather together to form a mass called a **slug**. This can weigh more than 2 pounds (1 kilogram). The slug creeps along the ground and eventually forms a tall fruiting body ▪ that releases spores ▪. The spores germinate to produce new amoebas.

Radiolarian

A protozoon with a silica skeleton

Radiolarians live in the sea. They usually have round cells with hundreds of pseudopods that collect food. The deepest parts of the seabed are covered by a thick layer of **radiolarian ooze**, composed of the skeletons of dead radiolarians. This forms because the skeletons are made of silica, a mineral that does not dissolve in deep water.

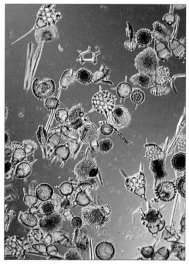

Microscopic sculptures
This light micrograph shows different species of radiolarian found in plankton. Tiny radiolarian skeletons form some of the most beautiful natural structures.

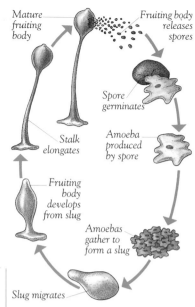

Mature fruiting body
Fruiting body releases spores
Spore germinates
Stalk elongates
Amoeba produced by spore
Fruiting body develops from slug
Amoebas gather to form a slug
Slug migrates

Life cycle of a slime mold
Slime mold amoebas come together to form a single mass, called a slug. This migrates toward the light, then forms a fruiting body that releases spores.

Foraminiferan

A protozoon with a perforated case

A foraminiferan, or **foram**, is a protozoon that lives in the sea. Its case, or shell, is made of the mineral calcium carbonate. The case has several connected chambers and is peppered with tiny holes. Microscopic threads, or pseudopods, project through the holes to collect food.

Foram shell

Paramecium

A group of species of protozoa that swim with the help of cilia

Paramecium is a highly active protozoon. It usually lives in fresh water and feeds on bacteria ▪. It has a slipper-shaped cell covered with thousands of tiny hairs called cilia ▪. These push the cell through the water.

Plasmodium

A group of species of protozoa that cause malaria

Plasmodium is a parasite that lives in the salivary glands of mosquitoes, and also in the human body. When a human is bitten by an infected mosquito, the parasites enter the body. They circulate in the blood and reproduce inside the liver and in red blood cells. This causes a disease called **malaria**. Every few days, the parasites break out of the red blood cells, releasing poisons that cause a fever.

Zooplankton

Planktonic organisms that live by taking in food

Zooplankton is the part of plankton ▪ made up of protozoa and tiny animals. Most of these organisms are microscopic, although some are visible to the naked eye. They float in water and live by eating other forms of life, or by filtering tiny particles of food from the water. Some of the organisms in zooplankton spend all their lives adrift. Others, such as crustaceans ▪ and sea urchins, live only like this when they are young. Later, they change shape, or undergo metamorphosis ▪, and take up different ways of life as adults.

See also

Single-celled algae

Algae live wherever there is water, light, and a supply of minerals. They use the Sun's energy to make food, and they themselves form food for other kinds of life. The smallest algae are tiny, single-celled organisms that are visible only through a microscope.

Algae

A group of simple plantlike organisms that makes its own food by photosynthesis

Like plants, algae (singular **alga**) are autotrophic ■, which means they produce their own food by photosynthesis ■. There are over 20,000 species ■ of alga, ranging from microscopic diatoms to giant seaweeds ■ over 328 feet (100 meters) long. Most algae live in water, and the larger ones reproduce by releasing spores ■.

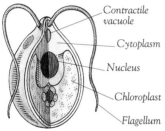

Contractile vacuole

Cytoplasm

Nucleus

Chloroplast

Flagellum

Single-celled pond alga
This cutaway of a single-celled alga shows the chloroplast, which traps the Sun's energy for use in photosynthesis.

Single-celled algae

A group of algae that consists of just a single cell

Single-celled algae are microscopic plantlike organisms. Many single-celled algae live in colonies; they are common in lakes and ponds. In summer, they often turn pond water green. Single-celled algae are usually classified as protists ■, while multi-celled algae are often classified as plants.

Plankton

Tiny organisms that float in water

The upper layers of seas and lakes are home to vast numbers of tiny organisms. Together, they form plankton, which consists of microscopic protists, algae, and multi-celled plants and animals. The plantlike organisms make up the part of plankton called phytoplankton, and the animal-like organisms make up zooplankton ■. Many of the animals are larvae ■. Most planktonic organisms just drift in the water, but some can swim.

Phytoplankton

A group of planktonic organisms that lives by photosynthesis

Every day, energy reaches the seas in the form of sunlight. The tiny organisms that make up phytoplankton collect this energy and use it to make food by photosynthesis. Phytoplankton forms the first link in most aquatic food chains ■, because it provides food for zooplankton.

Distribution of phytoplankton
This color-enhanced satellite picture shows the amount of phytoplankton in the seas. The red areas show the highest density, and the violet areas the lowest density.

Diatom

A single-celled alga with a silica case

Great numbers of diatoms live in the sea and in fresh water. They are the most numerous organisms in phytoplankton. A diatom is protected by a case made from the mineral silica. The case has two separate parts, or valves, that fit together like a box and its lid. This forms a space that protects the inside of the cell ■. Diatom cases are often intricately patterned. Some diatoms contain tiny droplets of oil that help them to stay afloat.

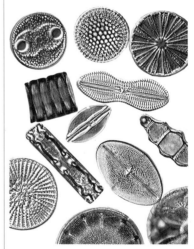

Marine diatoms
This light micrograph of single-celled marine diatoms shows the amazing variety and intricacy of diatom cases.

Diatomite

A powdery rock made of the cases of dead diatoms

When a marine diatom dies, its case falls to the bottom of the sea. In some places, diatom cases build up over a long time to form thick layers called **diatomaceous earth**. As these layers are compressed, they turn into a rock called diatomite. Diatomite is almost pure silica and is quarried for use as an abrasive, a filtering material, and an insulator.

Algal bloom

A rapid increase in the numbers of a species of alga

If conditions are favorable, a species of alga may suddenly increase to vast numbers, causing a population explosion. The algae reproduce rapidly until they run out of the minerals they need in order to survive. Algal blooms occur naturally in many lakes. They also happen if water becomes polluted ■ with nutrient minerals, such as phosphates ■.

Red tide

A toxic bloom of dinoflagellates

Dinoflagellates are algae that are common in warm seas. They produce some of the most powerful poisons in the natural world. During a red tide, a dinoflagellate species suddenly blooms and releases large amounts of poison into the water. The poison kills fish, and millions of dead fish may be washed up on the shore. Dinoflagellates are often eaten by filter feeders ■ such as mussels, and their poison may pass through the food chain.

Dinoflagellate

A kind of alga common in warm seas

Dinoflagellates are the second most important part of phytoplankton after diatoms. They usually have two whiplike tails, or flagella ■. One spins the cell around, while the other makes it move forward. Dinoflagellates often have an armor of plates made from cellulose ■. Some species of dinoflagellate have strange shapes and others are luminous.

Cellulose plates

—Flagellum

Armored cell
Ceratium *is a strange looking species of dinoflagellate with armor plates and spiky horns. The horns probably help stop it from sinking.*

Golgi body

Contractile vacuole

Euglenoid

Eye spot

—Flagellum

Attracted by light
Euglena gracilis *is a euglenoid with a sculpted outer shell, or pellicle, made of protein. It senses light with its eyespot and moves toward it with its flagellum so that it can carry out photosynthesis.*

Zooxanthella

A single-celled alga that often lives in partnership with animals

A zooxanthella is a dinoflagellate. Large numbers of these algae live inside the cells of corals ■ and other sea animals. The algae provide their animal partner with food through photosynthesis and in return, the animal gives the algae protection.

Euglenoid

An organism that has chloroplasts but no cell wall

A euglenoid has a mixture of plant and animal-like features. It contains chloroplasts ■ that enable it to make its own food by photosynthesis, but it can also eat food. Euglenoids live in fresh water, and move with long flagella.

Chloroplast

Outer shell or pellicle

Nucleus

Mitochondrion

Colony

A number of related organisms that live together

Many single-celled algae live in permanent groups called colonies. In some colonies, each cell is independent. In others, the cells share the work involved in staying alive. **Colonial** life-styles are found in many other kinds of organism, from bacteria ■ to insects ■.

Nonflowering plants

The earliest plants on Earth did not have flowers or produce seeds. They spread by shedding spores. Simple plants like this still exist, but now they share the Earth with their flowering relatives. The best places to see nonflowering plants are in damp, shady spots, and along the seashore.

Nonflowering plant

A plant that reproduces without growing flowers

Only flowering plants ▪, or angiosperms, reproduce by growing flowers. All other plants reproduce without them. Most nonflowering plants spread by shedding tiny packets of cells ▪, called spores ▪. Algae ▪, mosses, liverworts, gymnosperms ▪, and ferns ▪ are all nonflowering plants. They cannot survive in dry places. They live either in water or in places where there is plenty of moisture.

Seaweed

A marine alga

Seaweeds are algae that live in salt water. A large seaweed, such as a kelp, has a rootlike **holdfast** that anchors it either to rocks or to the seabed. The holdfast is connected to leaflike **fronds** by a rubbery **stipe**. Like all plants, seaweeds live by harnessing the energy in sunlight. The color of a seaweed depends on the photosynthetic pigments ▪ that it uses to trap the Sun's energy.

Seaweed selection

Most large seaweeds grow close to the shore, where they can anchor themselves in shallow water. A few float on the sea's surface.

Bladder wrack

Carrageen

Stipe

Air bladder

Sugar kelp

Leaflike frond

Thongweed

Holdfast

Dulse

Green algae

The largest and most diverse division of algae

Green algae make up a classification group ▪, or division, of plants called **Chlorophyta**. Their color comes from the green pigment chlorophyll ▪. Green algae live in many different habitats. Some grow in fresh water, and a few grow in the sea. Many others grow on damp surfaces such as tree trunks. The largest green algae are seaweeds, and the smallest kinds consist of just a single cell. There are about 6,000 species ▪ of green alga.

Blanketweed

A thread-forming alga

Blanketweeds are green algae that grow on the surface of still or stagnant water. Their cells are linked end to end, and they make long thread-shaped colonies ▪. The threads often float on the surface of the water in a slimy mass.

Green blanket

This dish contains a mass of blanketweed threads. They are formed by an alga called Spirogyra.

Red algae

A division of algae that contains red pigments

Red algae form the plant division **Rhodophyta**. Almost all species of red alga live in the sea. They grow on rocks below the tideline and also in deeper water. Some species can survive at a depth of 820 feet (250 meters), which is deeper than any other plant. Red algae get their color from pigments called **phycobilins**. These mask the green color of their chlorophyll. There are about 4,000 species of red alga.

Brown algae

A division of algae that contains brown pigments

Brown algae make up the plant division **Phaeophyta**. Nearly all brown algae live in the sea. They include kelps and other seaweeds that grow on rocky shores. Some species have gas-filled floats, or **air bladders**, that hold up their fronds to the sunlight. Brown algae contain chlorophyll and the pigment **fucoxanthin**, which gives them a dark green or brown color. There are about 1,500 species of brown alga, and most are found in cool water.

Kelp

A large brown seaweed

Kelps are brown algae that are common on rocky shores. They either grow on rocks below the low-water mark or on the seabed. Kelps are rich in minerals such as iodine, potassium, and phosphorus. In some parts of the world, they are harvested and used as a fertilizer.

Giant kelp

The largest species of kelp

Giant kelp (*Macrocystis pyrifera*) grows off the coast of California. It is the largest species of alga and can grow to a length of 328 feet (100 meters). It grows in shallow water, and its long fronds often float on the surface, buoyed up by air bladders. Giant kelp forms large underwater forests that are rich in marine life.

See also

Liverwort

The plant body, or thallus, of this liverwort grows closely pressed to the ground. Scattered over its surface are structures called gemma cups. These contain egglike clusters of cells, which are used in asexual reproduction. Raindrops dislodge and scatter the clusters, which form new plants.

Gemma cup

Thallus

Volvox

A group of species of microscopic green algae

Volvox is common in ponds. It forms ball-shaped colonies that contain up to 50,000 cells. The cells are set in jelly and make up a hollow ball. Each cell has two flagella ■ that beat to push the colony through the water. A mature *Volvox* colony often contains offspring colonies that tumble around inside it.

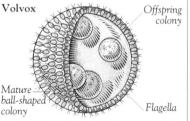

Volvox

Offspring colony

Mature ball-shaped colony

Flagella

Bryophyte

A liverwort, moss, or hornwort

Together, liverworts, mosses, and hornworts make up the plant division **Bryophyta**. Bryophytes are simple land plants that live in damp places. They usually grow close to the ground and do not have proper stems, leaves, or roots. Bryophytes are **nonvascular**, which means that they have no special channels for carrying water or nutrients.

Liverwort

A simple plant with a ribbonlike or leafy shape

Most liverworts live in damp, shady places. They are either flat or spreading with leaflike scales. Like all bryophytes, liverworts are anchored to the ground by rootlike cells called **rhizoids**. There are about 6,000 species of these simple plants.

Moss

A simple plant with leaflike scales

Mosses are small plants that often grow together in tight clumps. They usually live in damp places, although some can survive for long periods with little water. Many species of moss produce their spores in a capsule attached to a stalk. There are nearly 10,000 species of moss.

Mossy log
Many mosses grow in woodlands, either on rotting logs, like this one, or on the ground.

Simple vascular plants

The first plants lived in the sea and absorbed all the minerals they needed from the water around them. But on land, water and minerals are harder to reach. Vascular plants have developed internal pipelines that collect the substances they need from the soil, and carry them around the plant.

Vascular plant

A plant that has special channels for carrying water and nutrients

Ferns, club mosses, horsetails, gymnosperms ▪, and flowering plants ▪ are all vascular plants, or **tracheophytes**. This means that they have vascular systems ▪ made up of special groups of cells that operate like pipelines. These pipelines carry water and nutrients around the plant. Vascular plants have roots that collect nutrients from the soil, and stems that support their leaves.

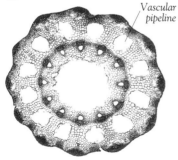

Vascular pipeline

Stem cross section
This cross section of a horsetail stem shows the vascular cells that carry water and nutrients around the plant.

Alternation of generations

A life cycle that alternates between two different forms

In the life cycle of a plant, two generations exist alternately. This means that there are two different forms of the plant within the same life cycle. One form of the plant, called the sporophyte, uses the kind of cell division called meiosis ▪ to produce the other form of the plant, known as a gametophyte. The gametophyte then uses a different kind of cell division, called mitosis ▪, to produce a new sporophyte.

The life cycle of a fern
There are two different plant forms in the life cycle of a fern. The sporophyte produces spores that grow into gametophytes. The gametophytes make sex cells, or gametes, that form new sporophytes after fertilization.

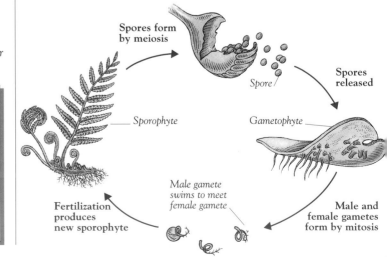

Spores form by meiosis

Spore

Spores released

Sporophyte

Gametophyte

Fertilization produces new sporophyte

Male gamete swims to meet female gamete

Male and female gametes form by mitosis

Sporophyte

The stage in a life cycle that produces spores

A sporophyte is diploid ▪, which means that it has a double set of chromosomes ▪. It produces large numbers of tiny spores ▪ by meiosis. The spores develop into gametophytes, which often live independently.

Gametophyte

The stage in a life cycle that produces gametes

A gametophyte is haploid ▪, which means that it has a single set of chromosomes. It is either male, or female, or both. It makes male or female sex cells ▪, or gametes, by mitosis. Fertilization ▪ takes place when a male and a female gamete come together. This produces a new sporophyte. In mosses and liverworts, the gametophyte stage is larger than the sporophyte stage. In most other plants, the sporophyte is the largest form in the life cycle.

Fern

A nonflowering plant with fronds that often uncoil as they grow

There are about 11,000 species ■ of fern that make up the division ■ **Pteridophyta**. Most ferns have leaves, or **fronds**, that are divided into many leaflets. They form spores on the underside of their leaves in structures called **sporangia**. The sporangia are often clustered together in a button-shaped structure called a **sorus**. Some ferns have sporangia on all their leaves, but others have them only on a few leaves, or on special stalks. Ferns are most common in the tropics, and they usually live in damp places.

Frond

Water fern

A fern that grows in water or on waterlogged ground

Water ferns look very different from most other ferns. They often have rounded fronds and a covering of water-repellent hairs. Floating water ferns grow on the surface of ponds and in ditches. If a floating fern is submerged, it bobs back up to the surface.

Tree fern

A large fern with a fibrous trunk

Tree ferns grow mainly in the tropics and subtropics. These ferns grow very tall and have large fronds grouped in a cluster, which makes them look like palm trees. The fronds of some tree ferns can be up to 16 feet (5 meters) long.

Large frond

Giant tree fern
Tree ferns like this one can grow to heights of over 65 feet (20 meters).

Club moss

A nonflowering plant that usually has small leaves arranged in a spiral around the stem

Club mosses are mosslike plants that grow in damp, shady places. They form the plant division **Lycopodophyta**. Most club mosses have creeping stems that bear upright branches. They make spores on special leaves called **sporophylls**. These are either spread along the branches, or clustered at their tips. There are about 1,000 species of club moss.

Giant club moss

An extinct club moss with a tall trunk

Giant club mosses once grew to a height of over 100 feet (30 meters). They had long trunks topped with a tight cluster of short branches. During the Carboniferous Period ■, giant club mosses formed dense forests over swampy ground. Dead club mosses built up layers of organic matter that were buried by sediment. After millions of years, this organic matter was turned into the carbon-rich fossil fuel ■ called coal.

Horsetail

A nonflowering plant with side branches arranged in rings

Horsetails have been on the Earth for millions of years. They are brushlike plants that are common in damp places. They make up the plant division **Sphenophyta**. Horsetails spread by shedding spores, and also by growing creeping underground stems, or rhizomes ■. A horsetail has two kinds of stem, or shoot. The **sterile shoots** have rings of narrow green branches. The **fertile shoots** often have no branches, and little or no chlorophyll ■. These shoots make the spores. There are 15 species of horsetail.

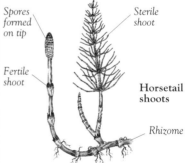

Spores formed on tip

Sterile shoot

Fertile shoot

Horsetail shoots

Rhizome

Nathanael Pringsheim

German botanist 1823–94

Nathanael Pringsheim specialized in the study of nonflowering, or "lower," plants. He was one of the first botanists to describe the alternation of generations, which he observed in algae ■. He was also one of the first botanists to examine chloroplasts, the structures inside plant cells that collect the energy in sunlight.

Gymnosperms

Gymnosperms were the first plants on Earth to reproduce by making seeds. Today, this small group of plants contains fewer than 1,000 species, but some of these are extremely hardy and long-lived.

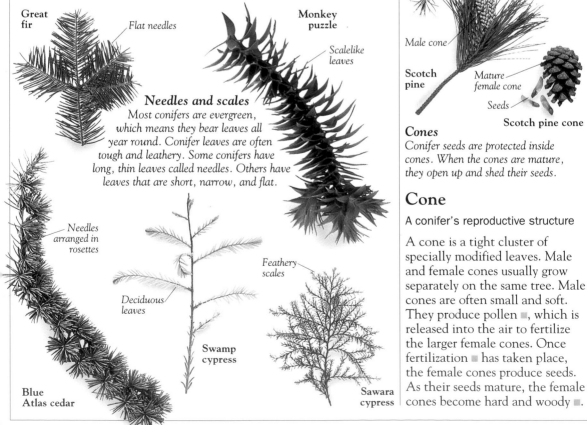

Young cones

Larch

Young cones

Douglas fir

Cypress

Young cones

Seed scales inside mature cone

Cedar cones

Gymnosperm

A plant with seeds that develop without a protective covering

Together with the flowering plants ▪, or angiosperms, gymnosperms make up a plant group called the **seed plants**, or **Spermatophyta**. The members of this group all reproduce by making seeds ▪. The word gymnosperm means "naked seed," because gymnosperm seeds are not enclosed inside an ovary ▪. Most gymnosperms are trees that form their seeds inside cones.

Conifer

A plant that reproduces by making cones

The conifers make up the division ▪ **Coniferophyta**, which contains about 550 species ▪. Conifers form dense forests in cool parts of the world, and they are also common on mountains. Some species also grow in warm places. Most conifers have evergreen leaves that can withstand drying winds. Leafshapes range from long, thin **needles** to short, flat **scales**.

Great fir

Flat needles

Monkey puzzle

Scalelike leaves

Needles and scales

Most conifers are evergreen, which means they bear leaves all year round. Conifer leaves are often tough and leathery. Some conifers have long, thin leaves called needles. Others have leaves that are short, narrow, and flat.

Needles arranged in rosettes

Deciduous leaves

Swamp cypress

Feathery scales

Blue Atlas cedar

Sawara cypress

Male cone

Scotch pine

Mature female cone

Seeds

Scotch pine cone

Cones

Conifer seeds are protected inside cones. When the cones are mature, they open up and shed their seeds.

Cone

A conifer's reproductive structure

A cone is a tight cluster of specially modified leaves. Male and female cones usually grow separately on the same tree. Male cones are often small and soft. They produce pollen ▪, which is released into the air to fertilize the larger female cones. Once fertilization ▪ has taken place, the female cones produce seeds. As their seeds mature, the female cones become hard and woody ▪.

Resin

A sticky sap produced by conifers

Many conifers produce resin to prevent insects from eating their wood. If the bark ▓ of a conifer is damaged, resin oozes out to protect the wound. Fossilized ▓ resin is called **amber**. Some amber contains prehistoric insects that were imprisoned in resin millions of years ago.

Amber jewelry
Amber is prized for its rich orange and pale yellow colors. People have used it to make beautiful jewelry for thousands of years.

Pine family

A family of conifers with needle-shaped leaves

Pines make up the family ▓ **Pinaceae** which contains about 200 species. Nearly all of these conifers have needles that grow in clusters of two or more. Besides **pines** (*Pinus*), this family includes **firs** (*Abies*), **spruces** (*Picea*), **hemlocks** (*Tsuga*), **Douglas firs** (*Pseudotsuga*), **larches** (*Larix*), and **true cedars** (*Cedrus*). The larch, also known as **tamarack**, is unusual because it is deciduous ▓, which means it loses all its leaves in the autumn.

See also

Bark 81 • Berry 95 • Deciduous 83
Dinosaur 109 • Division 56 • Family 56
Fertilization 160 • Flowering plant 72
Fossil 44 • Plant ovary 93 • Pollen 92
Seed 93 • Species 48 • Wood 81

Redwood family

A family of conifers that includes the world's biggest trees

The redwood family **Taxodiaceae** contains 15 species of conifer. Redwoods have needle-shaped or scale-shaped leaves and rounded cones. The redwood family includes two giants of the tree world – the **coast redwood** (*Sequoia sempervirens*), and the **giant redwood** (*Sequoiadendron giganteum*). Coast redwoods are the tallest trees in the world, and giant redwoods are the heaviest.

Conifer giants
The giant redwood grows in California. These conifers can grow over 262 feet (80 meters) high and measure up to 100 feet (30 meters) around the base.

Yew family

A family of conifers that do not have true cones

The 18 species of the yew family **Taxaceae** have seeds that form inside a fleshy jacket called an **aril**. These species are classified as conifers because the aril is part of the seed, not an ovary formed by the parent plant. The family includes **yews** (*Taxus*) and the **California nutmeg** (*Torreya californica*).

Cypress family

A family of conifers with needle-shaped or scale-shaped leaves

The cypress family **Cupressaceae** contains over 100 species. They include **cypresses** (*Cupressus*), **junipers** (*Juniperus*), and **false cedars** (*Thuja*). Cypresses have hard, rounded cones. Junipers have fleshy cones that look like berries ▓, and the cones of false cedars are small and woody.

Cycad

A gymnosperm shaped like a small palm tree

Cycads belong to the plant division **Cycadophyta**, which contains about 140 species. They first appeared over 300 million years ago and probably provided an important source of food for some dinosaurs ▓. Today, cycads are found mainly in the tropics. A cycad plant has long, divided leaves and large cones. The male and female cones grow on different plants.

Ginkgo

The last surviving member of an ancient division of conifers

Fanlike ginkgo leaves

The ginkgo, or **maidenhair tree** (*Ginkgo biloba*), is the only species in the plant division **Ginkgophyta**. It has fan-shaped leaves that are divided into two lobes. The female trees produce seeds in oval, fleshy fruits.

Summer foliage

Ginkgos are often planted in towns and cities because they can survive in polluted air.

Leaves shed in winter

Flowering plants

The flowering plants are the most widespread and successful plants on Earth. They live all over the world and have adapted to almost every kind of habitat, from sunbaked deserts to icy mountainsides.

New Zealand black beech

South American roble beech

Flowering plant

A plant that reproduces by growing flowers

A flowering plant carries out sexual reproduction ▪ by growing flowers ▪ that produce seeds. The seeds develop inside a protective structure called an ovary ▪. This gives flowering plants their other name – **angiosperms**. The term angiosperm means "vessel seed." Flowering plants make up the largest division ▪ of plants, called the seed plants, which also contains the gymnosperms ▪. This division contains over 250,000 species ▪, which are classified into around 300 groups, or families ▪.

Dicot

A flowering plant that has two cotyledons

Cotyledons

Young pumpkin plant

The largest group of flowering plants are the **dicotyledons**, or dicots. A dicot has seeds that contain two seed leaves or cotyledons ▪. Cotyledons either act as a food store, or open shortly after germination ▪ to fuel the seed's growth. Dicots have net-veined leaves, and flowers with parts that are usually divided into fours or fives. There are about 250 dicot families. Most trees are dicots.

Monocot

A flowering plant with one cotyledon

A **monocotyledon**, or monocot, has leaves with parallel veins and flower parts that are usually divided into threes or multiples of three. Most monocots are nonwoody, or herbaceous ▪, although some species, such as palms, grow into trees.

Magnolia family

A family of dicot plants with primitive flowers

The magnolia family **Magnoliaceae** is one of the oldest groups of dicot flowering plants. Species in this family have **primitive flowers**, which are flowers with many separate parts arranged in a spiral. There are about 230 species in the magnolia family. Most are trees or shrubs. They include **magnolias** (*Magnolia*), and the **tulip tree** (*Liriodendron tulipifera*).

Spiral arrangement

Hybrid magnolia

Chinese magnolia

Primitive flower

Beech family

A family of dicot plants that includes many trees

The beech family **Fagaceae** includes trees such as **beeches** (*Fagus*), **oaks** (*Quercus*), and **sweet chestnuts** (*Castanea*). Their flowers are often small hanging catkins and their fruits are in the form of nuts ▪. Beech family trees are an important source of timber in the northern hemisphere. This family contains about 1,050 species.

Buttercup family

A family of dicot plants that includes many weeds and garden flowers

Most species in the buttercup family **Ranuculaceae** have primitive flowers and divided leaves. The family includes **buttercups** (*Ranunculus*), and large numbers of garden plants such as **delphiniums** (*Delphinium*), and **anemones** (*Anemone*). Many members of the buttercup family are poisonous, and some species are used to make medicines. There are about 1,750 species in the buttercup family, most of which are herbaceous plants. The majority of these species grow in cool climates.

Cactus family

A family of dicot plants originally from the deserts of North and South America

The cactus family **Cactaceae** contains plants that have adapted to life in dry places. They are often protected by spines and carry out photosynthesis ▪ with their water-storing stems instead of with leaves. Most cacti are low-growing plants, although the biggest can reach a height of 65 feet (20 meters) or more. The cactus family contains about 1,650 species.

Spiral arrangement of petals and sepals

Flowers of the desert
Cacti usually have stemless flowers with many sepals and petals arranged in a spiral. Cacti often produce juicy berries.

Poppy family

A family of dicot plants that often grow on newly disturbed ground

The poppy family **Papaveraceae** includes plants that are quick to colonize patches of bare ground. Most members of the poppy family are annuals ▪, which means that they complete their life cycle in a single growing season. There are about 250 species in the poppy family. One species, the **opium poppy** (*Papaver somniferum*), is used to make pain-killing drugs.

Cabbage family

A family of dicot plants that contains important vegetables

The cabbage family **Cruciferae** (also known as **Brassicaceae**) includes many vegetable crops. **Cabbages, Brussels sprouts, cauliflowers**, and **broccoli** are all cultivated forms of one species, the **wild cabbage** (*Brassica oleracea*). There are about 2,200 species in the cabbage family, and they all have flowers with four petals, arranged like a cross.

Nightshade family

A family of dicot plants that includes potatoes and tomatoes

The nightshade family **Solanaceae** has many poisonous plants. It also includes widely cultivated species, such as the **potato** (*Solanum tuberosum*), the **tomato** (*Lycopersicon esculentum*), the **aubergine**, or **eggplant** (*Solanum melongena*), and the **pepper**, or **capsicum** (*Capsicum annuum*). There are about 2,600 species in the nightshade family, most of which are herbaceous.

Mint family

A family of dicot plants with square-shaped stems and paired leaves

In the mint family **Labiatae** (also known as **Lamiaceae**) plants have flowers with petals that are joined together to form a tube. The tube usually has two lips. There are about 6,500 species in the mint family. Many produce strong-smelling oils that are used to flavor food.

Rose family

A family of dicot plants that is often grown for fruit

Many species in the rose family **Rosaceae** are specially cultivated. They include **roses** (*Rosa*), and also **apples** (*Malus*), **pears** (*Pyrus*), **cherries** and **plums** (*Prunus*), and **strawberries** (*Fragaria*). These plants usually have flowers with four or five petals and many stamens. There are about 3,100 species in the rose family, many of which are trees or shrubs.

Crab apple — Stamens

Five-petaled flower

See also

Continued over page ➤

Gourd family

A family of dicot plants that includes melons and cucumbers

Gourds belong to a family ■ called **Cucurbitaceae**, which contains about 730 species. Plants in the gourd family are dicots ■. Most of them have trailing or climbing stems, and their flowers consist of five petals, which are often joined. Each flower is either male or female. Some gourd species ■ are dioecious ■, which means the male and female flowers grow on different plants. This family includes food plants such as **cucumber** (*Cucumis sativa*), **melon** (*Cucumis melo*), and **squash** (*Cucurbita pepo*).

Protea family

A family of dicot plants from the Southern Hemisphere

The protea family **Proteaceae** is one of the most widespread groups of plants south of the Equator. Most species of protea are trees or shrubs with tough, leathery leaves. Their individual flowers are small, but many hundreds are often packed together in large flowerheads, or inflorescences ■. There are about 1,300 species in the protea family. Many of these are cultivated as ornamental plants.

South African protea
The king protea has a huge flowerhead made up of hundreds of florets.

Disk florets

Oxeye daisy   \ *Ray floret*

Daisy family

A family of dicot plants with flowerheads that look like single flowers

The daisy family **Compositae** (also known as **Asteraceae**) is the largest family of flowering plants. It contains over 20,000 species, which grow all over the world. A daisy flower is **composite**, which means it is made up of many small flowers, or **florets**. The central flowers, or **disk florets**, are often tubular. The outer **ray florets** are long, flaplike petals. Some species have only a few florets in each flowerhead, while others usually have many hundreds. The daisy family includes crop plants such as **lettuce** (*Lactuca sativa*), and the **sunflower** (*Helianthemum annuus*), as well as many kinds of garden flowers.

See also

Pea family

A family of dicot plants with distinctive winged flowers

The pea family **Leguminosae** (also known as **Fabaceae**) includes many different species of **peas** and **beans**, which are important food crops. It is the third largest family of flowering plants, containing about 16,000 species. Plants in the pea family have flowers with five petals. One petal, called a **standard** or **banner**, forms a hood above the flower. Two other petals form a beak-shaped **keel**, and the remaining two form a pair of **wings**. The flower produces a fruit called a legume ■ that contains one or more seeds.

Standard   *Wing*

Keel

Wild pea

Parsley family

A family of dicot plants with umbrella-shaped flowerheads

The plants in the parsley family **Umbelliferae** (also known as **Apiaceae**) have small flowers with five petals. Their flowers are arranged in umbrella-shaped inflorescences called umbels. This family contains several plants that are important food sources, such as the **carrot** (*Daucus carota*), and the **parsnip** (*Pastinaca sativa*). Many other members of the parsley family are used for flavoring food or making medicine. This family contains about 3,000 species.

◄ *Continued from previous page*

Grass family

A family of monocot plants that includes the world's most important crops

The plants in the grass family **Gramineae** (also known as **Poaceae**) are monocots ■. Grasses are the most widespread flowering plants. Most species of grass are nonwoody, or herbaceous ■, but some species, such as **bamboos** (*Bambusa*), have woody stems. The flowers of a grass are very small and rely on wind pollination ■ to produce seeds. Grasses cultivated for their seeds, or **grain**, are called **cereals**. These include **bread wheat** (*Triticum aestivum*), and also **corn** (*Zea mays*), **oats** (*Avena sativa*), **rice** (*Oryza sativa*), and **sorghum** (*Sorghum bicolor*). The grass family contains about 8,000 species.

Couch grass

Orchid family

A family of monocot plants with highly specialized flowers

The orchid family **Orchidaceae** is the second largest family of flowering plants. An orchid's pollen ■ is produced in small beads called **pollinia**. Orchids have specially adapted ■ flowers that attract animal pollinators ■. Pollinia from the flowers fasten to the animal's bodies. Most orchids have very small seeds, which depend on symbiosis ■ with a fungus ■ for survival. There are over 18,000 species of orchid. Many are cultivated for their flowers.

Palm trees
Palms have round, fibrous trunks that do not usually have branches. Only the top of the trunk bears leaves.

Palm family

A family of monocot plants that grow mainly in the tropics

Most of the species in the palm family **Palmae** (also known as **Arecaceae**) are trees. They do not have branches, and their trunks get taller, but not wider, as they grow. The flowers of palms usually grow in hanging clusters. Palm fruits vary from small berries to large nuts. There are about 2,700 species in the palm family, many of which are cultivated for fiber and oils.

Orchid

Column dusts insect with pollen

Bright petals attract insect pollinators

Labellum forms an insect landing pad

Lily family

A family of monocot plants that are often grown for ornament

The lily family **Liliaceae** contains many species that have beautiful ornamental flowers. Most are herbaceous plants that grow from bulbs ■ or rhizomes ■, but a few species form small trees. There are about 4,500 species in the lily family, including **lilies** (*Lilium*), **onions** (*Allium*), **tulips** (*Tulipa*), and **aloes** (*Aloe*).

Wild tulips
These wild tulips are beautiful members of the lily family. They grow around the Mediterranean and also farther north.

Iris family

A family of monocot plants that are often cultivated for their flowers

Plants in the iris family **Iridaceae** have conspicuous flowers with parts that are arranged in threes. This family contains about 1,800 species, including many garden plants such as **irises** (*Iris*), **crocuses** (*Crocus*), and **gladioluses** (*Gladiolus*). Most grow from tubers or rhizomes.

Fungi

Fungi are neither plants nor animals. Some species look like plants, but they need to take in food like animals. Fungi absorb their food from organic matter, either living or dead, through networks of slender feeding threads.

Hyphae

Feeding threads
The black threads in this dead wood are hyphae clusters of the honey fungus.

Hypha

The feeding thread of a fungus

Most fungi produce long, slender threads that spread through living or dead matter. Each of these threads is a hypha (plural **hyphae**). A hypha often grows knoblike projections, called **haustoria**, that force their way into cells. The haustoria extract food from the cells to nourish the fungus.

Fungus

A single-celled or multicelled organism that absorbs its food

A fungus (plural **fungi**) absorbs simple food substances from the living or dead matter around it. The smallest fungi exist as microscopic single cells ■. Many fungi are multicelled organisms. However, they are often hidden inside their food, and usually become visible only when they form fruiting bodies. Fungi ■ make up their own kingdom.

Fly agaric

Cap

Spores form in gills

Developing toadstool

Stalk holds cap high enough to release spores into the air

Mycelium

A network of hyphae

If you break open a piece of rotting wood, you may notice layers of fine white threads. Each cluster is a mycelium (plural **mycelia**), a mass of hyphae that absorbs food substances.

Fruiting body

A structure that produces spores

Fungi grow fruiting bodies in order to reproduce. Their fruiting bodies can be smaller than a pinhead or bigger than a football. Each one releases tiny spores.

Saprotroph

An organism that lives by absorbing organic compounds from dead matter

A saprotroph, or **saprophyte**, feeds on dead organic matter. Saprotrophic fungi play a vital role in recycling nutrients ■. They break down dead matter, and convert it into a form that other living things can use.

Toadstool
The fly agaric fungus produces brightly colored toadstools, or fruiting bodies. Like many toadstools, they are very poisonous.

Biotroph

An organism that lives by absorbing organic compounds from living matter

Many fungi attack other living things, from plants to humans. These parasitic ■ fungi are called biotrophs. They absorb food from living cells in the form of organic compounds ■.

Toadstool

A fruiting body formed by some kinds of fungi

A toadstool is made up of a mass of hyphae. It produces millions of spores that are shed into the air, and these enable the fungus to spread. The structures that make the spores are on the underside of the toadstool. They are arranged either on vertical flaps called **gills**, or around hollows called **pores**.

Nature's recyclers
These are the fruiting bodies of a fungus that is breaking down dead wood.

Spore

A microscopic package of cells used in reproduction

A spore is similar to a seed ■, but is much smaller and simpler. It usually contains just one or a few cells, surrounded by a tough outer coat. Spores are produced by fungi, and also by nonflowering plants, such as mosses ■ and ferns ■. Most fungi release their spores into the air. The spores are so light that they can be carried high into the atmosphere, and they often travel great distances. If a spore lands in a suitable place, it germinates ■ and produces another fungus.

Spore print
If you place the cap of a toadstool on a piece of paper, the spores will slowly settle on the paper and produce a "print."

Fairy ring

A circular growth pattern produced by some fungi

When a fungal spore germinates on a lawn or field, it produces hyphae that grow out in all directions. The oldest hyphae eventually die because their food is used up, but new hyphae keep spreading outward. The result is a circle of hyphae that gets bigger and bigger. When the hyphae produce toadstools, the circular pattern is easy to see.

Fairy ring
The fruiting bodies of fairy ring fungi often appear overnight. This once led people to believe that they were magic circles left behind by fairies.

Mycorrhiza

A partnership between a fungus and the roots of a plant

A mycorrhiza (plural **mycorrhizae**) forms when a fungus invades the roots of a plant. The fungus takes nutrients from the plant, but the plant benefits because the fungus helps it to collect minerals from the soil. Mycorrhizae are an example of mutualism ■, a partnership of two species ■ in which both benefit. Mycorrhizae are found in many plants. Some orchids ■ cannot develop without the help of their fungal partners.

Lichen

A plantlike partnership between a fungus and an alga

A lichen is made up of fungal hyphae and single-celled algae ■. The algae live among the fungal hyphae and produce food by photosynthesis ■, which the fungus feeds on. The partnership between the fungus and the algae is so close that they live like a single organism. Lichens grow on all kinds of bare surfaces, from rocks to tree trunks. They grow very slowly, and may live for hundreds of years. Many species of lichen can grow only where the air is unpolluted.

Anton de Bary

German botanist 1831–88

Anton de Bary was one of the first **mycologists**, or scientists who study fungi. He classified many kinds of fungus, including microscopic species. He also discovered that lichens are formed by a partnership between fungi and algae. De Bary was the first person to use the word symbiosis ■ to describe a beneficial relationship between two species. This term now covers a wider range of relationships between different organisms.

Lichens
These orange and white lichens are growing on a limestone rock. Lichens eventually break down rocks and help to form soil.

See also

Cell 18 • Fern 69 • Fungi 57
Germination 93 • Moss 67
Mutualism 174 • Nutrient cycle 170
Orchid family 75 • Organic compound 24
Parasite 175 • Photosynthesis 84
Seed 93 • Single-celled algae 64
Species 48 • Symbiosis 174

Types of fungi

Fungi produce fruiting bodies to spread their spores from one food source to another. Each species of fungus has a particular kind of food and has evolved its own way of spreading spores. The fruiting bodies of fungi grow in a huge variety of shapes and sizes.

Mold

A fungus with a woolly growth form

A mold is made up of a mass of fungal threads, or hyphae ▪. It forms when a spore ▪ lands on a suitable food and germinates ▪. One of the most common kinds of mold is **pin mold** (*Mucor mucedo*), which lives on damp bread. Other kinds of mold grow on ripe fruit and on animal droppings.

Bracket fungus

A fungus with a fruiting body shaped like a shelf

Flat, shelflike fruiting bodies ▪ called brackets show that a tree is infected by a fungus. The brackets usually grow out horizontally from the tree trunk, releasing spores into the air. Some brackets become hard and woody and may last several years after their spores have been shed. These fungi are responsible for killing large numbers of trees.

Brackets build up in rings

Fungus shelves
These rounded bracket fungi have tiny pores on their undersides that shed spores into the air. They are often a sign that a tree is slowly dying.

Puffed away
This puffball is releasing a cloud of tiny spores into the air.

Puffball

A fungus with a fruiting body shaped like a ball

Every puffball begins life as a solid ball of cells ▪. The cells slowly dry out, and the outer skin of the ball becomes papery. If an animal or raindrop touches the skin, spores puff out through a hole in the top of the fruiting body.

Grass rust
The fruiting bodies of this microscopic rust fungus produce rust-colored streaks on summer grass leaves.

Rust

A microscopic fungus that infects some plants

Rusts are parasites ▪ that damage many kinds of plant. They often enter a plant through its leaf pores, or stomata ▪, and spread through the plant. Some rusts have a single host ▪ plant. Others have two hosts. For example, **wheat rust** (*Puccinia graminis*) infects wheat and barberry.

Mildew

A microscopic fungus that infects plants

Mildews are common pests of garden plants. They form white patches on leaves or fruit, and often make the leaves curl up. Mildew fungi do not usually kill their host plant, but they can seriously weaken it.

Mushroom

An edible fruiting body of a fungus

The term "mushroom" is a common name ▪ given to any edible fungus. Botanists do not classify mushrooms and toadstools ▪ into separate groups, but the name "toadstool" is generally given to poisonous fungi. Although mushrooms have a low food value, people eat species such as the **common mushroom** (*Agaricus bisporus*) for their flavor.

Dry rot

A species of fungus that infects and weakens timber

In some parts of the world, a fungus called dry rot (*Serpula lacrimans*) is a serious problem in houses. It infects dead wood and grows long hyphae that often spread over floors and walls to stretch from one piece of wood to another. If the fungus is left untreated, it may weaken the timber so much that it collapses.

Reaching out for food
This photograph, looking down on a basement floor, shows the hyphae of dry rot fungus spreading out in search of food.

Potato blight

A species of fungus that attacks potato plants

The potato blight fungus (*Phytophthora infestans*) produces dark patches on potato leaves, and eventually causes potatoes to disintegrate into a soft pulp. In 1846 and 1847, potato blight ruined almost the entire potato crop in Ireland and caused a widespread famine.

See also

Alcoholic fermentation 33 • Cell 18
Common name 56 • Fruiting body 76
Germination 93 • Host 175 • Hypha 76
Parasite 175 • Spore 77 • Stoma 82
Structural protein 30 • Toadstool 76
Transport system 86

Dutch elm disease

A fungal disease that attacks some species of elm tree

Dutch elm disease is caused by a species of fungus called *Ceratocystis ulmi*, which feeds on living elm wood. The fungus damages a tree's transport systems ▪. Infected trees often have wilted leaves and will die after several years. The fungus is spread by beetles that tunnel beneath the bark of elm trees.

Yeast

A microscopic, single-celled fungus

Yeasts are microscopic fungi that usually live as individual cells. They reproduce by **budding**, or growing new cells that separate from the parent. Yeasts carry out alcoholic fermentation ▪, which changes sugars into alcohol and carbon dioxide. This is used to make alcoholic drinks and also to make bread rise.

Budding yeast
Some of these yeast cells have small buds. The buds will eventually break away and become independent cells.

Ringworm

A fungus that lives in human skin

Ringworm fungi live by digesting keratin, a structural protein ▪ found in skin. They get their name because they form red ring-shaped patches, which were once thought to be caused by worms. Ringworm is more common in children than in adults. It does not cause any lasting damage.

White and black truffles

Truffle

An edible underground fungus that is prized for its flavor

The fruiting body of a truffle forms underground. Its spores spread when the fruiting body decays or when it is disturbed by animals. Truffles have a distinctive flavor and are prized as a great delicacy. Animals with a good sense of smell, such as dogs and pigs, are used to hunt for truffles.

Penicillium

A group of species of fungi used to flavor food and make antibiotics

Penicillium fungi grow on many damp substances. They are often used in cheesemaking to flavor cheese. These fungi also produce substances called **antibiotics**, which destroy bacteria. **Penicillin** is an antibiotic drug used to combat bacterial infections. It is produced from the fungus *Penicillium notatum*.

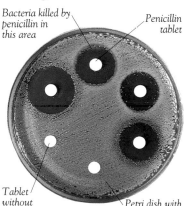

Bacteria killed by penicillin in this area
Penicillin tablet
Tablet without penicillin
Petri dish with bacterial colonies

Death zones
The clear circles around these penicillin tablets are zones where the penicillin has killed the surrounding bacteria.

Plant anatomy

The visible part of a land plant is the shoot, which stretches upward toward the light. The shoot is supported beneath the soil by a network of roots that is sometimes larger than the plant above ground.

Shoot

The part of a plant above ground

A plant shoot consists of a stem, buds, leaves ■, and flowers ■. A shoot normally grows toward the light, away from the pull of gravity. This kind of growth is an example of tropism ■.

Stem

The part of a plant that supports the buds, leaves, and flowers

A stem is made up of an outer layer, the **epidermis**, an inner layer, or **cortex**, and a central zone, the **pith**. It contains vascular ■ tissue ■ that carries water and nutrients around the plant. Some stems also act as food stores. Plants have many different kinds of stem. Some stems are short, while others are long and trailing, or partly underground.

Node

The part of a stem where leaves are attached

Most stems are divided up by nodes at regular intervals. On a stem, the space between nodes is called an **internode**.

Axil

The angle between a stem and its leaves or branches

Many plants grow buds or flowers at their axils. An **axillary** growth is a growth that sprouts out at an axil along the stem.

Root

The part of a plant that collects water and minerals

A plant's roots anchor it to the ground and supply it with water and minerals. Some roots also store food. The end of a root is covered by a **root cap** that protects the tip as it pushes through the soil. Behind the root tip are tiny **root hairs**. These are tubelike outgrowths of root cells ■. The hairs give the root a larger surface area for absorbing substances from the soil.

Tap root

A large main root

Seed plants have two different kinds of root system. Dicots ■ and gymnosperms ■ have a large tap root with smaller **lateral roots** spreading out from it. Monocots ■ have a mass of similar-sized roots that make up a **fibrous root** system. Most root systems are quite shallow, but plants that live in dry places have roots that reach far below ground level. A desert shrub called **mesquite** (*Prosopis juliflora*) has been known to produce roots up to 164 feet (50 meters) deep.

Plant structure

This tree mallow is a typical perennial plant. Its stem is partly woody, and it is anchored in the earth by a network of deep roots.

Flower

Tree mallow

Flower bud

Leaf

Leaf stalk, or petiole

Axillary growth at leaf node

Internode

Node

Stem

Pith

Cortex

Epidermis

Woody lower stem reinforced with lignin

Tap root

Lateral root

Rhizome

A creeping underground stem

Ginger rhizome

Many plants spread by growing rhizomes. A rhizome pushes its way through the soil and forms buds that grow into new stems above ground. Some grasses produce sharp-tipped rhizomes that can grow straight through other plants.

Tuber

A swollen underground stem

Sweet potato tuber

A potato is a well-known example of a tuber. It stores starch ■ from one growing season to be used in the next. The potato plant uses the starch to fuel its early growth.

Tuber

Corm

A thickened, upright underground stem that stores food

A corm is a swollen underground stem formed by certain plants, such as the crocus (*Colchium*). Unlike bulbs, corms do not contain fleshy scales inside.

Bulb

A shortened underground stem that stores food

Amaryllis bulb

A bulb is made up of layers of fleshy scales that are packed full of food. Plants use bulbs as they use tubers and corms – to store food to fuel early growth.

Cross section of bulb reveals fleshy scales

Bud

An undeveloped shoot that is protected by scales

A bud contains a tiny shoot that is packed into a small space. The shoot is protected by a covering of tough scales. The scales prevent the delicate shoot from dying during unfavorable conditions, such as in winter, or during the dry season. When conditions are right, the scales fold back, the bud bursts, and the shoot begins to grow.

Herbaceous plant

A plant with a nonwoody stem

A herbaceous plant has a stem that dies back at the end of each growing season. If the plant is perennial ■, its underground parts survive and produce new stems in the next growing season. Botanists often call herbaceous plants **herbs**. This can be confusing, because the word "herb" also describes the plants used to flavor food and make medicines.

Woody plant

A plant with a woody stem

Woody plants have tough stems that do not die back after each growing season. Their wood lets them grow tall without collapsing under their own weight. Woody plants are all perennial, which means that they live for many years. A **tree** is a tall woody plant that usually has a single main stem, or **trunk**. A **shrub** is a short woody plant that has several stems close to the ground.

Wood

A tissue that supports trees and shrubs

Wood is a tough tissue that is found in two kinds of seed plant – conifers ■ and dicots. It is made up of layers of xylem ■ cells. These cells are reinforced with a substance called **lignin**, which makes them rigid. Plants form wood in different ways, and produce different kinds of wood. Conifer wood is often called **softwood**, and dicot wood is known as **hardwood**. However, some kinds of hardwood, such as balsa, are actually softer than a softwood.

Pine tree trunk

Rings of xylem built up during each growing season

Bark

Bark

The tough outer skin of a woody plant

Bark is a protecting layer around the stem of a woody plant. The outer part of bark is dead, but beneath it there is a layer of living phloem ■ cells. As the stem grows, the outer bark stretches and often cracks or peels. Many woody plants have special pores, or **lenticels**, that let gases enter the bark to reach the cells inside the stem.

See also

Leaves

Leaves make food for plants. They collect energy from sunlight and use it to make food substances by photosynthesis. Leaves are often exposed to strong sunshine and dry winds, and have therefore evolved so that they can collect enough light without drying out.

Leaf

A plant organ that intercepts light

Lamina

A leaf consists of a thin, flat blade, called a **lamina**, which is attached to a stalk, or **petiole**. The lamina is made up of two layers of cells ■ – the epidermis on the outside surfaces, and the thicker mesophyll cells in between. *Midrib*
The leaf blade is strengthened by veins, which *Petiole* also transport substances to and from its cells. A large vein, or **midrib**, often runs along the center of the leaf. Smaller veins support the rest of the leaf's surface. The main function of a leaf is to trap the energy in sunlight for use in photosynthesis ■.

Epidermis

The outer layer of cells in a leaf

The upper and lower surfaces of a leaf are usually made up of a single layer of cells. The cells are covered by a waxy layer, called a **cuticle**, and sometimes by hairs. The wax and hairs help to prevent the leaf from losing too much water. The cells in the epidermis do not carry out photosynthesis.

Mesophyll

The cells inside a leaf

Mesophyll cells carry out photosynthesis. They contain large numbers of chloroplasts ■ that capture the energy in sunlight. In many plants, the mesophyll is made of an upper layer of column-shaped **palisade mesophyll cells**, which are packed tightly together. Beneath these are the more loosely packed **spongy mesophyll cells**.

Upper epidermis   *Waxy cuticle*

Palisade mesophyll cells

Chloroplasts

Spongy mesophyll cells

Air space

Stoma   *Guard cell*   *Lower epidermis*

Cross section of a leaf
Inside a leaf there are many air spaces. Gases move between the air and the mesophyll cells.

Stoma

A microscopic opening on the surface of a leaf

A stoma (plural **stomata**) allows gases to pass in and out of a leaf, so that its cells can carry out photosynthesis and respiration ■. A stoma is a tiny mouthlike slit. It is flanked by a pair of **guard cells** that can change shape to make the stoma open or close. During transpiration ■, a plant loses water vapor through its stomata. By opening or closing its stomata, the plant can control the rate at which it loses water.

Bract

A modified leaf

Bracts are usually smaller than a plant's ordinary leaves, and they can also be a different shape. Bracts often protect buds. A **stipule** is a bract at the base of a leaf. Stipules grow in pairs where a petiole joins a stem. In some plants, the stipules look like leaves. They can be as big, or even bigger, than the true leaves.

Compound leaf

A leaf divided into several parts

A compound leaf looks like several small leaves attached to the same stalk. Each of the small leaves is called a **leaflet**. In a **pinnate** compound leaf, the leaflets are undivided. A **bipinnate** compound leaf has leaflets divided into still smaller leaflets. A **simple leaf** is undivided.

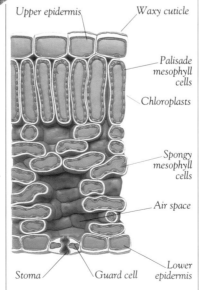

Pinnate leaf   **Bipinnate leaf**

Tendril

A modified leaf or stem that climbing plants use for support

A tendril is a long, threadlike organ. It reaches out from a plant, and wraps around any solid object that it touches. The rest of the tendril then coils up like a spring, pulling the plant close to the support.

Gourd plant tendril

Leaf vein

A strand of vascular tissue in a leaf

If you hold a leaf up to the light, you will be able to see its veins. Leaf veins are made of vascular ■ tissue. They supply a leaf with water and minerals, and carry away the food substances made in the leaf by photosynthesis. The pattern of veins in a leaf is called **venation**. Monocot ■ plants have **parallel-veined leaves** and dicot ■ plants have **net-veined leaves**.

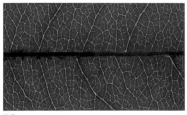

Net veins
In dicot leaves, a network of veins fan outward from the midrib.

Parallel veins
In monocot leaves, all the veins are parallel to the midrib.

Leaf arrangement

The positioning of leaves on a stem

Leaves grow in definite patterns to make sure that each leaf receives enough sunlight. These patterns vary from one kind of plant to another. Plants with **alternate leaves** have just one leaf per node ■. Plants with **opposite leaves** have two leaves at each node on opposite sides of the stem. Some plants have leaves that grow in rings at each node, called **whorls**.

| Alternate leaves | Opposite leaves | Whorled leaves |

Catching the light
Different leaf arrangements ensure that each leaf does not shade its neighbors.

Variegated leaf

A leaf with patches of different colors

The photosynthetic pigments ■ that trap sunlight are evenly spread out in most leaves. This gives the leaf an even color all over. In a variegated leaf, the pigments are unevenly spread, and some areas of the leaf may have no pigments at all. This can look very attractive, and although variegation occurs naturally in some plants, many ornamental plants are specially bred with variegated leaves.

Variegated holly leaf

Abscission

The process by which plants shed leaves, flowers, and fruits

Before a plant sheds a leaf, it absorbs any chemicals that it can recycle through the leaf's petiole. A layer of cells then grows across the base of the petiole, and the leaf falls off. In **deciduous plants**, all the leaves fall at the same time, leaving the plant bare. In **evergreen plants**, the leaves are shed and renewed all the time, so that the plant is never without leaves. Abscission is an important part of a plant's life cycle. It is controlled by plant hormones ■, such as ethylene and auxin. Small amounts of auxin in a plant prevent abscission, but large amounts encourage it. Leaves, flowers ■, and fruits ■ are all shed by this process.

Autumn sycamore leaves

See also

Photosynthesis

Plants can make their own food. They trap the Sun's energy with their leaves and use it to make food from simple substances. This process is called photosynthesis. Photosynthesis is vital to life on Earth because it provides food, either directly or indirectly, for almost every living thing.

Photosynthesis

A process that uses light energy to make food from simple chemicals

Photosynthesis means "putting together by light." It takes place in the chloroplasts ■ inside plant cells ■. During photosynthesis, a plant uses the energy in sunlight to carry out a chain of chemical reactions ■. It makes the food substance glucose ■ from molecules ■ of carbon dioxide and water. Oxygen is formed as a by-product. Glucose is packed with energy and plants use it to fuel their growth. Plants also use glucose to make starch ■, which acts as an energy store, and to make cellulose ■, which builds cell walls.

Light

A visible form of electromagnetic radiation

Sunlight is energy that travels from the Sun in the form of waves. The distance between one wave and the next is called a **wavelength**. Different wavelengths give light its different colors. Sunlight is a mixture of wavelengths that range through the **visible spectrum** from violet to red. In photosynthesis, plants use the energy in some wavelengths more than others. Plants collect about one ten-thousandth of the light energy that reaches Earth.

Sun

Photosynthetic reaction
In photosynthesis, a single molecule of glucose is formed by combining six water molecules and six carbon dioxide molecules using energy from the Sun. Six oxygen molecules are also formed.

Photosynthetic pigment

A chemical that collects the energy of sunlight

A plant traps the light it needs for photosynthesis with special chemicals called photosynthetic pigments. When light strikes a pigment molecule, the molecule absorbs some of the light's energy. It passes on the energy to other chemicals so that photosynthesis can take place.

Chlorophyll

The main photosynthetic pigment in green plants

Chlorophyll is the main pigment involved in photosynthesis. It is found in the chloroplasts inside plant cells. Chlorophyll gives plants their green color because it reflects green light, and absorbs red and blue light. There are several forms of chlorophyll. The most important form is called **chlorophyll a**. This is found in plants ■, green algae ■, and cyanobacteria ■.

Primary pigment

A pigment that fuels photosynthesis directly

Most plants contain several photosynthetic pigments. A primary pigment passes energy directly into photosynthetic reactions. In green plants, the primary pigment is chlorophyll a.

Water molecules

Carbon dioxide molecules

Leaf contains chlorophyll

Accessory pigment

A pigment that collects extra light energy

An accessory pigment collects extra energy from certain light wavelengths, and passes it on to a primary pigment. Accessory pigments include **carotenes** and **xanthophylls**, which are a red or orange color, and **phycobilins**, which are brown.

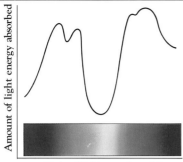

Chlorophyll absorption spectrum
The pigment chlorophyll absorbs very little green light. This is why most plants look green.

Absorption spectrum

A graph that shows which wavelengths of light a pigment absorbs most

Every pigment has a characteristic absorption spectrum. Chlorophyll a absorbs red and blue light, but very little green light. Carotenes absorb more green light, but very little red.

Thylakoid

A membrane-bound sac that contains chlorophyll

Thylakoids are flat, disk-shaped sacs found inside chloroplasts. They are piled in stacks called **grana**, which are separated by a space, or **stroma**. Each thylakoid is packed with chlorophyll. When light shines onto a leaf, it travels into the chloroplasts and strikes the thylakoids. The chlorophyll in the thylakoids traps the light energy, and photosynthesis begins.

Light reaction

A chemical reaction that can take place only in light

During the first part of photosynthesis, light energy splits up water molecules in a process called **photolysis**. This produces energy-carrying molecules such as ATP ■. These reactions happen inside a thylakoid and can take place only in light.

Dark reaction

A chemical reaction that can take place in the dark

During the second part of photosynthesis, energy from ATP molecules and other energy carriers is used to remove oxygen atoms from carbon dioxide molecules. The carbon atoms are then combined to form glucose. These reactions take place in the stroma of a chloroplast, and they do not need light.

Jan Ingenhousz

Dutch physiologist 1730–99

Jan Ingenhousz was one of the first scientists to investigate photosynthesis. In 1771, **Joseph Priestley** (1733–1804) discovered that plants give off oxygen. Ingenhousz followed up this discovery. He showed that plants take in carbon dioxide and release oxygen when light shines on them. In the dark, the opposite happens.

Carbon fixation

The conversion of carbon dioxide into organic compounds

All living things contain carbon ■, but only some can "fix" carbon, or turn it directly into complex organic compounds ■ such as glucose. Photosynthesis is the most important form of carbon fixation. Every year, plants fix about 110 billion tons of carbon.

Photosynthetic bacteria

A group of bacteria that can carry out photosynthesis

Some forms of bacteria also make their food by photosynthesis. **Purple bacteria** and **green bacteria** carry out a kind of photosynthesis that does not produce oxygen. Cyanobacteria carry out photosynthesis in a similar way to plants.

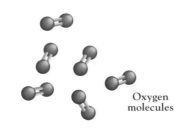

Glucose molecule

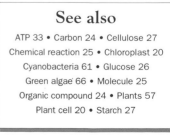

Oxygen molecules

Plant transport systems

Inside living things, substances are constantly moving from place to place. Nutrients are carried to where they are needed, and waste products are transported away. Many plants have systems of microscopic pipelines to move substances around.

Transport system

A system that moves substances around a living thing

Every living thing needs to move food substances and waste products from place to place. Substances travel short distances within and between cells ■ by diffusion ■, osmosis ■, and active transport ■. Over greater distances, substances are carried by special transport systems. A circulatory system ■ carries substances around an animal's body. A vascular system carries substances inside a plant.

Vascular system

A system that carries water and nutrients throughout a plant

A plant's vascular system consists of two kinds of **vascular tissue**, called xylem and phloem. The tissue ■ is made up of clusters of cells that work together. In herbaceous plants ■, the xylem and phloem cells are arranged in vertical clusters called **vascular bundles**. Simple plants, such as mosses ■, do not have these special transport systems.

Sap

A liquid that transports dissolved substances in plants

Sap is the liquid inside xylem and phloem cells. It is made up of water and dissolved substances such as minerals ■ and sugars ■. **Cell sap** is the fluid contained in a plant cell's vacuole ■.

Xylem

A tissue that carries water and minerals from roots to leaves

Xylem cells form part of a plant's transport system. They carry water and minerals from the roots to the rest of the plant. The water-carrying xylem cells are cylindrical or spindle-shaped. They are joined together to form tubes that reach all the way up the plant. Each cell has a thick cell wall ■, which is reinforced by lignin, the substance found in wood. Xylem cell walls contain holes that allow water to move between cells. In mature xylem, the water-carrying cells are dead.

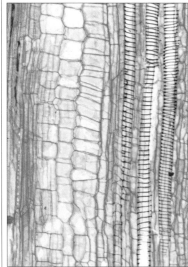

Xylem and phloem cells
This light micrograph shows phloem cells (on the left) and xylem cells (on the right). Xylem cells are often strengthened by spiral reinforcements. Phloem cells are not reinforced in this way.

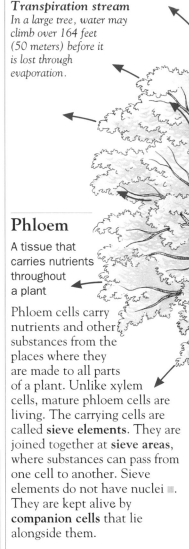

Transpiration stream
In a large tree, water may climb over 164 feet (50 meters) before it is lost through evaporation.

Phloem

A tissue that carries nutrients throughout a plant

Phloem cells carry nutrients and other substances from the places where they are made to all parts of a plant. Unlike xylem cells, mature phloem cells are living. The carrying cells are called **sieve elements**. They are joined together at **sieve areas**, where substances can pass from one cell to another. Sieve elements do not have nuclei ■. They are kept alive by **companion cells** that lie alongside them.

Transpiration

The loss of water vapor from a plant through evaporation

The leaves of a plant constantly lose water vapor through tiny pores called stomata ■. The water is replaced by water from the soil, which enters the plant's roots and rises up the stem. This forms a continuous column of water called a **transpiration stream**. Transpiration always occurs in the same direction. It is brought about by root pressure and transpiration pull.

Water evaporates through leaves

Transpiration pull draws water up

Root pressure forces water upward

Water flows into roots from soil

Transpiration pull

A force that draws water up through a plant

Water moves up a plant mainly because it is pulled from above. The pull begins when water evaporates from the mesophyll ▪ cells in the leaves and causes a drop in water potential ▪. This makes water move into the mesophyll cells from xylem cells nearby. Water molecules have a strong attraction for each other, or **cohesion**. Once they start moving, they draw other water molecules with them. This forms a continuous column of water in the xylem. The column is also supported by **capillary action**, which makes water creep upward when it is in a narrow space.

Transpiration rate

The rate at which water is lost from a plant

The transpiration rate of a plant depends on many factors. These include the temperature, the water content, or **humidity**, of the air, and how windy it is. All plants can control their transpiration rate by opening or closing their stomata. Plants that live in dry, windy places also have other adaptations, such as small leaves or a covering of hairs, to reduce water loss.

See also

Root pressure

The pressure that forces water upward from a plant's roots

When roots absorb minerals from the soil, the minerals are concentrated inside their xylem cells. Osmosis then causes water to flow into the cells from the soil. This creates pressure that forces water up the stem. Root pressure is not produced in all plants: it can push water upward for only a short distance.

Wilting

Loss of shape caused by shortage of water

Plants rely on water to keep their shape. The water that is drawn into their cells by osmosis creates turgor pressure ▪, which makes the cells rigid. If a plant loses more water through its leaves than it takes in with its roots, its cells lose their turgor and become limp. This causes the plant to wilt. If the plant stays in this state for long it will die.

Translocation

The movement of nutrients around a plant

During translocation, a plant moves nutrients from the place in which they are made, called a **source**, to the place where they are used, called a **sink**. Unlike transpiration, translocation happens in two directions, both up and down the plant. It takes place through the phloem.

Guttation on morning leaves
The leaves of this lady's mantle plant are edged by water droplets that were produced by guttation during the night.

Guttation

The discharge of water from a leaf

Sometimes a plant's roots force water up the stem faster than the water can evaporate from the leaves. When this occurs, drops of water are squeezed out of the edges of the leaves. This usually happens on still, windless nights, when evaporation is slow.

Plant growth

Unlike animals, plants cannot move around to seek out food or better conditions. However, they can use special kinds of growth to reach toward light and raw materials, and to react to their changing environment.

Growth

An increase in size

Living things grow mainly by increasing the number of their cells ■ through cell division ■. Many animals stop growing once they have reached a certain size. This is called **determinate growth**. Plants show a mixture of determinate and **indeterminate growth**. Indeterminate growth continues as long as conditions are favorable. For example, a plant's leaves, flowers, and fruits usually grow to a fixed size, but its roots and stems may continue to grow throughout its life. Plants grow by cell division but, unlike animals, they can also grow by making existing cells bigger.

Meristem

A tissue that contains cells that are able to divide indefinitely

Some of the cells in a plant stop dividing, once they are mature. But the cells in a plant's meristem tissues ■ continue to divide throughout its life, like the cells beneath human skin ■.

Apical meristem

A meristem at the apex of a root or stem

An apical meristem is a cluster of cells at the tip of a root or stem. As the cells divide, the root or stem becomes longer. This increase in length is called **primary growth**. Some plants grow only by primary growth.

Growth begins
A seedling's cells divide rapidly as it germinates. Early growth is fueled by the seed's food reserves.

Food stored in seed

Apical meristem at top of shoot

Taking shape
Cells divide at the seedling's meristems. These are at the tips of the shoot and roots.

Leaves make food to fuel growth

Apical meristem at root tip

Maturing plant
Once a part of a stem or root has formed, it stops growing. Cells continue to divide at the plant's growing tips.

Growing tip

Roots supply plant with water and minerals

Cambium

A meristem just beneath the surface of roots and stems

Cambium is also called **lateral meristem**. It forms between the xylem ■ and phloem ■ cells, and creates a continuous layer over a plant's roots and stems. As the cells in the cambium divide, they form new layers of xylem and phloem. This process is called **secondary growth**, and makes the stems and roots fatter.

Growth ring

A growth layer formed during a single growing season

If you look at a sawn tree trunk, you will see a series of rings in the wood. Each ring is a band of secondary growth, produced during a single growing season. Growth rings usually form at the rate of one a year, and their width shows how much growth occurred in a particular season. By analyzing growth rings, a scientist called a **dendrochronologist** can estimate a tree's age, and the conditions that it experienced each year.

Growth rings

Apical dominance

The suppression of branching growth by the tip of a stem

In many plants, the main stem grows more quickly than the side branches, so the plant becomes tall and narrow. A plant grows like this because the apical meristem at the tip of its stem produces plant hormones that suppress the growth of buds farther down. If the tip is cut off, the hormone supply stops, and the lower buds start to grow. Gardeners often cut off the tips of certain kinds of plant to make the plants more bushy.

Plant hormone

A substance produced by one plant cell that has an effect on another

Plant hormones affect the way plant cells develop and grow. There are five hormone groups. The **auxins**, **cytokinins**, and **giberellins** cause cells to divide or become longer. **Abscisic acid** is a hormone that suppresses growth. **Ethylene**, which is also called **ethene**, causes fruit to ripen, and fruit and leaves to fall.

Tropism

The growth of a plant in response to an outside stimulus

If you grow seedlings by a window, they bend toward the light. The uneven light causes an uneven distribution of the plant hormone auxin at the stem tips. This makes the tips bend as they grow. A response to light is called **phototropism**. Plants also display other kinds of tropism. **Geotropism** is a response to gravity, and **thigmotropism** is a response to touch. A tropism is either positive or negative. A **positive tropism** is growth toward a stimulus, and a **negative tropism** is growth away from it.

Shoot reaches toward light

Phototropism
Stems grow toward the light, so that the plant can collect energy for photosynthesis.

Geotropism
Roots grow toward the pull of gravity. This gives them good anchorage and the best chance of finding water.

Roots reach down into the ground

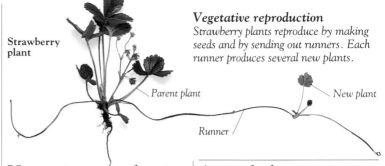

Strawberry plant

Parent plant

Runner

New plant

Vegetative reproduction
Strawberry plants reproduce by making seeds and by sending out runners. Each runner produces several new plants.

Vegetative reproduction

A form of growth that produces new plants

Many perennial plants reproduce by growing parts that eventually become new plants. These parts include underground tubers ■ and rhizomes ■, and small bulbs ■ called **bulbils**. A **runner** is a stem that grows out over the ground, and then forms an independent plant. Vegetative reproduction produces new plants that are genetically identical to the parent plant.

Growing from buds
Some plants, such as the Mexican hat plant, produce small buds that drop off and become new plants. Bud / \ Leaf

Photoperiodism

A response triggered by the changing lengths of day and night

Many plants flower at the same time every year. This happens because they contain a light-sensitive chemical called **phytochrome**, that detects the changing length of the day. Plants respond to changing day length in different ways. A **long-day plant** flowers only when there are many hours of daylight. A **short-day plant** flowers when the days are shorter. **Day-neutral plants** are not affected by changes in day length.

Annual plant

A plant that completes its life cycle in a single growing season

An annual plant puts all its energy into rapid reproduction. It flowers quickly and dies after producing seeds. Annual plants normally have shallow roots, and are quick to make use of bare ground.

Biennial plant

A plant that completes its life cycle in two growing seasons

A biennial plant spends its first growing season making food with its leaves and building up a root system. In the second growing season, the plant uses its food reserves to produce flowers and seeds, and then it dies.

Perennial plant

A plant that lives for more than two growing seasons

A perennial plant lives for several years. It may flower every year, or just once in its lifetime. Herbaceous ■ perennials have stems that die down every year. Woody ■ perennial plants have stems that stay alive and grow longer each season.

See also

Bulb 81 • Cell 18 • Cell division 40
Herbaceous plant 81 • Phloem 86
Rhizome 81 • Skin 141 • Tissue 23
Tuber 81 • Woody plant 81 • Xylem 86

Flower structure

Whatever their size, shape, or color, all flowers are made up of the same basic parts. These parts perform a flower's most important function, which is to bring about pollination to produce seeds for reproduction.

Flower

A structure that contains the organs for sexual reproduction in flowering plants

The main function of a flower is to bring about pollination ▪ so that seeds can be formed. A flower is made up of rings, or **whorls**, of different parts. Some of these parts produce the male or female sex cells ▪. Other parts, such as petals, protect the flower, or attract pollinators. A flower is attached to a swelling, or **receptacle**, at the end of a stem.

Sepal

An outer flap that protects a flower bud

A ring of sepals makes up a flower's **calyx**. Sepals are normally green and they form a case that protects the flower bud. In some flowers, the sepals are big and brightly colored to attract pollinators. In other flowers, the sepals fall to the ground when the flower opens.

Petal

An inner flap that often helps to attract animal pollinators

A ring of petals forms a flower's **corolla**. The petals can be joined together to produce a variety of shapes, including tubes and funnels, or they can be separate. Flowers that rely on animal pollination often have large, bright petals, and may be scented. Flowers that use wind pollination usually have small petals, or no petals at all. The corolla and the calyx make up a flower's **perianth**.

Pistil

The female parts of a flower

A pistil, or **gynoecium**, is the seed-bearing part of a flower. It is made up of organs called carpels. A flower may contain one or more carpels.

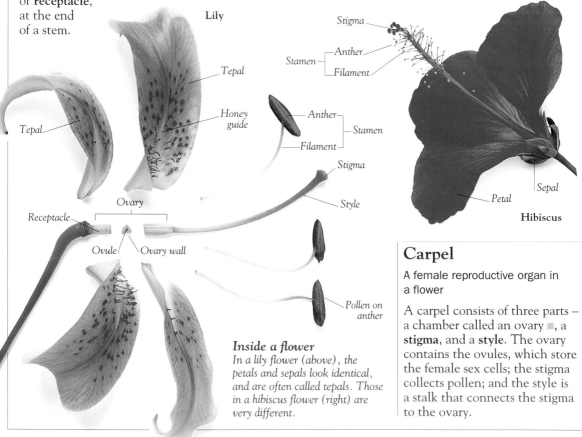

Lily

Tepal

Tepal

Honey guide

Receptacle

Ovary

Ovule   Ovary wall

Stamen — Anther — Filament

Anther — Stamen

Filament

Stigma

Style

Pollen on anther

Stigma — Anther — Filament

Inside a flower
In a lily flower (above), the petals and sepals look identical, and are often called tepals. Those in a hibiscus flower (right) are very different.

Stigma

Sepal

Petal

Hibiscus

Carpel

A female reproductive organ in a flower

A carpel consists of three parts – a chamber called an ovary ▪, a **stigma**, and a **style**. The ovary contains the ovules, which store the female sex cells; the stigma collects pollen; and the style is a stalk that connects the stigma to the ovary.

Stamen

A male reproductive organ in a flower

A stamen consists of an **anther** and a **filament**. The anther produces pollen in compartments called **pollen sacs**. When the pollen is ripe, the sacs split open to release the pollen. The filament connects the anther to the rest of the flower. Together, the stamens make up the flower's male parts, or **androecium**.

Inflorescence

A group of flowers on a stem

Some plants have single flowers on long stems. Others have flowers clustered together in groups, called inflorescences, or **flowerheads**. In some plants, such as members of the daisy family ■, an inflorescence can look like a single flower. The inflorescence of a daisy is called a **capitulum**. A **spike** has stalkless flowers on a single upright stem. A **raceme** is similar, but its flowers have short stalks. An **umbel** is an umbrella-shaped inflorescence, and a **catkin** is a spike that hangs downward.

Varieties of inflorescence

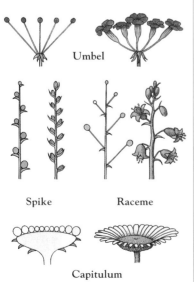

Umbel

Spike   Raceme

Capitulum

Regular flower

A flower that is radially symmetrical

A poppy ■ is a regular, or **actinomorphic**, flower. It has a round outline that can be divided into two equal halves in several different ways. Regular flowers have the simplest form of flower structure. The first flowers to evolve were shaped in this way.

Regular flowers

Tulip

Poppy

Rose

Monoecious plant

A plant that has male and female organs in separate flowers

The word monoecious comes from the Greek for "one house." Monoecious plants, such as the cucumber, have male and female organs in different flowers on the same plant. **Hermaphrodite** plants, such as poppies, have male and female organs in the same flower.

Dioecious plant

A plant that has either male or female flowers

Dioecious is from the Greek for "two houses." In dioecious plants, male and female flowers grow on separate plants. The **kiwi fruit** (*Actinidia sinensis*) is a dioecious plant. For these plants to produce fruit, the flowers on the female plant must receive pollen from a male plant.

Irregular flower

A flower that is bilaterally symmetrical

A pea ■ flower has a complicated outline, and it can be divided into equal halves in only one way. It is a typical irregular, or **zygomorphic**, flower. Irregular flowers are often pollinated by a particular kind of insect or other animal.

Irregular flowers

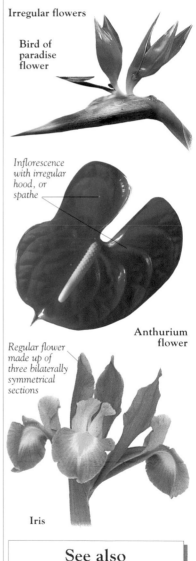

Bird of paradise flower

Inflorescence with irregular hood, or spathe

Anthurium flower

Regular flower made up of three bilaterally symmetrical sections

Iris

See also

Daisy family 74 • Pea family 74
Plant ovary 93 • Pollination 92
Poppy family 73 • Sex cell 41

Pollination & seeds

Before a flower can produce seeds, it must be pollinated. For this to happen, pollen has to travel from the male part of a flower to a female part. When a pollen grain lands on a suitable flower, an extraordinary chain of events begins, which results in the production of seeds.

See also

Dicot 72 • Fertilization 161
Grass family 75 • Gymnosperm 70
Monocot 72 • Nucleus 19
Photosynthesis 84 • Plant cell 20
Sex cell 41 • Spore 77
Tissue 23 • Variation 42

Pollination

The transfer of pollen from the male parts of flowers to the female parts

Pollen grain

Pollination is the process that brings male and female sex cells ▧ together so that fertilization ▧ can occur. Pollen contains male sex cells. It is produced by a flower's male parts, the anthers. Pollen is usually carried to the female parts, or stigmas, of a flower by animals or by the wind.

Pollen

Dustlike particles that contain male sex cells

Pollen is made up of microscopic **pollen grains**; it often looks like yellow or orange dust. Each grain of pollen has a tough outer wall, patterned with bumps and pits. Pollen is produced by a flower's anthers. It contains the male nuclei ▧ that fertilize the female sex cells. Fertilization occurs when a pollen grain lands on the stigma of a suitable flower.

Nectar

A sugary liquid produced by animal-pollinated flowers

Nectar is produced by small glands in a flower, called **nectaries**. The sweet nectar attracts animals, which help spread the plant's pollen as they feed on different plants.

Cross-pollination

The pollination of one plant by another plant of the same species

Many plants have both male and female organs and are capable of pollinating themselves, or **self-pollination**. However, this does not produce much genetic variation ▧, and plants have evolved different methods of cross-pollination. This involves transferring pollen from one plant to another, and requires an agent, or **pollinator**, to carry the pollen from flower to flower.

Large scented petals

Animal pollination

A kind of pollination that is carried out by animals

Many flowering plants depend on animals to carry their pollen between flowers. The most common animal pollinators are insects, but birds and bats also pollinate flowers. Animal-pollinated flowers usually have sticky pollen that glues itself to visiting animals. Flowers attract animals with their bright colors and sweet scents.

Pollen is collected in special baskets on the bee's hind legs

Animal pollinator
A nectar-gathering bee is dusted with pollen from the flower's stamens.

Wind pollination

A kind of pollination that is carried out by the wind

Wind-pollinated plants usually have drab, feathery flowers and dry, dustlike pollen. When the flowers are ripe, they scatter their pollen into the air. The wind carries the pollen from one plant to another. Wind-pollinated plants include grasses ■ and most gymnosperms ■.

Wind pollination
Pollen grains from these hazel catkins are being scattered into the air by the wind.

Water pollination

A kind of pollination that is carried out by water

Most flowering plants that live in water flower above the surface and are pollinated by animals or by the wind. Some pondweeds flower at the surface, and the water floats their pollen from one flower to another.

Plant ovary

A female structure that contains the ovules

In flowering plants, the ovary is a chamber inside which the **ovules** form. An ovule is a collection of cells ■ on a short stalk. It is attached to a part of the ovary called the **placenta**. The ovule has a protective layer of cells around it. The outer cells surround an inner cluster of cells called an **embryo sac**. One of these inner cells is the female sex cell, or **ovum**. A small hole called the **micropyle** allows the pollen tube to enter the ovule.

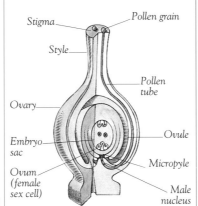

Fertilization
Chemicals guide the growing pollen tube to the embryo sac.

Pollen tube

A tube that grows from a pollen grain and into an ovule

When a pollen grain lands on the stigma of a suitable flower, it begins to grow. It produces an extremely fine tube that grows down through the style. The pollen tube pushes through the micropyle of the ovule until it reaches the embryo sac. Two male nuclei then travel down the tube. One fertilizes the ovum, and one fertilizes two other female nuclei to produce the endosperm. This is called **double fertilization**, and it is found only in flowering plants.

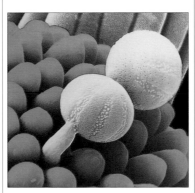

Pollen tubes
This color-enhanced electron micrograph shows two pollen grains on the surface of a flower's stigma. A pollen tube has started to grow out of one of the grains.

Seed

A reproductive structure containing an embryo plant and a food store

A seed is formed by a fertilized ovule. It is bigger than a spore ■, and much more complex. A seed contains an **embryo**, which is the beginning of a plant. It also has all the food supplies needed to fuel the plant's early growth. The food is stored in a tissue ■ called the **endosperm**. In some plants, food is also found in the seed leaves, or cotyledons. A ripe seed is surrounded by a hard coat called a **testa**.

Cotyledon

A seed leaf

A cotyledon is a small leaf that is packed inside a seed. Some cotyledons store food and remain below ground when the seed germinates. Others open above ground and produce food by photosynthesis. A plant's cotyledons often look quite different from its other leaves. A monocot ■ has one cotyledon, while a dicot ■ has two.

Germinating bean

Germination

The start of growth in a seed or spore

When conditions are right, a seed takes in water and begins to grow. A root, or **radicle**, breaks through the seed coat, and begins to grow down into the soil. Shortly afterward, a stem, or **plumule**, begins to grow upward. Seeds germinate in two different ways. In **hypogeal germination**, cotyledons stay below ground. In **epigeal germination**, the cotyledons emerge aboveground and begin to make food by photosynthesis ■.

Fruits

The term "fruit" refers to anything that contains seeds, from a coconut to a cucumber. Fruits can be succulent and juicy or hard and dry. Plants use fruits as a way of scattering their seeds far and wide.

—Seeds scatter

Exploding fruit

Himalayan balsam

Fruit

A ripened ovary that contains a flower's seeds

When a flower's ovary ▪ has been fertilized ▪, it forms seeds that develops into a fruit. If the plant uses animals to spread its seeds, the fruit wall, or **pericarp**, often becomes succulent and juicy. If seeds are carried by the wind, the fruit wall is usually hard and dry.

Seed dispersal

The scattering of a plant's seeds

A seed needs light, water, and minerals to grow into a new plant. To avoid overcrowding, a seed must be dispersed away from the parent plant. Plants that use **animal dispersal** have fruits with hooks that cling to an animal's fur, or fruits that are good to eat. When an animal eats a fruit, the seeds often pass through its body unharmed. Plants that use **wind dispersal** have fruits that blow away on parachutes or tiny sails. **Mechanically dispersed** fruits explode or burst and flick the seeds away. Plants that use **water dispersal** have seeds and fruits that float.

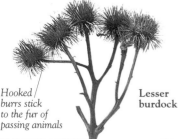

Hooked burrs stick to the fur of passing animals

Lesser burdock

Simple fruit

A fruit that forms from a single ovary

There are many kinds of simple fruits, such as berries, drupes, and nuts. Each fruit is formed from a single ovary.

Achene

A dry fruit with a single seed

An achene is one of the simplest types of indehiscent fruit. It has a single seed that lies in a space inside the fruit. The seed is surrounded by a dry fruit wall, or pericarp. Plants in the buttercup family have achenes.

Strawberry

A strawberry is a false fruit. Its surface is covered with tiny achenes.

Schizocarp

A dry fruit that breaks up into enclosed, one-seeded units

Maple trees (*Acer*) are examples of plants that have schizocarpic fruits. Each fruit contains two winged seeds. When they are ripe, the seeds break apart and flutter to the ground separately. These one-seeded units are called **mericarps**. Plants in the parsley family ▪ also have fruits that split in this way.

Dehiscent fruit

A dry fruit that splits or bursts open to release its seeds

Some fruits break open when they are ripe. This can happen very suddenly, so that the seeds are flicked away from the parent plant. These fruits are called dehiscent. **Indehiscent** fruits are ones that do not break open.

Strawberry

Sepal

Swollen receptacle

Poppy seeds

Achene

Capsule

A dry fruit that develops from several ovaries joined together

Poppy capsule

A capsule contains many seeds. Plants in the poppy family ▪ grow capsules. If you break open a poppy capsule, you can see the partitions formed by neighboring ovaries. A poppy capsule often has a circle of holes that lets the seeds escape. Some other flowers have capsules with lids that flip up to release the seeds.

Poppy

Legume

A dry fruit that opens along two sides

One of the most common kinds of legume is a pea pod. It forms from a single ovary and releases its seeds by splitting along two sides. The plants in the pea family ■ grow legumes, or pods, of many shapes and sizes. Some are over 5 feet (1.5 meters) long.

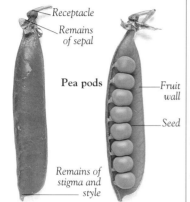

Receptacle
Remains of sepal
Pea pods
Fruit wall
Seed
Remains of stigma and style

Compound fruit

A fruit that develops from several ovaries

Many plants have fruits that develop from several ovaries. The ovaries join together to form compound fruits. An orange is made up of several segments, each of which has formed from a single ovary. In an **aggregate fruit**, such as an orange or blackberry, the ovaries all belong to one flower. A **multiple fruit**, such as a pineapple, has ovaries from several flowers.

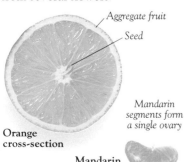

Aggregate fruit
Seed
Mandarin segments form a single ovary
Orange cross-section

Mandarin segment

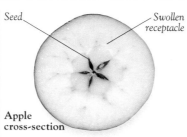

Seed
Swollen receptacle
Apple cross-section

False fruit

A fruit that develops from an ovary and other flower parts

Apples and strawberries are both false fruits. Their juicy flesh is actually a swollen receptacle, rather than part of an ovary. In an apple, the true fruit is the core. In a strawberry, the fruits are tiny achenes scattered over the fleshy surface.

Berry

A succulent fruit with many seeds

Berries have soft flesh and many seeds. The juicy flesh attracts animals that eat the berries and disperse the seeds. Many plants grow berries, including tomatoes, grape vines, and even bananas.

Cape gooseberry

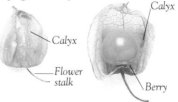

Calyx
Calyx
Flower stalk
Berry

Outside view   **Inside view**

Drupe

A fleshy fruit containing hard seeds

Drupes develop from one or more carpels ■ that are fused together. They contain one or many seeds that are protected by a very hard pericarp. Plums, cherries, and peaches are all kinds of drupe.

See also

Carpel 90 • Fertilization 161
Parsley family 74 • Pea family 74
Plant ovary 93 • Poppy family 73

Nut

A hard, dry fruit with a single seed

In a nut, the seed is surrounded by a hard fruit wall, or pericarp. The pericarp protects the nut's embryo and food store, or **kernel**. Many trees grow nuts. In some trees, each nut sits on a fleshy swelling or a cup, and the nut drops off when it is ripe. In others, the nuts develop inside a case, which sometimes has spines. When the nuts are ready to fall, the case usually splits open. Many smaller plants grow tiny nuts called **nutlets**.

Follicle

A dry fruit that opens along one side

A follicle develops from a single ovary. When the fruit is ripe, it splits open along one side only to release the seeds. Follicles often occur in groups, or clusters. The **larkspur** (*Consolida regalis*) and delphiniums (*Delphinium*) are two garden plants that produce this kind of fruit.

Plums

Simple invertebrates

An invertebrate is an animal that does not have a backbone. Many are small water-dwellers that spend their adult lives in one place. Invertebrates make up over nine-tenths of all animal species.

See also

Arthropod 100
Phylum 56 • Species 48

Invertebrate

An animal without a backbone

There are over 30 phyla ■ of invertebrate. Most invertebrates are small and slow moving. Many are **sessile** during their adult lives, which means that they stay in one place. Invertebrates are mostly found in the sea and in fresh water, although one group, the arthropods ■, has also been particularly successful on land.

Comb jelly

An invertebrate with long, trailing tentacles

Comb jellies are small, jellylike animals that drift in the sea. They belong to the phylum **Ctenophora**. Most comb jellies catch their food by trailing two long tentacles in the water. These are covered with sticky cells.

Sponge

An invertebrate that draws in water through a system of pores

Sponge skeleton

Sponges belong to the phylum **Porifera**, which contains about 5,000 species ■. A sponge's body is riddled with tiny holes, or pores. Water is drawn in through the pores by **collar cells,** which act like sieves. It travels through the sponge and passes out through a larger vent, the **osculum.** The sponge filters out food particles from the water. A sponge's cells are supported by a skeleton made of tiny struts, called **spicules**.

Cnidarian

An invertebrate with a digestive cavity that has only one opening

The cnidarians form the phylum **Cnidaria** or **Coelenterata**, which has over 10,000 species. Cnidarians have two different body forms. A **polyp** lives with one end of its body attached to something solid. A **medusa** moves by contracting its bell-shaped body. Both forms catch food with armlike **tentacles** that have stinging threads called **nematocysts**. The tentacles draw food into a **digestive cavity**.

Cross section of a jellyfish

Bell-shaped body — *Digestive cavity*

Mouth lobe — *Tentacle*

Mouth

Jellyfish

A cnidarian with a bell-shaped body

A jellyfish has tentacles that trail from the rim of its bell-shaped body. **Mouth lobes** trail from the center. A jellyfish swims by contracting and relaxing its bell to push against the water.

Coral

A cnidarian that often lives in large groups

Coral polyps have cylinder-shaped bodies. Some protect themselves by building hard cases of calcium carbonate. When these corals die, their cases can form **coral reefs**.

Hydra

A group of species of cnidarian found in fresh water

Most cnidarians live in the sea, but *Hydra* lives in fresh water. A *Hydra* polyp has a hollow trunk. Its mouth is at one end and is surrounded by a ring of tentacles. *Hydra* captures small animals by trailing stinging tentacles in the water. It can reproduce asexually.

Sea anemone

A cnidarian with a suckerlike foot

Sea anemones usually live alone. They have thick bodies and long tentacles with stinging cells. They attach themselves to rocks with a **basal disk**, which works like a sucker. Sea anemones feed on small animals.

Anemones
An anemone folds in its brightly colored tentacles when the tide recedes.

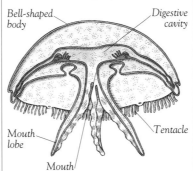

Worms

The word "worm" often refers to any animal that has a long, soft body without legs. There are many different kinds of worm, all of which are shaped to suit different lifestyles.

Flatworm

A ribbonlike worm without a segmented body

Flatworms have a flattened body with just one opening, the mouth. They make up the phylum ■ **Platyhelminthes**, which has over 10,000 species ■.

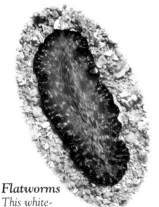

Flatworms
This white-streaked flatworm comes from the Marshall Islands in the Pacific Ocean.

Planarian

A free-living flatworm with tubelike mouthparts

Planarians live either in water or in damp places. They creep over solid surfaces using muscles and cilia ■ on their flat undersides. A planarian's mouth is halfway down its body, and it eats by pushing out a long tube, called a **pharynx**. Many planarians can reproduce asexually ■.

See also

Asexual reproduction 160 • Cilium 19
Deposit feeding 117 • Host 175
Parasite 175 • Phylum 56 • Species 48

Tapeworm

A parasitic flatworm that lives in the digestive system of its host

A tapeworm is a parasite ■. It lives inside the body of an animal, called the host ■. An adult tapeworm has a tiny head, or **scolex**. Its long, flat body is divided into sections, called **proglottids**. Hooks and suckers on the worm's head grip the inside of a host's intestines. Tapeworms absorb food from their host's gut. They make millions of eggs, which are slowly released when their oldest body sections leave their host's body.

Annelid worm

A worm with a segmented body, a mouth, and an anus

Annelid worms make up the phylum **Annelida**, which has about 12,000 species. Their bodies are made up of segments. Each segment has a set of muscles. It may also have flaps or bristles that help the worm move.

Bristleworm
A bristleworm is an annelid; it has a segmented body. This species lives in shallow seawater.

Leech

An annelid worm with a sucker at each end of the body

Leeches often feed on the blood of other animals. They attach themselves with suckers and use small teeth to make a cut. When a leech feeds, it produces an **anticoagulant**, a substance that stops blood from clotting. Some leeches eat small invertebrates.

Earthworm

An annelid worm that feeds on organic matter in soil

An earthworm's rounded body has rows of small bristles, called **chaetae**. It moves using two sets of muscles to make its segments change shape. Earthworms are deposit feeders ■. They get their food from the soil.

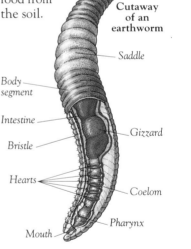

Cutaway of an earthworm

Saddle
Body segment
Intestine
Gizzard
Bristle
Hearts
Coelom
Pharynx
Mouth

Roundworm

An unsegmented worm that is covered by a hard cuticle

Roundworms make up the phylum **Nematoda**, which contains at least 15,000 species. Roundworms have a cylindrical body covered by a hard outer layer called a **cuticle**. They live in different kinds of habitat, and many are parasites of plants or animals, including humans.

Mollusks

Mollusks have soft, moist bodies that are often protected by hard shells. Most are slow-moving animals, although octopuses and squid can shoot through the water with a burst of speed.

See also

Cell 18 • Class 56 • Filter feeding 117
Gill 122 • Invertebrate 96
Jet propulsion 144 • Lung 124
Phylum 56 • Shell 136 • Species 48

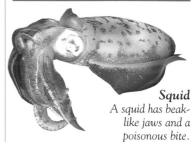

Squid
A squid has beak-like jaws and a poisonous bite.

Mollusk

A soft-bodied invertebrate that is often protected by a hard shell

Mollusks make up the phylum ■ **Mollusca**, which contains about 100,000 species ■. The mollusks are the second largest group of invertebrates ■. Most mollusks have shells ■ and live in water, although some live on land. Many are hermaphrodites, which means that they have both male and female parts. The three main mollusk groups are gastropods, bivalves, and cephalopods.

Gastropod

A mollusk with a suckerlike foot

The **garden snail** (*Helix aspersa*) is a typical gastropod. It moves by creeping along on its muscular foot and is protected by a coiled shell. A snail has a mouthpart called a **radula**, which has rows of tiny teeth. Land snails have lungs ■ and breathe air, while snails that live in water breathe with gills ■. A **slug** is similar to a snail, but usually does not have a shell. Gastropods make up the class ■ **Gastropoda**, which includes over four-fifths of all mollusk species.

Bivalve

A mollusk with a two-part shell

Bivalves belong to the class **Bivalvia**. They live in water and are usually either slow-moving or stay in one place. Most bivalves live by filter feeding ■. Their bodies are protected by a shell made of two hinged halves, or **valves**. These can be pulled together by a powerful **adductor muscle**. **Oysters**, **clams**, and **mussels** are bivalves.

Cock's comb oyster

Painted tree oyster

Camp Pitar-venus

Siphon

A tube that carries water to a mollusk's gills

Some mollusks, particularly bivalves, live buried in sand or mud on the seabed. They use siphons to draw water over and through their gills, so they can breathe and feed.

Cephalopod

A mollusk with a large head and a ring of tentacles

Cephalopods include animals such as **octopuses**, **squid**, and **cuttlefish**. Unlike most other mollusks, cephalopods are often fast-moving and are effective hunters. They catch other animals using sucker-bearing tentacles and they move by a form of jet propulsion ■, which involves squirting water through a siphon.

Chromatophore

A cell containing pigments

Most cephalopods can change color to match their background. They do this by using chromatophores. These are cells ■ with tiny bags of **pigment**, or color, inside them. The bags can be stretched or squashed to alter the cell's color.

Garden snail
This cutaway model of a snail shows how its digestive system is protected inside its shell.

Shell

Lung

Anus

Salivary gland

Eye

Crop

Sensory tentacle

Mouth

Reproductive organ

Stomach

Reproductive gland

Foot

Echinoderms & sea squirts

The word echinoderm means "spiny skinned." Echinoderms often have a distinctive five-part body plan, arranged like the spokes of a wheel. Sea squirts are distant relatives of vertebrates.

Echinoderm

An invertebrate with an internal skeleton and fivefold symmetry

Echinoderms are unlike all other animals. Their bodies are usually divided into five equal parts, and they have skeletons ■ made of hard plates, called **ossicles**, just beneath the skin. Most echinoderms have lots of small, sucker-tipped **tube feet**. Echinoderms live in the sea and include animals such as starfish, sea cucumbers, and sea urchins. They make up the phylum ■ **Echinodermata**, which has about 6,500 species ■.

Starfish

A star-shaped echinoderm with broad arms

Starfish live in shallow water. The undersides of their arms are covered with rows of fluid-filled tube feet, which they use for moving and feeding. Many starfish eat bivalves. A starfish can slowly pull apart the halves of a bivalve's shell, squeezing its stomach into the tiny opening to digest the bivalve's soft body.

See also

Larva 166 • Phylum 56
Skeleton 136 • Species 48
Vertebrate 104

Brittlestar

An echinoderm with slender arms and a central disc

Brittlestars live on the seabed and feed on dead animals. Unlike true starfish, brittlestars have slender, flexible arms. They move by hooking their arms around anything solid and pulling themselves along.

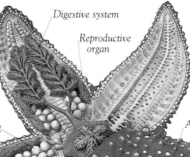

Digestive system

Reproductive organ

Chamber connecting to tube foot

Arm

Ossicles

Fluid-filled pipe

Tube foot

Starfish
This cutaway model of a starfish shows the fluid-filled pipes that connect the starfish's many tube feet.

Sea cucumber

A cucumber-shaped echinoderm with a ring of tentacles

Instead of arms or spines, sea cucumbers have tentacles and five rows of tube feet. They lie lengthways on the seabed, and collect food with their tentacles.

Sea urchin

An echinoderm that has a spiny, rounded skeleton

A sea urchin's body is protected by a hard case called a **test**, made of interlocking plates. The test is covered with protective spines. Most sea urchins are round and live on rocks. Those that live in sand or mud in shallow water have flatter bodies.

Sea urchins
A sea urchin scrapes food off rocks using five hard teeth on its underside.

Sea squirt

A bottle-shaped invertebrate that has a tadpole-like larva

Sea squirts are small animals that belong to the phylum **Chordata**. This large phylum contains all animals, including vertebrates ■, that have a flexible skeletal rod, called a **notochord**, running down their bodies. A sea squirt only has a notochord during the first stage of its life cycle, when it is a larva ■. An adult sea squirt is a sessile animal, which means that it spends its life in one place.

Sea squirts
A sea squirt lives by pumping water through its body to filter food particles.

Arthropods

The arthropods are one of the most successful invertebrate groups. There are over 1 million known species on land and in water. Arthropods vary greatly in size and appearance, but all have jointed bodies protected by a tough outer case.

Arthropod

An invertebrate with a jointed body case

An arthropod is an invertebrate ■. Its body is usually segmented, and is covered by a tough, waterproof body case, or exoskeleton ■. The exoskeleton is made up of separate plates. Flexible joints between the plates allow the animal to move. During their lives, arthropods must shed this exoskeleton several times in order to grow to adult size. This process is known as molting. The phylum ■ **Arthropoda** is the largest and most successful in the Animal Kingdom. The major groups of arthropods are crustaceans, arachnids, and insects ■. Of these three groups, the insects are by far the largest.

Lobster
A lobster is a decapod. It hunts by walking slowly over the seabed. If threatened, it can swim backward by flicking paddle-shaped swimmerets and its broad tail.

Water flea
A water flea, or Daphnia, swims by flicking its feathery antennas. This female water flea contains two fertilized eggs.

Crustacean

An arthropod with jointed legs and two pairs of antennas

Crustaceans make up the superclass **Crustacea**, which contains about 32,000 species ■. They get their name from the hard case, or "crust," that encloses the body. A typical crustacean has compound eyes ■, two pairs of antennas ■, and several pairs of jointed legs. Crustaceans vary greatly in size. As they grow into adults, most crustaceans undergo metamorphosis ■. Crustaceans usually live in seawater. Only a few, such as **woodlice**, live on land.

Decapod

A crustacean with five pairs of walking legs

Decapods make up about one-third of all crustacean species. They include **crabs**, **lobsters**, and **shrimps**. A decapod's body is divided into two regions. At the front of the body, the head and **thorax** are fused together to make up the **cephalothorax**. A hard shield called a **carapace** protects the cephalothorax. The more flexible abdomen, which is at the back of the body, is sometimes tucked underneath. Decapod means "ten-legged," and most decapods have five pairs of walking legs. They also have two pincers, which may be different sizes.

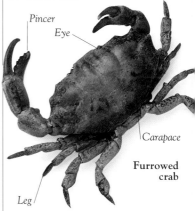

Pincer

Eye

Carapace

Furrowed crab

Leg

Crabs
A crab is protected by a shieldlike carapace. Its abdomen is folded beneath its body.

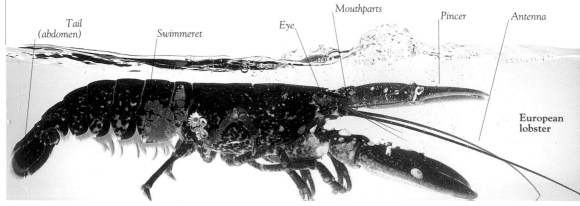

Tail (abdomen)

Swimmeret

Eye

Mouthparts

Pincer

Antenna

European lobster

Krill

A marine crustacean that lives in the Antarctic Ocean

Krill (*Euphausia superba*) are small shrimplike animals that feed on plankton ■ in the sea. They live in giant shoals that may contain billions of animals. Krill are an extremely important part of Antarctic food chains ■ and provide food for birds and several kinds of marine mammal ■, including whales.

Arachnid

An arthropod with four pairs of walking legs

Arachnids include spiders, mites, scorpions, and other similar animals. Together, they make up the class ■ **Arachnida**, which contains at least 70,000 species. Like crustaceans, arachnids have a cephalothorax and an abdomen. However, unlike crustaceans, most arachnids live on land, have only four pairs of walking legs, and no compound eyes.

Mite

A small arachnid that sucks fluid from plants, animals, or dead remains

Mites usually have rounded or flattened bodies and legs that grip. Most live on land, but a few live in water and are good swimmers. A **tick** is a mite that sucks blood from animals. Some ticks transmit diseases.

See also

Antenna 156 • Carnivorous 116
Class 56 • Compound eye 153
Enzyme 31 • Exoskeleton 136
Food chain 172 • Insect 102
Invertebrate 96 • Mammal 112
Metamorphosis 166 • Phylum 56
Plankton 64 • Protein 30 • Species 48

Spider

An arachnid with poisonous fangs

Spiders are the largest and most successful arachnids, with about 30,000 different species. All spiders are carnivorous ■ and have powerful fangs that release deadly poison into their prey. A spider pumps digestive enzymes ■ into its victim, and sucks up the nutritious fluid that is formed. Some spiders catch their food by spinning **webs** of silk, made from protein ■. The silk is squeezed out through nozzles called **spinnerets**. Spiders that do not make webs often jump on their prey.

Chilean red-leg spider

Spinneret

Abdomen

Cephalothorax

Feeler

Jaws

Scorpion

An arachnid with pincers and a poisonous stinger

Scorpions live mainly in warm parts of the world. They catch other animals with their strong claws, or **pincers**, then paralyze their prey with a poisonous sting. A female scorpion is a careful parent. She gives birth to live young and carries them on her back until they are big enough to look after themselves.

Pincer

Centipede

An arthropod with poison claws and a long, flattened body

Centipedes are many-legged hunters that live in soil and feed on small animals. A centipede has a pair of legs on each body segment. They kill their prey with two **poison claws** situated behind the head. Centipedes make up the class **Chilopoda**, which has about 3,000 species.

Millipede

An arthropod with a cylindrical body and many pairs of legs

Millipedes have cylindrical bodies with two pairs of legs on each segment. The largest millipedes have over 500 pairs of legs, although many have far fewer than this. Millipedes live mainly in soil or under dead bark, and they feed on decaying plants. They belong to the class **Diplopoda**, which contains about 8,000 species.

Poisonous stinger

Scorpion

Exoskeleton made of flexible plates

Insects

Almost every habitat on land contains insects. They make up three-quarters of all the animal species on Earth, and every year about 10,000 new species of insect are identified.

Antenna

Locust

Insect

An invertebrate with six legs and a body divided into three parts

Insects make up the class ■ **Insecta**, which contains at least 800,000 species ■. An insect is an invertebrate with a segmented body that can be divided into three parts. The mouthparts and the sense organs, which often include a pair of compound eyes ■, are situated on the **head**. The **thorax** has three pairs of legs and, in most insects, one or two pairs of wings. The **abdomen** contains the digestive system and reproductive organs.

Wingless insect

A primitive insect without wings

Wingless insects are small, and many do not have antennas ■ or eyes. They undergo incomplete metamorphosis ■, which means they change shape gradually as they grow into adults. Wingless insects, such as **silverfish**, live in damp places.

Winged insect

An insect that has wings

Winged insects form the subclass **Pterygota**, which contains over nine-tenths of all insect species. Most have two pairs of wings, called **forewings** and **hindwings**, and all undergo metamorphosis ■, which means they change shape abruptly or gradually as they mature. During evolution ■, some winged insects, for example many ants, have lost their wings.

Airborne hunter
Unlike most insects, a dragonfly cannot fold its wings. It rests with them at right angles to its body.

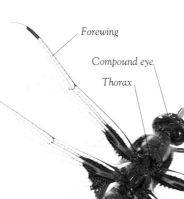

Forewing

Compound eye

Thorax

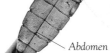

Hindwing

Abdomen

Termite

A social insect with biting mouthparts, often without wings

Termites are social animals ■ that live together in colonies. A colony is made up of different termite groups, called **castes**. Each caste carries out different tasks. The **queen** lays eggs, the **workers** look after the eggs and collect food, and the **soldiers** defend the nest. Termites often build large nests from mud or wood and feed on plant material. They undergo incomplete metamorphosis as they become adults. Termites belong to the order ■ **Isoptera**, which contains about 2,000 species.

Grasshopper

An insect with powerful back legs and leathery forewings

Grasshoppers, together with **crickets**, make up part of the order **Orthoptera**, which contains over 20,000 species. Insects in this order can fly, but usually move by jumping. Most communicate with sounds made by stridulation, which involves rubbing a small roughened surface on their hind legs against their front wings. They have powerful jaws and feed on plants and animals. They develop by incomplete metamorphosis. The **locust** (*Locusta migratoria*) is a form of grasshopper.

Dragonfly

Dragonfly

A predatory insect that has two pairs of stiff wings

Dragonflies are hunters. They are skillful fliers and catch insects in midair by holding their legs together to form a basket. They have the largest compound eyes of all insects, and can see moving objects several yards away. Dragonflies undergo incomplete metamorphosis. A young dragonfly, or nymph ■, lives in water. It has a big head, thick body, and no wings. The nymphs catch their prey with a set of hinged mouthparts called a **mask**. Dragonflies make up part of the insect order **Odonata**, which has over 5,000 species.

Bug

An insect with piercing mouthparts and thickened forewings

In biology, a bug is a particular kind of insect. Bugs belong to the order **Hemiptera**, which contains about 50,000 species. These "true bugs" live on plants or animals. They have a long, jointed feeding tube for piercing and sucking their food. All bugs develop by incomplete metamorphosis.

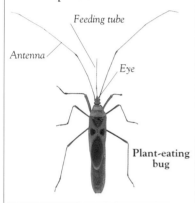

Feeding tube

Antenna

Eye

Plant-eating bug

Beetle

An insect with hardened forewings

Beetles belong to the order **Coleoptera**, which is the largest order of insects. There are nearly 400,000 species of beetle. A beetle's forewings are modified into two curved plates, called **elytra** (singular **elytron**). The delicate hindwings used for flying are protected beneath the elytra. Beetles undergo complete metamorphosis ■. Young beetle larvae, or grubs, often burrow through their food.

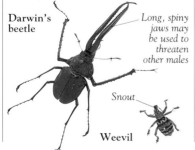

Darwin's beetle

Long, spiny jaws may be used to threaten other males

Snout

Weevil

Fly

An insect that has only one pair of working wings

A true fly is an insect that belongs to the order **Diptera**, which contains about 90,000 species. This order includes the **housefly** (*Musca domestica*), **horseflies** (family **Tabanidae**), **mosquitoes** (family **Culicidae**), and **tsetse flies** (family **Glossinidae**). True flies use only their forewings for flight. Their hindwings have evolved into tiny club-shaped organs called **halteres**. These help the insect balance in flight. Flies feed on many things, and their mouthparts are adapted for sucking or piercing. All true flies develop by complete metamorphosis, and their legless larvae are often called **maggots**.

Wasp

An insect that has forewings and hindwings which hook together

Wasps belong to the order **Hymenoptera**, which numbers about 100,000 species, and also includes **bees** and **ants**. Many of these insects are social animals, which means they live in large groups. Wasps eat a variety of food, and many species of small wasp are parasites ■ of other insects. The females have a long egg-laying tube, called an **ovipositor**. This may be adapted to form a poisonous stinger. Like bees and ants, wasps undergo complete metamorphosis.

Butterfly

An insect that has large wings and is covered with tiny scales

Together with **moths**, butterflies make up the order **Lepidoptera**, which contains about 150,000 species. Butterflies and moths have a covering of scales over their wings, bodies, and legs. They undergo complete metamorphosis. Their caterpillars ■, or larvae, usually live by chewing plant food. An adult butterfly has a tubelike **proboscis** that it uses to suck liquids such as nectar from flowers. The proboscis can be coiled up when it is not in use.

Swallowtail butterfly

Swallowtail butterfly caterpillar

True leg

Head

Prolegs

Caterpillars
A caterpillar has three pairs of true legs and four pairs of stumpy prolegs.

See also

Antenna 156 • Caterpillar 167 • Class 56

Complete metamorphosis 167

Compound eye 153 • Evolution 44

Incomplete metamorphosis 166

Metamorphosis 166 • Nymph 166

Order 56 • Parasite 175

Social animal 159 • Species 48

Fish

Leopard shark

Fish are the most successful group of vertebrates They live almost anywhere there is water. Fish are perfectly equipped for their underwater life with slippery scales and a streamlined body. Most have balloonlike swim bladders that help keep them afloat.

Vertebrate

An animal with a backbone

A vertebrate has a body that is supported by a backbone. A backbone is made up of separate units, called vertebrae ■, that link together to form a column. Most vertebrates have highly developed sense organs and nervous systems ■, so they can react to their surroundings. Vertebrates form the subphylum **Vertebrata**, which contains over 40,000 species ■. They make up the largest part of the phylum ■ Chordata. Fish, reptiles, birds, mammals, and amphibians are different kinds of vertebrate.

Fish

A vertebrate that lives in water and breathes through gills

A fish is a vertebrate that lives in water. Fish are ectotherms ■, which means their body temperature changes with that of their surroundings. Most fish take in oxygen by breathing through gills ■. They move through water using their tail, and are usually protected by a coat of hard scales ■. The scales are often covered in a slippery fluid called **mucus** which helps the fish slide through the water. There are three groups of fish – the jawless fish, the cartilaginous fish, and the bony fish. These groups make up the superclass **Pisces**, which contains over 20,000 species.

Jawless fish

A primitive fish with a jawless mouth

Most fish have mouths with hinged jaws ■, but jawless fish have simple, suckerlike mouths. Jawless fish were the first fish to evolve, over 400 million years ago. The only kinds of jawless fish alive today are lampreys and hagfish. They make up the superclass **Agnatha**, which contains about 70 species.

Lamprey

A parasitic jawless fish

Lampreys live in fresh water and in the sea. The adults have long bodies and round mouths with sharp teeth. They are parasites ■ that live by attaching themselves to other fish and sucking their blood. Young lampreys change into adults by metamorphosis ■. **Hagfish** are jawless fish that live on dead animals. They have no eyes; their long bodies are covered with slimy mucus. A hagfish has a special tongue with sharp teeth for burrowing into dead fish.

Suckerlike mouth
This picture of a sea lamprey's mouth shows the round sucker and sharp teeth.

Cartilaginous fish

A fish with a skeleton made of cartilage instead of bone

Nearly all cartilaginous fish are hunters that live in salt water. They include **sharks**, **skates**, and **rays**. These fish all have hinged jaws and skeletons made of a strong, flexible tissue called cartilage ■. Their skin is covered with rough, toothlike scales that feel like sandpaper. Skates and rays have flattened bodies and wide pectoral fins. There are about 700 species of cartilaginous fish and they make up the class ■ **Chondroichthyes**.

Tail fin

Scales

Anal fin

Shark

A cartilaginous fish with a long, streamlined body

Most sharks are ferocious predators ■. They are powerful swimmers and have jaws armed with sharp teeth. A shark's streamlined body is perfect for swimming, but a shark often has to keep moving to stay afloat because it has no swim bladder. However, sharks do have large, oil-filled livers that help with flotation. The largest sharks, the **basking shark** (*Cetorhinus maximus*) and the **whale shark** (*Rhincodon typus*) eat plankton ■ and are harmless to humans.

Bony fish

A fish with jaws and a skeleton made of bone

Bony fish have skeletons made of bone, and swim bladders to keep them afloat. Their gills are covered by a flap called an **operculum**. There are over 20,000 species of bony fish, and they make up the class **Osteichthyes**. Bony fish range in size from huge **sunfish** (*Mola mola*), which can weigh up to 2 tons (about 2 tonnes), to tiny **gobies** (*Trimmatom*), which can be less than 0.4 inch (1 centimeter) long.

Opercular bones protect gills

First dorsal fin

Second dorsal fin

Bony fish skeleton
This is a skeleton of an Atlantic cod, which is a typical bony fish.

Tail fin

Hinged jaw

Pectoral fin

Pelvic fin

Bony spine

Anal fin

Dorsal fin

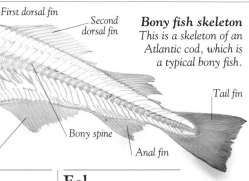

Gill cover

Koi carp
A typical example of a bony fish is the koi carp. Koi carp have been bred to produce bold colors.

Lungfish

A fish that breathes air through organs that are similar to lungs

Lungfish are unusual fish with long bodies and short, stumpy fins. They live in warm, swampy places and they breathe air with organs that work like lungs ■. Many lungfish survive the dry season by sealing themselves in chambers of mud. They are the only living relatives of fish that were widespread millions of years ago.

Eel

A bony fish with a snakelike body

An eel has a long, slippery body, which is usually without scales. It has a continuous fin that runs along its back, around its tail, and along its underside. There are about 350 species of eel, including the **conger** (*Conger conger*) and the ferocious **moray** (*Muraena helena*). They make up the order **Anguilliformes**.

Deep-sea fish

A fish that lives at depths of the sea, where there is no light

At great depths there is not enough light to support plant life. Fish that live in the deep sea must feed either on waste that falls from the surface or on each other. Many deep-sea fish are **bioluminescent**, which means they make their own light. They use this light mainly to draw prey toward them. The female **angler fish** (*Lophius piscatorius*) has a luminescent lure that dangles over its mouth. If another fish comes to inspect the lure, the angler suddenly swallows it.

Swim bladder

A gas-filled bag that helps a fish to float in the water

A swim bladder is a balloonlike organ ■ that contains gas. It allows a fish to be **neutrally buoyant** in the water, which means that it does not rise or sink. Near the surface, the pressure of the water is much less than it is farther down. When a fish dives, it increases the amount of gas in its swim bladder so that the bladder will not be squashed by water pressure.

Flatfish

A bony fish that lies on one side

Flatfish feed on the seafloor. As they mature, they undergo an extraordinary change of shape, or metamorphosis. A young flatfish swims in open water until eventually it settles on the seabed. It then lies on one side, and the eye facing the seabed slowly moves around so that both eyes are on the top side. Flatfish form the order ■ **Pleuronectiformes**, which includes the **winter flounder** (*Psuedopleuronectes americanus*).

See also

Cartilage 137 • Class 56
Ectotherm 133 • Gill 122 • Jaw 119
Lung 124 • Metamorphosis 166
Nervous system 148 • Order 56
Organ 23 • Parasite 175 • Phylum 56
Plankton 64 • Predator 174
Scale 141 • Species 48 • Vertebra 138

Amphibians

Axolotl

The amphibians were the first vertebrates to develop legs instead of fins and to move onto dry land. Today, amphibians are at home both on land and in water. They usually live in damp places, where their thin skins will not dry out.

Amphibian

A vertebrate that lives partly in water and partly on land

Amphibians are ectothermic ■ vertebrates ■. There are about 3,000 species ■ of amphibian and they make up the class ■ **Amphibia**. Amphibians spend at least part of their lives in water and undergo metamorphosis ■ as they grow up, which means that their bodies change shape. A typical amphibian begins its life as a larva ■ or tadpole ■, which breathes through gills ■. It then develops legs and begins to breathe mainly through its lungs. Most amphibians can also exchange gases through their damp skins. Some retain their gills throughout life.

Tetrapod

A vertebrate with four limbs, or an animal that has evolved from one

Amphibians were the first animals to develop four limbs for walking. This successful body pattern was handed on through evolution ■ to reptiles, birds, and mammals. Some tetrapods, such as caecilians and snakes, have gradually lost their legs, and have developed other ways of moving. In birds, the front limbs have become wings. Almost all tetrapods have pentadactyl limbs ■, which are limbs that have five digits.

Salamander

An amphibian with a long body and tail

Salamanders have long bodies, short thin legs, and cylindrical tails. They usually spend their adult life on land and breathe by absorbing oxygen through their damp skin. Some species, such as the **fire salamander** (*Salamandra salamandra*), ooze poisons when they are attacked, and their skin is brilliantly colored to warn predators. The **Chinese giant salamander** (*Andrias davidianus*) is the largest of all amphibians. It can reach a length of 5 feet (1.5 meters). Salamanders belong to the order ■ **Urodela**, which also includes the newts. This order contains about 450 species.

Bright warning spots

Damp skin absorbs oxygen

Spotted salamander

Newt

A long-bodied amphibian that spends much of its life in water

Newts are close relatives of salamanders. They usually have webbed tails, and spend most of their adult lives in water. Like salamanders, newts often carry out elaborate courtship displays during the breeding season in order to attract a mate.

Axolotl

A salamander that can reproduce without fully maturing

The axolotl (*Ambystoma mexicanum*) is an unusual salamander that lives in Mexico. It has pink skin and bright red gills. Unlike most amphibians, the axolotl can reproduce before it has developed an adult body. This is called **neoteny**. Axolotls do sometimes grow up. When this happens, they lose their gills and take up life on land.

Frog

An amphibian with strong legs and no tail

Unlike salamanders and newts, frogs lose their tails as they grow up. Their bodies become short and compact, and their back legs develop powerful muscles for jumping. They have large mouths and are all meat-eating, or carnivorous ■. Frogs usually live close to water, so they can jump into it if danger threatens. Together with toads, frogs make up the order **Anura**, which has about 2,500 species.

Sticky pads on toes for gripping

Tree frog

A frog with toes that have sticky pads

Tree frogs live mainly in warm parts of the world. Their long, thin toes have round, sticky pads that give them a good grip. Many tree frogs lay their eggs above ground in nests made of folded leaves or foam. When the eggs hatch, the tadpoles drop into water on the ground.

Big eyes for spotting prey

Large, webbed fingers form a parachute for gliding

Arrow-poison frog

A tropical frog that protects itself with a deadly poison

Tiny arrow-poison frogs live in the rain forests of South and Central America. Their skins produce a deadly poison and they are brilliantly patterned to warn predators. Forest people use the poison of these frogs to smear on the heads of their arrows, which is how the frogs get their name. Female arrow-poison frogs usually lay their eggs on land in batches of less than 10. After the tadpoles have hatched, the male carries them on his back and takes them to a pool in a tree hole.

Red-eyed tree frog

Flying tree frog
This red-eyed tree frog feeds on insects, which it stalks through the branches of the rain forest. It can glide between leaves and trees spreading out its webbed toes to form a kind of parachute.

Caecilian

An amphibian without legs

Caecilians live in tropical climates and spend their lives either in water or in soil. They have long, wormlike bodies with no legs, and their skin is often covered with tiny scales. Most caecilians have tadpoles that develop in water. Caecilians make up the order **Apoda**, which contains about 150 species.

Midwife toad

A toad with an unusual method of parental care

The midwife toad (*Alytes obstetricans*) lives in western Europe. Unusually for amphibians, midwife toads mate on land. The female lays about 50 eggs. After fertilization ■ the male carefully wraps the eggs around his back legs. He carries them for up to one and a half months, then puts them in water when they are ready to hatch.

Male toad carries eggs on its back legs

Flying frog

A frog that glides on its outstretched feet

Flying frogs live in the forests of Southeast Asia. They have slender bodies and unusually long toes. Flying frogs cannot really fly, but they are very good at gliding. When a flying frog jumps from a tree, it spreads its toes wide. The webbing between its toes turns each foot into a parachute, and the frog drops gently through the air until it reaches another tree trunk.

Toad

A tailless amphibian with powerful legs and a dry skin

Toads are similar to frogs, but they spend much more of their adult lives away from water. A toad's skin is dry and is covered with bumps, which are commonly known as warts. The skin produces poisons, which helps protect a toad from attack. Frogs usually have a smoother, more moist skin.

Midwife toad

Reptiles

The reptiles once dominated life on Earth. They were the first animals to become fully suited to life on land. One of their most important adaptations was a new kind of egg – one that could be laid on land without drying out.

Eye swivels

Toes grip

Chameleon

A tree-dwelling lizard with a prehensile tail

Madagascan chameleon

Chameleons hunt insects ■ by stealth and are well adapted for this way of life. A chameleon's skin can change color to blend in with its surroundings, and its eyes move independently to seek out food. Its toes are specially shaped for climbing trees, and it has a prehensile tail that can grip branches by wrapping around them. Chameleons catch prey by shooting out their long tongues.

Hatching rat snake

Reptile

A vertebrate with scaly skin and sealed eggs

A reptile is a vertebrate ■ with a tough skin of waterproof scales ■. Reptiles are ectothermic ■. To become active, a reptile must warm itself by basking in the sun, and they therefore cannot live in cold parts of the world. Reptiles lay **cleidoic** or **amniotic** eggs ■. This means the eggs are sealed with a strong membrane, or amnion, that stops them drying out. Young reptiles hatch as miniature versions of their parents. Reptiles form the class ■ **Reptilia**, which contains about 6,000 species ■.

Lizard

A land-dwelling reptile that usually has four legs

Most lizards are swift predators that hunt smaller animals. They often have long tails for balance and feet with sharp claws. Some lizards, such as the **slow-worm** (*Anguis fragilis*), have no legs at all. Together with snakes, lizards form the order ■ **Squamata**, which has over 5,000 species.

Gecko

A nocturnal lizard with flat toes

Geckos live in warm parts of the world, and they feed on insects. A gecko has a flattened body, large eyes, and special sticky toes, which are covered with small bristles. The bristles can grip most surfaces, so that a gecko can walk up walls, and even across ceilings. Most reptiles are silent animals, but geckos have noisy calls.

Iguana

A long-legged lizard that often has a crest on its back

Iguanas are large lizards that live mainly in North and South America. Many are brightly colored, and they often have elaborate courtship ■ displays. The **basilisk lizard** (*Basiliscus plumifrons*) is one of the few reptiles that can run on two legs. It uses its long tail for balance, and it can even run across water. The **marine iguana** (*Amblyrhynchus cristatus*) is the only species of lizard that lives in the sea. It lives on the Galápagos Islands and feeds on seaweed.

Carapace

Plastron

Red-eared terrapin

Turtle

A reptile with a shell

A turtle's body is protected by a bony shell that consists of a domed upper part, the **carapace**, and a flat lower part, the **plastron**. Large scales, made of the structural protein ■ keratin, cover the shell. Instead of teeth, a turtle has jaws ■ with hardened edges, like a bird's beak. Turtles belong to the order **Chelonia**, which contains about 250 species. These include **terrapins**, which are small water-dwelling turtles, and **tortoises**, which live on land.

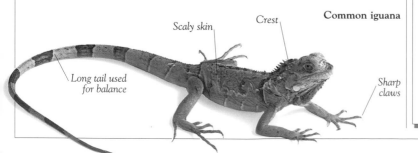

Scaly skin

Crest

Common iguana

Long tail used for balance

Sharp claws

See also

Carnivorous 116 • Class 56
Courtship 159 • Ectotherm 133
Egg 161 • Family 56 • Insect 102
Jacobson's organ 156 • Jaw 119
Mass extinction 51 • Order 56
Scale 141 • Species 48
Structural protein 30 • Vertebrate 104

Snake

A legless reptile with loosely connected jaws

Snakes are closely related to lizards, but they have lost their legs during evolution. Snakes are carnivorous ▪, and have jaws that can stretch wide apart to swallow large prey. Many snakes kill their prey using a poison, or **venom**. They inject venom through hollow teeth called **fangs**, or with teeth that have special grooves. A snake "smells" the air around it by using its forked tongue to press airborne particles against a sensory pit on the roof of its mouth. This pit is called a Jacobson's organ ▪.

Boa constrictor

A large snake that kills by coiling around its prey

The boa constrictor (*Constrictor constrictor*) is a snake that kills its prey by coiling around it and squeezing it until the prey suffocates. Boa constrictors belong to the family ▪ **Boidae**. This family includes **pythons**, and the huge **anaconda** (*Eunectes murinus*), which can measure up to 25 feet (8 meters) long.

Puff adder

A snake with hinged fangs

The puff adder (*Bitis arietans*) is one of the world's most deadly snakes. It has hollow fangs that hinge forward as it strikes, to inject a lethal venom into its victim. The puff adder belongs to the **viper** family, which also includes the **common viper** or **adder** (*Vipera berus*), and the **Gaboon viper** (*Vipera gabonica*).

Muscular body for coiling around prey

Indian python

Skin pattern camouflages snake in trees

Loosely hinged jaws can be stretched apart to swallow prey

Constrictor killer
Pythons catch their prey by hanging in trees and waiting for a victim. They grip their prey with strong teeth and squeeze it to death before swallowing it.

Crocodile

A water-dwelling reptile with armored skin

Crocodiles belong to the ancient order **Crocodilia**. This contains about 21 species, including **alligators**, which are similar to crocodiles, and **gavials**, which have much narrower jaws. A crocodile is a ferocious carnivore that is well adapted to life in water. It can close its nostrils when it dives, and it has a powerful tail for swimming. Female crocodiles lay their eggs in nests and are careful parents.

Tuatara

The last surviving member of an ancient order of reptiles

The tuatara (*Sphenodon punctatus*) is a lizardlike reptile that lives in New Zealand. It is the only living member of the order **Rhyncocephalia**, which dates back millions of years to the Triassic Period. Unusually for reptiles, tuataras can keep active in temperatures as low as 55° F (13° C). They grow very slowly and can live for over 50 years.

Dinosaur

An extinct reptile

Dinosaur means "terrible lizard" in Greek. The dinosaurs were a group of reptiles, some of which were huge in size, that lived on the Earth millions of years ago. However, not all big reptiles were dinosaurs. The dinosaurs were part of a larger group of reptiles called **archosaurs**. This group included the ancestors of today's crocodiles and birds, as well as the **pterosaurs**, which were giant flying reptiles. Most archosaurs died out in the mass extinction ▪ at the end of the Cretaceous Period.

Powerful tail

Nile crocodile

Ferocious jaws

Horny scales

Birds

Birds are the most powerful and widespread flying animals. Some birds use their wings for short bursts of flight. Others stay in the air for weeks or months at a time, collecting the food they need on the wing.

Bird

An animal with feathers

A bird is an endothermic ▦ vertebrate ▦. Birds are the only animals that have feathers and, apart from bats, they are the only vertebrates capable of powered flight ▦. Birds do not have teeth, and their jaws ▦ have evolved into a beak or **bill**. Birds reproduce by laying eggs with a hard covering called an **eggshell**. There are about 8,600 species ▦ of bird, and they live on land, in fresh water, and at sea.

Feather

A flap made of fine keratin strands

Bird feathers are made of the tough structural protein ▦ keratin. Each feather consists of thousands of tiny strands, or **barbs**, that are hooked together by **barbules** to give most feathers a flat surface. A bird has several different kinds of feather. Long, stiff **flight feathers** grow on its wings ▦ and tail, and enable the bird to fly. **Contour feathers** cover the bird's body, and give it a streamlined shape. Fluffy **down feathers** grow close to a bird's skin to keep it warm.

Tail feather

Wing feather

Contour feathers

Down feather

Nest

A shelter built by an animal

Like many animals, birds usually protect their eggs by laying them in a nest. Some birds build very simple nests on the ground. Their young are normally well developed, or **precocious**, when they hatch because they must be able to escape from danger. Other birds build more elaborate nests in trees. When their young hatch, they are often blind and helpless, or **altricial**.

Parrot

A bird with a hooked beak and feet that can grip

Scarlet macaw

Parrots form the order ▦ **Psittaciformes**, which contains just over 300 species. Parrots live mainly on plant food and have strong toes that enable them to grip their food with one foot while they eat. Parrots are very colorful birds, and many species are collected for their brilliant plumages. As a result, some species of parrot have become endangered. The **parakeet**, or **budgerigar** (*Melopsittacus undulatus*) is a small seed-eating parrot.

Perching bird

A bird with toes that grip

Perching birds, or **passerines**, usually have small, light bodies, and four-toed feet. Three of their toes point forward, and one points backward. This enables a perching bird to grip tightly with its feet and perch easily on branches. Perching birds make up the order **Passeriformes**, which includes over half the world's bird species. Among them are **weaverbirds**, **sparrows**, **finches**, **starlings**, and **crows**.

Cuckoo

A bird that often lays its eggs in the nests of other birds

There are over 100 species of cuckoo. About half of them are brood parasites ▦, which means that they trick other birds into raising their young. A female cuckoo lays its eggs in other birds' nests and then flies away. The young cuckoo is then raised by its "foster parents." Cuckoos belong to the order **Cuculiformes**, which contains about 150 species. The **roadrunner** (*Geococcyx californianus*) of North America is an unusual cuckoo that hunts on the ground.

Owl

A predatory bird that usually hunts by night

Owls are adapted for hunting in the dark. They have large, forward-pointing eyes that give them binocular vision ▦. They also have such good hearing that many owls can catch their prey in complete darkness. There are about 130 species of owl. They belong to the order **Strigiformes**.

Bird of prey

A bird that hunts animals

Most birds of prey are powerfully built predators. They catch prey with sharp-clawed toes called **talons** and use strong, hooked beaks to tear up their flesh. Birds of prey find their food mainly by sight. They have forward-pointing eyes to give them clear binocular vision. When it spots an animal, a bird of prey dives towards its victim at great speed. The **peregrine falcon** (*Falco peregrinus*) can dive at speeds of up to 180 miles (290 kilometers) per hour. **Eagles**, **hawks**, and also **vultures**, which feed on dead animals, are all birds of prey. They belong to the order **Falconiformes**, which has about 280 species.

Powerful wings

Hooked beak

Sharp talons

Kestrel
A kestrel is a typical bird of prey. It has sharp talons to catch small mammals and insects, and a hooked beak to pull apart animals that are too big to be swallowed whole.

Hummingbird

A bird that drinks nectar

A hummingbird is a tiny, often brilliantly colored bird. Its wings are specially adapted ■ for hovering ■, and it drinks nectar from flowers through a tubelike beak. With **swifts**, hummingbirds form the order **Apodiformes**, which has about 300 species. The **bee hummingbird** (*Calypte helenae*) measures 2 inches (5 centimeters) long, and is the smallest bird in the world.

See also

Flightless bird

A bird that has lost the ability to fly

During the process of evolution ■, birds have developed many different ways of life. For some birds, the ability to fly has stopped being an advantage. Over many generations their wings have slowly become smaller, until they can no longer be used for flight. Flightless birds include **ostriches**, **emus**, **kiwis**, and **penguins**. The **African ostrich** (*Struthio camelus*) is the world's largest bird, and can grow to over 6.5 feet (2 meters).

Waterfowl

A bird with webbed feet and a blunt, flattened beak

Ducks, **geese**, and **swans** are all waterfowl, or **wildfowl**. They are specially suited to life on or near water. Waterfowl keep their feathers waterproof by covering them with oil from large **oil glands**. They also have webbed feet that act as paddles when they swim through the water. Ducks and swans usually feed on plants and small animals in the water, but geese graze on land. There are about 160 species of waterfowl, and they make up the order **Anseriformes**.

Wader

A bird with long legs and a long, pointed beak

Waders, or **shorebirds**, include birds such as **curlews**, **plovers**, and **sandpipers**. They usually live along coastlines, or on damp ground inland. Waders feed mainly on small animals. They find their food either by striding out into water, or by probing into the mud. Many waders have beaks with sensitive tips and can feel food they cannot see. Along with **gulls** and **terns**, they make up the order **Charadriiformes**, which contains about 150 species.

Long beak for searching out food

Long legs for wading

Avocet
The avocet is one of the few waders that has a strongly upturned beak.

Mammals

Mammals live in almost every kind of habitat, from rivers and oceans to jungles and deserts. They are one of the most diverse of all animal groups – a bat and a zebra look very different, but they are both mammals.

Furry body

Finger bones

Fruit bat

Mammal

An animal with hair that feeds its young on milk

Mammals are endotherms ■ and make up one of the most diverse animal groups. They have hair on their bodies, although sometimes not very much, and they suckle their young on milk. There are about 4,000 species of mammal, and together they make up the class ■ **Mammalia**. Humans belong to a group of mammals called the primates ■.

Milk

A liquid food made by a female mammal

Milk is produced by a female mammal's **mammary glands**. It provides all the nutrients that a young mammal needs before it is able to find food for itself. Some mammals **suckle** their young for just a few days, but large mammals, such as elephants, feed their young for many months.

Monotreme

A mammal that lays eggs

There are only three species ■ of monotreme – the **duck-billed platypus** (*Ornithorhyncus anatinus*), and two species of **spiny anteater**. Together, they make up the order ■ **Monotremata**. Monotremes are unusual mammals because they lay eggs ■. After hatching, the young feed on the mother's milk.

Marsupial

A mammal that develops inside its mother's pouch

There are about 250 species of marsupial and they make up the order **Marsupialia**. This order includes **kangaroos** and **wallabies**, **opossums**, and the **koala** (*Phascolarctos cinereus*). Female marsupials have a short gestation period. They give birth to poorly developed young, which then grow up inside a pouch, called a **marsupium**.

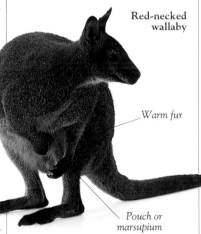

Red-necked wallaby

Warm fur

Pouch or marsupium

Placental mammal

A mammal that develops inside its mother's body

A placental mammal develops inside its mother's uterus ■, where it is nourished through a spongelike organ called a placenta ■. Placental mammals make up the class **Eutheria**, which has about 3,750 species. This is the largest mammal group.

Bat

A placental mammal capable of powered flight

A bat's wings consist of thin flaps of skin stretched between long finger bones. The smallest bats feed on flying insects, which they find by echolocation ■. This involves sending out pulses of high-pitched sound and listening for the echoes that bounce back. **Flying foxes** and **fruit bats** are larger, and live on fruit, pollen ■, and nectar. Bats make up the order **Chiroptera**, which has about 950 species.

Elephant

A placental mammal with a trunk

Elephants are the largest land-dwelling mammals. They eat plants and collect food with a long, muscular nose, or **trunk**. The two elephant species – the **Indian elephant** (*Elephas maximus*), and the **African elephant** (*Loxodonta africana*) – are the only members of the order **Proboscisoidea**.

Insectivore

A primitive placental mammal with short, sharp teeth

Insectivores include **hedgehogs**, **shrews**, and **moles**. Together they form the order **Insectivora**, which contains about 350 species. Insectivores have poor eyesight and hunt insects and small creatures mainly by smell.

Whale

A placental mammal that lives in water

Whales are air-breathing mammals that have adapted to a life in water. Their front legs have become flat **flippers** and their back legs have disappeared. A whale's tail is made of two paddles called **flukes**. The largest whales are the **baleen whales**, which are filter feeders ■. They live on plankton ■, which they filter from seawater with a curtain of fringed plates, called **baleen plates**. **Toothed whales** do not have baleen and feed on fish and other animals. The **sperm whale** (*Physeter catodon*), **porpoises**, and **dolphins** are all toothed whales. There are 79 species of whale and they make up the order **Cetacea**.

Ungulate

A placental mammal with hoofed feet

Most ungulates walk on the tips of their toes, which end in a hard **hoof**. Hooves are made of the structural protein ■ keratin. Ungulates are plant-eating, or herbivorous ■, animals. There are about 200 species of ungulate and they make up two different orders. **Odd-toed ungulates** have one or three working toes. They belong to the order **Perissodactyla**, which includes **horses**, **zebras**, and **rhinoceroses**. **Even-toed ungulates** usually have two working toes and they belong to the order **Artiodactyla**. This includes **pigs**, **camels**, and **cattle**.

Rodent

A placental mammal with gnawing teeth

Rodents are usually small mammals with sharp incisor ■ teeth that never stop growing. A rodent uses its teeth like chisels to chip at its food. There are over 2,000 species of rodent, including **squirrels**, **rats**, **mice**, and **porcupines**. Together, they form the order **Rodentia**, which is the largest order of mammals.

Porcupine

Seal

A mammal that feeds in water

Most seals live in the sea, although some live in large lakes. They have streamlined bodies and webbed feet that are shaped like paddles. Seals feed on many kinds of animals. They do not spend all their time in water, and usually give birth on land. Seals belong to the order **Pinnipedia**, which contains 34 species.

See also

Adaptation 46 • Carnivorous 116
Class 56 • Echolocation 154 • Egg 161
Endotherm 133 • Filter feeding 117
Herbivorous 116 • Incisor 118 • Order 56
Placenta 163 • Plankton 64 • Pollen 92
Primate 114 • Species 48
Structural protein 30 • Uterus 162

Carnivore

A placental mammal with specially shaped teeth that usually lives by hunting

The term carnivore is often used to refer to any meat-eating predator. But in classification, a carnivore is not just a carnivorous ■ animal, but also a member of the order **Carnivora**. There are about 240 species of carnivore including **wolves**, **cats**, **foxes**, and **bears**. Carnivores have teeth adapted for gripping and cutting flesh, although some eat plant food as well as meat. The **giant panda** (*Ailuropoda melanoleuca*) is an unusual carnivore that has adapted ■ to a diet of plants.

Common zebra

Odd-toed ungulate
The zebra is an odd-toed ungulate that belongs to the horse family. Zebras live on the plains of Africa. No one knows for certain why zebras have a striped coat.

Hoof

Primates

Monkeys, apes, and humans all belong to the same group of animals – the primates. Most species of primate live in trees and have forward-pointing eyes, long arms, and gripping fingers. Most primates are quick to learn and as a group they are more intelligent than other mammals.

Long legs for sprinting

Patas monkey
The patas monkey is an Old World monkey that lives mainly on the plains of Africa. It has long legs and can sprint at speeds of up to 34 mph (55 km/h).

Primate

A mammal with flexible fingers and toes and forward-pointing eyes

Primates are mammals ■ that either live in trees or have evolved ■ from tree-dwelling ancestors. A typical primate has long fingers and toes, which it uses to grip objects. It also has flat nails instead of claws. A primate has big, forward-pointing eyes that provide good binocular vision ■. This is essential for judging distances when jumping from branch to branch. There are about 180 primate species ■. They make up the order ■ **Primata**. This order is split into two groups – prosimians and anthropoids.

Prosimian

A primitive tree-dwelling primate with grasping hands

The first primates to evolve were probably small tree-dwellers with good eyesight, much like today's **tree shrews** from the order **Scandentia**. Their descendants include **lemurs** (family **Lemuridae**), **lorises** (family **Lorisidae**), and **tarsiers** (family **Tarsiidae**). Prosimians are mainly nocturnal, which means they are active at night. They eat leaves, insects, and young birds. Prosimians live in Southeast Asia, Africa, and Madagascar.

Anthropoid

A primate with a rounded head and a bare face

Most of the primates in the world are anthropoids. They are often big animals and include monkeys, apes, and humans. Many anthropoids have large, complex brains. They are usually intelligent and learn quickly. Most anthropoids live in trees, but some species have adapted to a life on the ground. Some anthropoids are noisy animals that communicate with one another with howls and hoots. They also use facial expressions as a way of communicating.

Bushbaby
A bushbaby is a type of prosimian. Its large eyes help it find prey in the dark and judge the distances between branches.

Large sensitive ears pick up the sound of moving insects

Grasping hands

Long, bushy tail

Monkey

An anthropoid primate that usually lives in trees

Monkeys are large or medium-sized primates. Most have tails and live in trees. A few, such as baboons, have no tails and live mainly on the ground. Monkeys eat almost anything, including birds, flowers, frogs, fruit, insects, leaves, nuts, and lizards. They can be divided into two groups – Old World monkeys and New World monkeys.

Old World monkey

A monkey with closely set nostrils

Old World, or **catarrhine**, monkeys belong to the family ■ **Cercopithecidae**. A typical Old World monkey is large, and has close-set nostrils that point downward. Unlike New World monkeys, very few have prehensile tails. Old World monkeys come from Africa or Asia. They include **colobuses** (*Colobus*), which spend nearly all their lives in trees, and **macaques** (*Macaca*), which live both in trees and on the ground. The biggest Old World monkeys are **baboons** (*Papio*), which live mostly on the ground.

New World monkey

A monkey with widely set nostrils and a prehensile tail

New World, or **platyrrhine**, monkeys have widely spaced nostrils that face forward. All New World monkeys live in trees, but vary greatly in shape, size, and color. They come from Central or South America, and form two families: the **Cebidae** family, which includes **cebid monkeys**; and the **Callitrichidae** family, which includes **tamarins** and **marmosets**. Most tamarins and marmosets are small day-active, or diurnal, animals. They scamper through the trees like squirrels, and feed on fruit, insects, and spiders. Cebid monkeys include the **black spider monkey** (*Ateles paniscus*), and the **red howler monkey** (*Alouatta seniculus*). Most have long **prehensile tails** that are specially adapted ▦ for wrapping around branches or for grasping other objects. They also use their tails for balance.

Ape

A primate that can move on its back legs

Apes are primates that do not have tails. They have partly or fully opposable thumbs, which are flexible thumbs that can be used to grip objects. All apes are capable of bipedal locomotion ▦, or walking on two legs, although most apes cannot walk like this for long distances. In classification ▦, apes are divided into three families – the gibbons, the great apes, and the hominids ▦. Humans are the only living species of hominid.

Gibbon

An ape that uses its arms to swing through trees

Gibbons are the smallest apes. They spend almost their entire lives in trees and often live together in small family groups. Gibbons have loud calls that can be heard from a long way off. A gibbon's arms are much longer than its legs. It moves through the trees at high speed by swinging on its arms. This movement is known as **brachiating**. Gibbons make up the family **Hylobatidae**, which contains six species.

Large, forward-pointing eyes for judging distances

Opposable thumb for gripping

Long flexible tail used for balancing

Squirrel monkey
The squirrel monkey is a New World monkey from the jungles of South America. It has a long flexible tail that it uses for balance as it leaps from branch to branch.

Chimpanzee
The chimpanzee lives in the forests and grasslands of tropical Africa. It is the primate most closely related to humans.

Great ape

A large ape that lives in trees or on the ground

The great apes belong to the family **Pongidae**, which contains just four species – the **orangutan** (*Pongo pygmaeus*), the **gorilla** (*Gorilla gorilla*), the **chimpanzee** (*Pan troglodytes*), and the **pygmy chimpanzee** (*Pan paniscus*). Great apes are powerfully built animals, and the males are often larger than the females. Orangutans are slow-moving tree-dwellers that usually live alone. Gorillas and chimpanzees are more social animals ▦, and tend to live in small groups. Comparisons of DNA ▦ show that chimpanzees are the closest living relatives of humans.

See also

Adaptation 46 • Binocular vision 153
Bipedal locomotion 54 • Classification 56
DNA 34 • Evolution 44
Family 56 • Hominid 54
Mammal 112 • Order 56
Social animal 159 • Species 48

Feeding

Plants can make their own food, but animals have to eat in order to survive. Different diets and ways of feeding have evolved to suit each animal's lifestyle and nutritional needs.

Feeding

The process of taking in food

Animals and other heterotrophic ▪ organisms have to take in food from their surroundings in order to survive. They do this by feeding, or **ingestion**. Once an organism has ingested some food, the food is gradually broken down by a process called **digestion**. A single-celled organism, such as an amoeba ▪, usually feeds by surrounding and then engulfing its food. Multicelled organisms have special body parts that help them to feed. In humans, these body parts include jaws and teeth.

Fuel for life
Like all animals,
a tortoise
needs a
steady
intake of
food to
survive.

Diet

The type and amount of food eaten by an animal

Some animals have a varied diet, while others eat a very narrow range of food. A koala, for example, lives entirely on eucalyptus leaves. The amount of food an animal needs depends on its size and metabolic rate ▪. A tortoise has a low metabolic rate. In proportion to its size, it eats far less than a shrew.

Omnivorous

Plant-eating and meat-eating

Animals that eat a diet of both plants and meat are known as **omnivores**. Omnivorous animals include humans, hedgehogs, bears, and many other kinds of mammal. Their digestive systems can break down both plant and animal food.

Nutrition

The process by which living things obtain raw materials to sustain life

All living things need raw materials, or nutrients ▪, to build up organic matter, or to provide energy. Heterotrophic organisms, including humans, obtain most of their nutrients from food. **Macronutrients** are nutrients such as carbohydrates ▪, which we need in large amounts. **Micronutrients** are nutrients such as vitamins ▪, which we need in only small amounts.

Herbivorous

Plant-eating

Animals that eat only plant food are called **herbivores**. Cows, caterpillars, and tortoises are all herbivorous animals. Herbivores often have special teeth for grinding plant material. Many also have digestive systems that contain microorganisms which break down the cellulose ▪ in plants. Herbivores often have to consume large amounts of plant food to obtain enough nutrients.

Carnivorous

Meat-eating

An animal whose diet consists mainly or entirely of meat is called a carnivore ▪. Most carnivorous animals are predators and survive by hunting other animals. They have strong jaws and well-developed carnassial ▪ and canine ▪ teeth. Carnivores often spend a long time finding food, but meat is full of nutrients, so many can survive for long periods between meals.

Fluid feeding

Feeding by sucking liquids

Fluid feeders live on liquid food and are usually small animals. Most fluid feeders have special tubelike mouthparts through which they can suck up liquids. These mouthparts often have sharp tips that can pierce plant stems or skin. Mosquitoes, aphids, and hummingbirds ▪ are all fluid feeders.

Feeding on fluids
Mosquitoes pierce the skin of their victims and suck the victim's blood.

Detritivorous

Feeding on dead remains

When dead plants and animals decay, their remains often form small particles called **detritus**. A **detritivore**, or **detritus feeder**, is an animal that feeds on these particles. Detritivores are common on the seafloor, and include animals such as sea cucumbers ▪ and brittlestars ▪.

Filter feeding

Feeding by sieving food from water

Water is often full of food. A **filter feeder** is an animal that collects this food from the water around it. Some filter feeders, such as barnacles and sea squirts, collect their food by staying in one place and pumping water through fine sieves. Other filter feeders trap food while they are on the move. Baleen whales, for example, trap krill ▪ with horny baleen plates in their mouths.

Deposit feeding

Obtaining food from surrounding substances

An earthworm is a **deposit feeder**. As it tunnels through the ground, it eats the soil in front of it. The earthworm's digestive system breaks down the organic matter in the soil, and the rest is passed out as waste. Deposit feeders live in or on their food and can only survive in surroundings with adequate nutrients.

Baleen whale

Water and krill in

The whale's mouth fills up with water and krill. When the whale closes its jaws, both water and krill are trapped.

Water out

Baleen plates

Water is squeezed out through the baleen plates. The krill is trapped in the comblike plates and is eaten.

Tentacles used for feeding

Cilia

Undersea fans
Fanworms are salt-water relatives of earthworms that live in tubes. To feed, a fanworm opens out a "fan" of fine tentacles. Tiny hairs on the tentacles collect small particles of food, and carry them to the worm's mouth.

Tube made from mud and sand, held together with mucus

Mouth is hidden in center of tentacles

Teeth & jaws

Animals use their teeth for cutting and crushing food and also for catching prey or for defending themselves. Teeth are usually the hardest parts of an animal's body, and they are firmly anchored in the jaw.

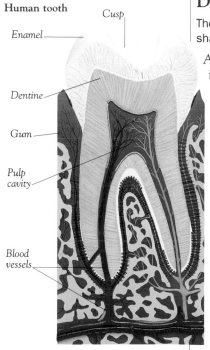

Human tooth

Cusp

Enamel

Dentine

Gum

Pulp cavity

Blood vessels

Tooth

A hard structure that grinds food

Many vertebrates ■ have teeth, but mammals ■ are alone in having teeth that are shaped to work in different ways. A tooth is covered by a hard substance called **enamel**. Below this is a layer of bony **dentine**, and finally a **pulp cavity**, which is a space containing nerves and blood vessels. The tooth is anchored to the jaw by one or more **roots**. Some animals, such as sharks, have teeth that are constantly being replaced. Others, such as rabbits, have teeth that keep growing. This prevents them from becoming worn down.

Dentition

The number, arrangement, and shape of teeth in the mouth

An animal's dentition reflects its diet ■ and its way of life. For example, humans have teeth that are specially adapted to an omnivorous ■ diet. Human teeth grow in two sets. The 20 **milk teeth**, or **deciduous teeth**, are later replaced by 32 **adult teeth**, or **permanent teeth**. Many mammals, have four main kinds of teeth – incisors, canines, premolars, and molars.

Dental formula

A way of showing how teeth are arranged

A dental formula shows the type and number of teeth on each side of an animal's jaw.

	Incisors	Canines	Premolars	Molars
Upper jaw	2	1	2	3
Lower jaw	2	1	2	3

Dental formula
The numbers in the dental formula above represent, from left to right, the numbers of incisors, canines, premolars, and molars on each side of the human upper and lower jaws.

Incisor

A tooth with a cutting edge

Incisors are chisel-shaped teeth at the front of the jaw. Mammals use incisors for biting into food and slicing it up. Rodents ■ use their incisors for gnawing through food and other material. Many mammals also use their incisors for grooming their fur.

Canine

A tooth that grips and pierces

A canine tooth has a single point and is often used for holding prey. Hunting mammals, such as cats and dogs, have long, sharp canines for stabbing meat. Human canines are shorter and blunter.

Molar

A tooth that chews

Molars are positioned near the back of the jaw. They have deep roots and ridges, or **cusps**, for crushing or grinding food. The **premolars** are just in front of the molars and often slightly smaller. In humans, the last four molars to appear, or **erupt**, are called **wisdom teeth**, or **third molars**. Molars are not present in the milk teeth.

Upper jaw

Lower jaw

Incisor   Canine   Premolar   Molar

Carnivorous dentition

A dog's teeth allow it to grip its prey and to slice up meat. Its jaw can move up and down, but not sideways.

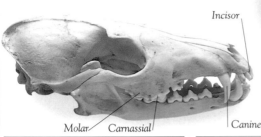

Incisor

Molar Carnassial

Canine

Incisor

Canine

Diastema (gap)

Molars

Carnassial

A tooth formed from the last premolar and first molar

Carnassials are found in dogs and other carnivorous ■ mammals. They have a pointed edge, and work like shears. Unlike incisors, carnassials are near the hinge of the jaw. Their position allows them to close with great force, so they can slice through meat, or crack open bones.

Tusk

A tooth that projects beyond the jaw

Tusks are specialized teeth that extend from the upper or lower jaw. They are used for digging up food or for defense. An elephant's tusks are very long incisors, while the tusks of a walrus are long canines. Both are made of **ivory**, a hard substance which is a form of dentine. The swordlike tusk of the male **narwhal** (*Monodon monoceros*) is an upper left incisor with spiral grooves.

Jaw

A bone that is used to bite or chew

A jaw is a bone that often bears teeth. In mammals, the lower jawbone, or **mandible**, hinges with the skull ■ at two points, called **temporomandibular joints**. Powerful muscles pull the jawbone upward. Mammals have just one bone in their lower jaw, but other vertebrates have several bones. The "missing" jaw bones of mammals have evolved into ear ■ ossicles, which are used in hearing. The upper jaw is known as the **maxilla**. It does not move.

Herbivorous dentition

A sheep has no incisors or canines in its upper jaw and instead cuts grass against a hard pad. It chews by moving its jaw sideways and up and down.

Diastema

A toothless gap in the jaw

In herbivorous ■ mammals, such as rodents, the cutting teeth (incisors) at the front of the jaw are separated from the chewing teeth (molars) at the back of the jaw by a gap called the diastema. Food can be collected in this gap before it is broken up and chewed.

Denticle

A toothlike scale found in the skin of some fish

Many cartilaginous fish ■ feel rough because their skin is covered with small, sharp scales. These are very similar to teeth, and teeth probably evolved ■ from them.

Tusks

The tusks of an elephant are the largest teeth in the animal kingdom. They are often used for stripping bark.

Digestive system

The digestive system breaks down food into simple substances that the body can use. In vertebrates, it consists of a tube and a number of linking organs, including the liver.

Digestive system

A system of organs that works together to digest food

All vertebrates ■, including humans, have similar digestive systems. A tube called the **alimentary canal**, or **gut**, runs from the mouth to the **anus**. During **digestion**, food is broken down into soluble substances by enzymes ■ in the alimentary canal. These substances diffuse ■ into cells ■ by a process called **absorption**, and are then transported around the body.

External digestion

A kind of digestion that takes place outside an organism

When a spider catches a fly, it injects enzymes into its victim. These partly digest the fly's tissues, and the spider eats the nutritious fluid that is produced. This is called external digestion.

Mouth

The entry to the alimentary canal

In the mouth, food is usually cut up or chewed by teeth ■. This is called **mastication**. In mammals, food is also partly digested by saliva from the salivary glands.

See also

Blood 128 • Cell 18 • Cellulose 27
Diffusion 22 • Enzyme 31 • Glycogen 27
Herbivorous 116 • Hormone 134
Lymphatic system 131
Microorganism 60 • Protein 30
Starch 27 • Tooth 118 • Vertebrate 104

Human digestive system

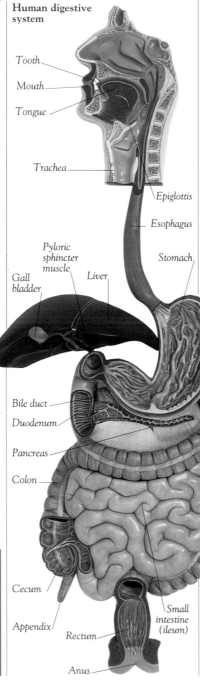

Tooth
Mouth
Tongue
Trachea
Epiglottis
Esophagus
Pyloric sphincter muscle
Stomach
Gall bladder
Liver
Bile duct
Duodenum
Pancreas
Colon
Cecum
Appendix
Rectum
Small intestine (ileum)
Anus

Salivary gland

A gland that produces saliva

When food enters the mouth, the salivary glands produce a digestive juice called **saliva**. This watery liquid helps food pass through an animal's body. Saliva contains the enzyme **amylase**, which begins the digestion of starch ■.

Esophagus

A muscular tube that leads to the stomach

When an animal swallows food, muscles in the esophagus contract and push the food towards the stomach. The esophagus tightens behind the food, and loosens in front of it. This is called **peristalsis**. Food passes through the whole alimentary canal in this way.

Stomach

A curved chamber in the alimentary canal

Powerful muscles churn up food in the stomach. The cells lining the stomach produce **gastric juice**. This contains **hydrochloric acid**, which helps to digest food, and the enzyme **pepsin**, which breaks down proteins ■. A muscular valve at the base of the stomach, called the **pyloric sphincter**, keeps food in the stomach until it is ready to move on.

Small intestine

A long tube in which food is digested and absorbed

Food from the stomach enters the small intestine. In humans, this is made of two main parts, the **duodenum** and the **ileum**. The lining of the duodenum produces digestive enzymes, and the lining of the ileum absorbs food substances.

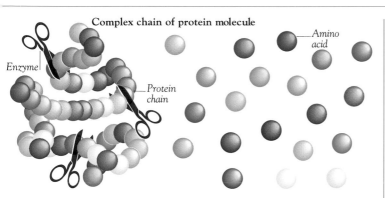

Complex chain of protein molecule

Enzyme

Protein chain

Amino acid

Villus

A projection from the lining of the small intestine

A villus (plural **villi**) is one of millions of tiny projections that line the small intestine. They give the small intestine lining a huge surface area across which digested food substances can be absorbed. These pass through the villi into the blood ▦ or the lymphatic system ▦.

Pancreas

An organ that produces hormones and digestive enzymes

The pancreas secretes **pancreatic juice**, which contains digestive enzymes. Pancreatic juice is alkaline and counteracts the acid made by the stomach. The pancreas also makes insulin and glucagon, hormones ▦ that control blood sugar levels. It is connected to the duodenum.

Liver

An organ that stores food substances and produces bile

The liver is an organ that carries out hundreds of chemical reactions and stores vital chemicals such as vitamins and glycogen ▦. The liver produces **bile**, a liquid that breaks down, or **emulsifies**, fats. Bile is stored in the **gall bladder** and released into the small intestine through the bile duct when it is needed.

Digestion in progress
Enzymes work like chemical scissors to break down complex molecules.

Large intestine

A large tube that absorbs water from digested food

After digested food has passed through the small intestine, it enters the large intestine. The **colon** forms most of the large intestine. This tube absorbs large amounts of water from undigested remains, which are then expelled as **feces** through the anus.

Cecum

A pouch at the beginning of the colon

In some herbivorous ▦ animals, the microorganisms ▦ needed to break down cellulose ▦ are found in the cecum. The cecum is less important in humans. Connected to it is a narrow dead-end tube called the **appendix**.

Crop

A special pouch in a bird's esophagus

A bird's crop is a temporary storage area. When a bird eats, food travels into the crop. The crop stretches as it fills up, and passes the food to the stomach.

Gizzard

A chamber that grinds up food

Animals that swallow their food without chewing it often have a gizzard. A gizzard is a chamber with muscular walls. When the muscles contract, they grind up the food so it can be digested. Some birds swallow small stones that lodge in their gizzards and help break down food.

Ruminant

A plant-eating mammal with a four-chambered stomach

Ruminants have special stomach chambers to digest plant food. When a ruminant swallows, food passes into the largest stomach, the **rumen**, where microorganisms break down cellulose. The animal regurgitates the partly digested food, called **cud**, and chews it for a second time. The food then passes through the other stomach chambers, the **reticulum**, the **omasum**, and **abomasum**, where digestion is completed.

Digestive system of a cow

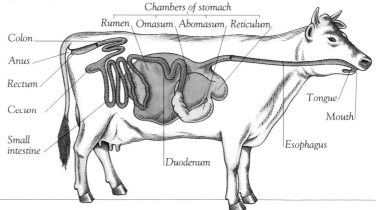

Chambers of stomach

Rumen, Omasum, Abomasum, Reticulum

Colon

Anus

Rectum

Cecum

Small intestine

Duodenum

Tongue

Mouth

Esophagus

Gas exchange

All animals need to take in oxygen and expel carbon dioxide. Small animals can exchange these gases through their body surface alone. However, larger animals need special organs, such as lungs or gills, to increase the amount of gas they can exchange.

Gas exchange

The movement of gases between cells and their surroundings

Gas exchange involves the movement of carbon dioxide and oxygen by diffusion ■. The gases move across respiratory surfaces to any areas where they are less concentrated.

Fish out of water
A mudskipper breathes air by holding pools of water in its gills.

Surface-to-volume ratio

The ratio between an organism's surface area and its volume

The smaller an animal is, the bigger its surface-to-volume ratio. A flatworm, for example, has a large surface area compared to its volume. This allows sufficient gas exchange to keep its cells alive. Bigger animals, such as humans, have a much smaller surface-to-volume ratio. Special respiratory organs provide the extra surface area they need to exchange gases.

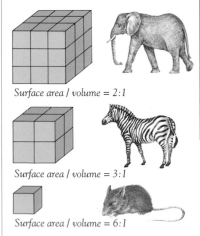

Surface area / volume = 2:1

Surface area / volume = 3:1

Surface area / volume = 6:1

Respiratory organ

An organ that aids gas exchange

A respiratory organ normally has a large surface area packed into a small space. Its surface is usually thin and moist and richly supplied with blood ■. Oxygen diffuses through the surface of the organ and into the blood, and carbon dioxide diffuses in the opposite direction. Respiratory organs include lungs ■, gills, and the tracheae of insects. Amphibians absorb gases through their skin ■, which acts as a respiratory organ. Most amphibians also have lungs.

A shrinking surface
These stacks of building blocks show how surface area changes with volume. A large animal, such as an elephant, has a relatively small surface area.

Gill

A respiratory organ that works in water

A gill is a collection of thin flaps that exchange gases with the surrounding water. Most animals that live in water, including mollusks, insects, and fish have gills. A fish's gills consist of flaps called **lamellae** fixed to arches of cartilage ■ or bone ■. A fish takes in water through its mouth. As the water moves over the lamellae, oxygen diffuses into the fish's blood. Carbon dioxide from the blood diffuses out through the gills and into the water. Fish gills are enclosed in a cavity behind the fish's head, but in other animals, the gills project outside the body. Many filter feeders ■, such as **clams**, **oysters**, and **basking sharks**, also use their gills to collect food.

Fish gill
A fish's gills exchange gases with a stream of moving water.

Water in | Mouth
Pharynx | Gill lamella | Operculum
Water out

See also

Blood 128 • Bone 137
Cartilage 137 • Diffusion 22
Filter feeding 117
Lung 124 • Muscle 142
Skin 141 • Vertebrate 104

Countercurrent flow

A system of currents that flow in opposite directions

In many respiratory organs, blood flows in one direction, while air or water flows in the opposite direction. This is called countercurrent flow, and it ensures that gases are exchanged efficiently and continuously. By using countercurrent flow, a fish's gills can extract up to 90 percent of the oxygen in the water flowing past them.

Tracheal system

A system of air tubes through the body of an insect

In vertebrates ■, blood carries gases through the body. However, in insects, gases move through a system of narrow air-filled tubes called **tracheae**. The tracheae branch into tiny **tracheoles** that are small enough to supply individual cells. Gases usually spread through the tracheal system by diffusion, although some insects have muscles ■ that pump air through their tracheae and air sacs.

Spiracle

A respiratory opening in an insect's body

A spiracle is a tiny air hole that allows air to enter an insect's tracheae. It is surrounded by a ring of muscle that enables the spiracle to open and close. A land-dwelling insect has several pairs of spiracles on the sides of its thorax and abdomen.

Spiracle

Trachea

Abdomen

Bird respiratory system
A bird's air sacs enable the bird to get the most oxygen from each breath. Birds have the most efficient respiratory systems of all vertebrates.

Lung

Air sacs

Air sac

A reservoir of air in an animal's body

An air sac holds air, but is not directly involved in gas exchange. Instead, it supplies air to the places where gas exchange takes place. Birds have several air sacs connected to their lungs. When a bird inhales, some air travels to the lungs and the rest flows into the rear air sacs. When the bird exhales, air in the rear air sacs flows through the lungs to the front air sacs, and is breathed out. During breathing, air moves straight through a bird's lungs, and most of its oxygen is extracted. Some insects have air sacs connected to their tracheal systems.

Book lung

A respiratory organ in arachnids

Spiders and scorpions exchange gases through book lungs that lie on the underside of the abdomen. A book lung is made up of thin flaps of tissue, rather like the pages of a book. These are separated by air spaces. Oxygen from the air flows through the flaps and into the blood. Carbon dioxide flows in the opposite direction. Many spiders also have **tracheal tubes** which carry air into the body. These are similar to the tracheae of insects, but less extensive.

Breathing underwater
Water spiders breathe air. They collect air and store it in an underwater bubble.

Air sac *Thorax*

Antenna

Tracheal system
Tiny air-filled tracheae run through an insect's body. Air passes into the tracheae through pores called spiracles.

Lungs

Lungs are organs at the center of the respiratory system. They bring air and blood close together so that gases, mainly oxygen and carbon dioxide, can travel from one to another.

Cutaway human lung

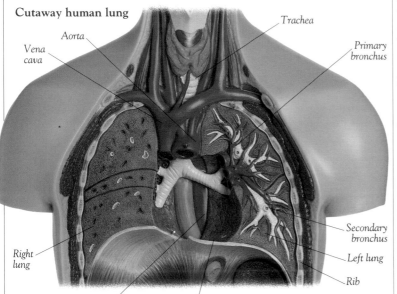

Aorta

Vena cava

Trachea

Primary bronchus

Right lung

Secondary bronchus

Left lung

Rib

Heart   Diaphragm

Lung

A respiratory organ

Lungs are the organs ■ that most vertebrates ■ use to exchange gases ■. Inside the lungs, air and blood ■ are separated by a lining that is two cells thick. This lining allows the exchange of oxygen and carbon dioxide to take place.

Breathing

The forced movement of air into and out of a lung

Most animals have to pump air into and out of their lungs in order to get enough oxygen. During breathing, muscles around the lungs contract and relax, causing the lungs to change shape. This sucks air into or blows air out of the lungs.

Air in

Inhalation
When an animal breathes in, the **diaphragm** *muscles pull the diaphragm downward. The ribs lift upward and outward. This increases the volume of the thoracic cavity, and air is sucked into the lungs.*

Diaphragm contracts

Air out

Exhalation
When an animal breathes out, the diaphragm and muscles connected to the ribs relax. This reduces the volume of the thoracic cavity, and forces air out of the lungs.

Diaphragm relaxes

Trachea

A passageway leading to the lungs

The trachea, or **windpipe**, is a short tube that runs from the throat to the lungs. Air passes down the trachea into the lungs. The trachea is reinforced by C-shaped bands of cartilage ■. Tiny cilia ■ cover the lining of the trachea. They constantly beat upward to clear away inhaled dust and other particles.

Bronchus

A passageway leading from the trachea and into a lung

Inside the chest, the trachea divides into two large tubes. Each tube is called a bronchus (plural **bronchi**), and carries air to one lung. Inside the lung, the bronchi divide into many branches, much like branches on a tree trunk. The smallest branches, called **bronchioles**, lead to tiny pockets called alveoli.

Alveolus

A sac in which gas exchange takes place

An alveolus (plural **alveoli**) is a tiny air-filled sac. Clusters of alveoli are situated at the end of the bronchioles, and contain the respiratory surfaces necessary for gas exchange to take place.

Alveoli
In an alveolus, blood is separated from the air by a barrier that is two cells thick.

Oxygen

Carbon dioxide

See also

Blood 128 • Cartilage 137
Cilium 19 • Gas exchange 122
Organ 23 • Vertebrate 104

Heart

The pumping action of the heart keeps blood circulating around an animal's body. The human heart pumps blood through 50,000 miles (80,000 kilometers) of blood vessels and beats about 100,000 times every day.

Heart

A hollow muscular pump that forces blood around the body

The heart is a hollow muscular organ ■ that contains one or more chambers. Some animals have more than one heart. For example, earthworms have ten.

Atrium

A chamber that admits blood to the heart

The human heart has four muscular chambers. These chambers are arranged in two pairs that work side by side. An atrium (plural **atria**) is one of the two upper chambers. The left atrium takes in oxygenated blood from the lungs and the right atrium takes in deoxygenated blood from the body. When the atria contract, they pump blood into the ventricles.

Ventricle

A chamber that expels blood from the heart

When the ventricles contract, they force blood out of the heart and into arteries ■. In the human heart, the left ventricle is bigger than the right because it pumps blood around the whole body. The right ventricle pumps blood only to the lungs.

See also

Artery 126 • Muscle 142
Organ 23

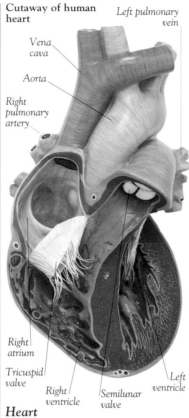

Cutaway of human heart

Left pulmonary vein

Vena cava

Aorta

Right pulmonary artery

Right atrium

Tricuspid valve

Right ventricle

Semilunar valve

Left ventricle

Heart

Blood from the lungs flows into the heart via the pulmonary veins, and out to the body via the aorta. Blood from the body flows into the heart via the vena cava, and out to the lungs via the pulmonary artery.

Pulse

The momentary expansion of an artery following a heartbeat

A pulse is created by the expansion of arteries throughout the body. In humans, this can be clearly felt in the wrist or neck. A normal **pulse rate** is between 70 and 90 beats per minute.

Heart valve

A valve that makes blood flow in one direction

Heart valves are flaps that open and close when the heart beats. They allow blood to flow in one direction only. The human heart has two sets of valves. The **tricuspid** and **bicuspid** valves prevent blood flowing backward from the ventricles to the atria. The **semilunar** valves prevent blood in the arteries flowing back into the ventricles.

Heartbeat

A single cycle in the heart's pumping action

The heart chambers contract in a fixed sequence. Each chamber undergoes a contraction phase, called a **systole**, and a relaxation phase, called a **diastole**. The heartbeat is triggered by a small area of muscle ■ in the heart, called the **sinoatrial node**, or **pacemaker**. It produces electrical impulses that spread across the heart and make its chambers contract in the correct sequence.

Diastole
Deoxygenated blood (blue) flows to the right side of the heart. Oxygenated blood (red) flows to the left.

Atrial systole
The two atria contract at the same time, forcing blood into the ventricles.

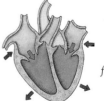

Ventricular systole
The ventricles contract, forcing deoxygenated blood into the lungs and oxygenated blood around the body.

Circulatory systems

A circulatory system carries blood in a constant cycle around an animal's body. Its complex system of tubes supplies every cell with the substances it needs to survive.

Circulatory system

A system that maintains a constant flow of blood throughout an animal's body

A circulatory system transports blood ▪ to all parts of an animal's body. Blood carries nutrients ▪ and oxygen to the body's tissues ▪ and takes away waste products. It also circulates heat throughout the body. The blood often flows through a system of tubes called **blood vessels** and is kept moving by the pumping action of the heart ▪. The smallest organisms rely on diffusion ▪ to transport substances through their bodies.

Open circulatory system

A circulatory system in which blood flows through body spaces

Most arthropods ▪ and mollusks ▪ have open circulatory systems. In an open circulatory system, the heart pumps blood into short blood vessels. The blood then flows out of the vessels and circulates through open spaces in the body before returning to the heart. In this kind of circulatory system, the blood flows slowly and its pressure is low.

See also

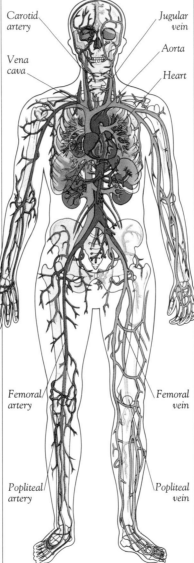

Carotid artery
Jugular vein
Aorta
Vena cava
Heart
Femoral artery
Femoral vein
Popliteal artery
Popliteal vein

Human circulatory system
This diagram shows the major blood vessels in the human circulatory system. On the left side only the arteries (red) are shown, and on the right only the veins (blue) are shown.

Closed circulatory system

A circulatory system in which blood always flows through blood vessels

All vertebrates ▪, including humans, have closed circulatory systems. In a closed circulatory system, the heart pumps blood around the body through a network of finely branched blood vessels. The vessels pass close to every living cell ▪ in the body. The heart, blood, and blood vessels form an animal's **cardiovascular system**.

Blood pressure

The pressure of blood in a circulatory system

Blood pressure varies throughout a circulatory system. It is high in the arteries leading from the heart, and becomes lower as the blood travels through the narrow capillaries and then the veins. Blood pressure is an important indicator of the body's health, and can be measured by an instrument called a **sphygmomanometer**.

Artery

A blood vessel that carries blood away from the heart

Arteries carry blood to all parts of the body. They divide into small branches called **arterioles**. An artery has thick, muscular walls because the blood inside it is under high pressure. The walls of an artery stretch and contract with every heartbeat ▪, creating a pulse ▪.

Cutaway of a main artery

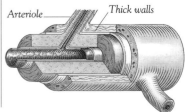

Arteriole
Thick walls

Capillary

An extremely fine blood vessel that supplies individual cells

Capillaries receive blood from arterioles. They are finer than a human hair, and pass close to almost every cell in the body. A capillary has very thin walls, which allows substances from the blood to pass from to the surrounding tissues and cells, or back in the other direction.

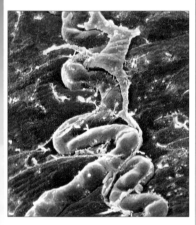

Microscopic capillary
This color-enhanced electron micrograph shows a capillary in muscle tissue.

Vein

A blood vessel that carries blood back to the heart

After blood has flowed through a capillary, it passes into fine vessels called **venules**. These lead into veins that carry the deoxygenated blood back to the heart and lungs. The blood inside a vein is under low pressure, so a vein has thinner walls than an artery. It also has valves to stop the blood from being pulled backward by gravity.

Cutaway of a main vein

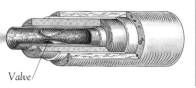

Valve

Double circulation

A circulatory system that is split into two separate loops

In some animals, blood circulates in a single loop from the heart, around the body, and back again. This is called a **single circulation**. However, in birds ■ and mammals ■, blood flows alternately through the lungs ■ and then around the body, in a figure-eight pattern. This is called a double circulation. After completing each loop, the blood returns to a different side of the heart. The blood that flows through the lungs is pumped at a lower pressure than the blood that flows through the body. In humans, blood cells can complete both loops in less than a minute.

Pulmonary circulation

The circulation from the heart to the lungs and back again

The blood flowing from the body back to the lungs is a dark red color. It is low in oxygen and high in carbon dioxide. As the blood passes through the lungs, it releases its carbon dioxide and collects oxygen, which makes the blood turn bright red again. The blood then returns to the heart, so that it can be pumped around the body with its fresh supply of oxygen.

Systemic circulation

The circulation from the heart around the body and back again

In the systemic circulation, oxygen-rich blood from the lungs is pumped around the body by the heart. As the blood travels through the body's tissues, it releases its oxygen and collects waste carbon dioxide. The systemic circulation has many branches. One of these is the **coronary circulation**, which supplies blood to the heart.

Single circulation

In a fish, blood flows around the body in a single loop.

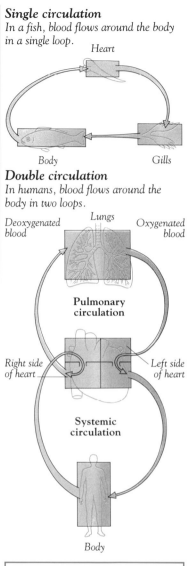

Heart

Body   Gills

Double circulation

In humans, blood flows around the body in two loops.

Deoxygenated blood   Lungs   Oxygenated blood

Pulmonary circulation

Right side of heart   Left side of heart

Systemic circulation

Body

Ibn an-Nafis

Arab doctor and anatomist (died 1228)

Ibn an-Nafis was the first person to show that blood flows through the lungs, forming a circulatory system. However, his ideas did not reach western scientists, and it was not until 1628 that the English doctor **William Harvey** (1578–1637) showed that blood circulates throughout the whole body.

Blood

Blood is a fluid that circulates around an animal's body. It carries oxygen and nutrients from digested food to the body's cells and carries away their waste products for disposal. Blood also helps fight germs that invade the body.

Blood

A complex liquid that supplies and maintains the body's cells

The cells ■ of large animals, such as humans, are very specialized. They cannot gather their own food, and they cannot dispose of waste products easily. Instead, they rely on blood to do this for them. Blood flows close to all the body's cells, helping to maintain the conditions needed to keep the cells alive. Blood makes up just under 10 percent of the body's weight. An adult human, for example, has between 7 and 10 pints (4 to 6 liters) of blood.

Red blood cell

A blood cell that carries oxygen

A single drop of blood contains millions of cells. Most of these are red blood cells, or **erythrocytes**, which contain the protein hemoglobin. Red blood cells collect oxygen from one part of the body, and carry it to another. They also carry some carbon dioxide, although most of this is dissolved in the plasma. Red blood cells are made in the bone marrow. Unlike most other cells, they do not have nuclei. They live for about four months, and are destroyed in the liver.

Red blood cells
This color-enhanced electron micrograph shows human red blood cells.

White blood cell

A blood cell that combats infections

White blood cells, or **leukocytes**, combat infections. They engulf bacteria ■ and other foreign organisms, and help to produce antibodies ■. White blood cells are larger than red blood cells. They can squeeze through the walls of capillaries ■ to reach the site of an infection.

White blood cells
*This color-enhanced electron micrograph shows a **neutrophil**, the most common kind of white blood cell. Neutrophils are formed in the bone marrow.*

Blood plasma

The fluid part of blood

The blood of all vertebrates ■ contains cells, but if these are removed, a straw-colored liquid called plasma is left behind. Plasma contains water, salts, and digested food substances, as well as many different proteins ■. These include fibrinogen, which is involved in clotting, **albumins**, which help to give blood its thickness, and antibodies. In humans, plasma makes up just over half of the blood's volume.

Blood group

A class of blood with characteristic proteins

Blood contains proteins on the surface of its red cells and in its plasma. These proteins can vary between animals of the same species ■. Two individuals that share the same proteins are said to belong to the same blood group. There are four major human blood groups – A, B, AB, and O – and over 200 minor groups. If blood from two groups is mixed, the different proteins can produce an immune response. This makes the red blood cells clump together, or **agglutinate**. Before giving blood to someone during a **blood transfusion**, doctors must therefore select the correct blood group to ensure agglutination does not occur.

See also

Antibody 130 • Bacteria 60
Capillary 127 • Cell 18
Invertebrate 96 • Molecule 25
Pathogen 130 • Protein 30
Species 48 • Vertebrate 104

Hemoglobin

An iron-containing protein that carries oxygen

Hemoglobin is found in the red blood cells of vertebrates and in the blood plasma of some invertebrates ▪. Molecules ▪ of hemoglobin combine readily with oxygen and carbon dioxide, enabling these gases to be transported in the bloodstream. Hemoglobin is one of several kinds of carrier proteins, or **blood pigments**.

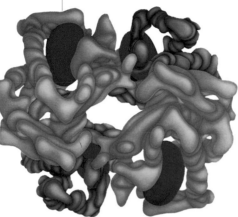

Hemoglobin
A hemoglobin molecule forms a reversible bond with oxygen molecules. It allows the blood to carry much more oxygen than it otherwise could.

Platelet

A cell fragment that helps blood to form clots

Platelets, or **thrombocytes**, are small cell fragments that do not have nuclei. They help repair damaged blood vessels and prevent bleeding. When platelets reach the site of a cut, they change shape and stick together.

Blood clot

A solid plug formed when a blood vessel is damaged

Clotting, or **coagulation**, stops pathogens ▪ entering the body and prevents too much blood being lost from a wound. It involves a series of chemical reactions that converts the soluble plasma protein **fibrinogen** into the insoluble protein **fibrin**. Fibrin forms a mesh of fibers, making a clot or **scab**. In the disease **hemophilia**, the clotting system does not work properly, and small cuts and bruises can cause extensive bleeding.

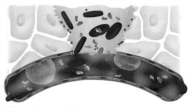

Blood vessel damage
When a blood vessel is cut, platelets near the wound stick together to form a temporary plug.

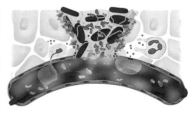

Clot formation
The platelets trigger the production of a protein called fibrin by the blood. This creates a tangled network of threads.

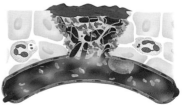

Tissue repair
The threads bind the red blood cells into a clot, or scab. This stays in place until the skin and blood vessel underneath have repaired themselves.

Deoxygenated blood
Blood that is low in oxygen is a dull red color.

Oxygenated blood
Hemoglobin carrying oxygen gives blood a bright red color.

Blood plasma
Plasma contains many different dissolved substances.

Fighting disease

An animal's body is a biological battleground. Microorganisms settle on it and try to break in, while the body retaliates and tries to fend them off. Using a battery of special defenses, the body normally manages to keep the invaders in check.

Immune response

Virus

Antigens on the surface of invading viruses trigger an immune response

Antigen

Antibodies attach to antigens on virus

Antibody

Antibodies neutralize antigens

Disease

A breakdown in the body's stable state

An animal's body is usually kept in a stable condition by the control systems of homeostasis ▪. However, this stable state sometimes breaks down, and the body stops functioning normally. This breakdown is called disease. An **infectious disease**, such as measles, is one that is triggered by an infection, or by the growth of pathogens. A **noninfectious disease** is one that is triggered by other factors, such as inherited characteristics.

Pathogen

A disease-producing organism

A pathogen is an organism that causes disease by invading the body and destroying some of its cells ▪ and tissues. The most common pathogens are viruses ▪, bacteria ▪, and fungi ▪. Pathogens also include protists ▪ such as the parasite that causes malaria. Microorganisms ▪ that are usually harmless on the surface of an animal's body can become **pathogenic**, or disease-causing, once they enter the body itself.

Nonspecific resistance

Defense systems that attack a wide range of pathogens

Nonspecific defense systems respond in the same way to all invading organisms. They provide a variety of physical and chemical barriers against infection. For example, tears wash away pathogens from the eyes. Tears also contain an enzyme ▪ called **lysozyme** which attacks the cell walls ▪ of some harmful bacteria. Sweat and saliva also contain this enzyme. The body also produces cells called **phagocytes** that engulf invading foreign cells.

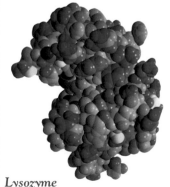

Lysozyme
This computer-generated image shows the structure of a single lysozyme molecule.

Immune system

Specific defenses against disease-causing organisms

Unlike nonspecific resistance, the immune system produces substances that are specifically selected to attack a particular invading pathogen. The immune system recognizes specific foreign cells when they enter the body, and produces special chemicals called antibodies to fight them. The immune system also "remembers" invading pathogens, and responds even faster if they reappear.

Antibody

A protein that locks on to a specific foreign substance

An antibody is a special protein that circulates in the blood. When a pathogen enters the body, antibodies lock onto the foreign substances, or **antigens**, on the pathogen's surface. This **immune response** makes the invader harmless. Antibodies are produced by special white blood cells, called lymphocytes. Lymphocytes can make antibodies against millions of potential antigens.

See also

Bacteria 60 • Capillary 127 • Cell 18
Cell wall 20 • Enzyme 31 • Fungus 76
Homeostasis 132 • Joint 137
Microorganism 60 • Protists 57
Virus 61 • White blood cell 128

Immunity

Resistance to a pathogen or a foreign substance

Immunity is the result of an immune response. Once the body has been infected with a pathogen, it "memorizes" the pathogen's antigens. If the pathogen strikes again, the body quickly increases its production of antibodies, and stops the pathogen from causing illness.

Lymphocyte

A type of white blood cell found in the lymphatic system

Lymphocytes are white blood cells ■ that are involved in the immune system. Some lymphocytes, called **macrophages**, engulf specific invaders and destroy them. Others, called **B cells**, make antibodies.

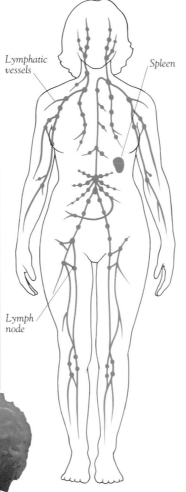

Lymphocyte
This color-enhanced electron micrograph shows a macrophage (blue) engulfing an invading yeast cell (yellow).

Lymph node

A bean-shaped swelling in a lymphatic vessel

Lymph nodes occur at intervals along lymph vessels, and also in clusters in areas such as the groin. Each one has a network of fibers that filter out bacteria and other foreign substances. In mammals, the lymph nodes often swell up if the body is fighting infection. When this happens, the nodes are called "swollen glands."

Lymphatic vessels

Spleen

Lymph node

Lymphatic system

Lymphatic system

A system of channels that drains fluid and fights infections

The lymphatic system drains fluid from the body's tissues into the blood. It also harbors lymphocytes, which fight infection. The system consists of a network of dead-end channels that reach throughout the body. The channels contain **lymph**, a fluid that seeps out of blood capillaries ■. The lymphatic system collects the fluid, and returns it through **lymph vessels** to the blood. Lymph vessels contain valves, and lymph is pushed through them by movements of the body.

Autoimmune disease

A disease in which the body attacks its own cells

Sometimes the immune system breaks down, and the body starts to attack its own tissues. One of the most common autoimmune diseases is **rheumatoid arthritis**. In this disease, antibodies attack antigens in the joints ■, making them inflamed and difficult to move.

Rheumatoid arthritis
This color-enhanced X-ray shows a person with rheumatoid arthritis in their hands. Inflamed joints restrict movement.

Allergy

An excessive immune response to an antigen

Allergies are the result of the immune system working too vigorously, and harming the body as a result. Allergies are triggered by substances called **allergens**. Allergens affect people in different ways. Many trigger immune responses that release a substance called **histamine**. Histamines often cause inflammation and they can make breathing difficult. One very common allergy is **hay fever**, which is triggered by contact with pollen. Hay fever can be controlled by **antihistamine** drugs, which counteract the effects of histamine. Allergic reactions range from mild inflammation to a very serious condition called **anaphylactic shock**, which can lead to heart failure and death.

Homeostasis

The term homeostasis means "staying the same." Homeostasis involves control systems in an animal's body that make sure conditions inside the body remain stable.

Homeostasis

The maintenance of stable conditions in a cell or a living thing

Every living thing has an **internal environment** that must be kept within certain limits within a changing **external environment**. This allows the animal's metabolism ▪ to operate in stable conditions. Stability is achieved by control systems that detect and respond to unwanted changes in an animal's body.

Feedback system

A control system that corrects unwanted changes

The mechanical thermostat that controls heating in houses is an example of a feedback system. It senses changes in temperature and switches the heating on and off to maintain a constant temperature. An animal's body has feedback systems. Like a thermostat, most of them work by **negative feedback**. This means that they detect and reverse any unwanted changes.

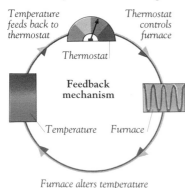

Temperature feeds back to thermostat

Thermostat controls furnace

Thermostat

Feedback mechanism

Temperature *Furnace*

Furnace alters temperature

Excretion

The process of eliminating waste

All living things form waste products, such as carbon dioxide, water, salts, and **nitrogenous waste**, which contains nitrogen. Waste has to be removed, because if it builds up, it can interfere with the body's metabolism. In vertebrates ▪, the main **excretory organs** are the skin ▪, lungs ▪, and kidneys. Some invertebrates ▪ do not have excretory organs, while others have very simple ones, such as the contractile vacuole ▪ of the amoeba.

Kidney

An excretory organ that eliminates waste and controls water content

Kidneys remove waste from the blood ▪, and regulate its water content. A kidney works by removing water and waste from the blood at the same time. It replaces most of the water, but expels the waste products in a concentrated solution called **urine**. The amount of water excreted by the kidneys is controlled by hormones ▪ secreted by the pituitary gland.

Cortex

Bowman's capsule

Collecting duct

Nephron

Loop of Henle

Medulla

Ureter

The kidney
The kidney is a complex filtering system that removes water and waste from blood.

Nephron

A filtering unit in the kidney

A human kidney contains about one million tiny filtering units, called nephrons, packed closely together. A nephron is a long narrow tube. At one end is a closed cup called a **Bowman's capsule**. Water and dissolved waste enter the nephron from a tiny knot of blood vessels in the capsule, called a **glomerulus**. The water and waste then travel down a long loop, called the **loop of Henle**. Most of the water is returned to the blood, either through the walls of the loop, or of the adjoining collecting duct. The waste passes through the duct into the **ureter**. This empties into the **bladder**, which collects urine before it is expelled.

Endotherm

An animal that keeps its body warm through its metabolism

All animals generate heat through their metabolism. In an **endothermic** animal, heat from the metabolism circulates in the blood to keep the body at a constant warm temperature. This temperature is usually higher than that of the animal's surroundings. All mammals ■ and birds ■ are endotherms and are often called **warm-blooded animals**. They are also known as **homeotherms**.

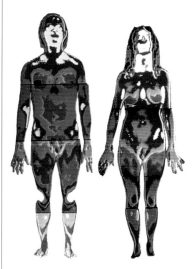

Human heat map
This thermal image shows the surface temperatures of a man and a woman. The hottest parts are shown in red, the coolest parts are shown in blue.

Ectotherm

An animal whose temperature changes with its surroundings

Ectotherms are often called **cold-blooded animals**. Their bodies are not necessarily cold, but their temperature rises and falls with that of their surroundings. Reptiles ■, fish ■, amphibians ■, and all invertebrates are **ectothermic** animals. An alternative name for an ectotherm is a **poikilotherm**.

Thermoregulation

The control and adjustment of body temperature

Most animals can control their body temperature. Ectothermic animals, such as lizards and snakes, control their temperature by their behavior. They bask in sunshine to raise their body temperature, or move into shade to lower it. Endothermic animals control their temperature mainly through bodily changes such as sweating, shivering, and vasodilation. A region of the brain called the hypothalamus ■ monitors the body's temperature and corrects any unwanted changes before they cause cooling or overheating.

Sweating

The secretion of moisture from the skin to cool the body

Many mammals, including humans, can cool their bodies by sweating. This involves secreting a salty fluid called **sweat** from the skin. As sweat evaporates, it cools the body's surface. Sweat, or **perspiration**, is produced by **sweat glands** below the skin and reaches the skin's surface via tiny tubes called **sweat ducts**. Mammals that have few sweat glands, such as dogs, lose heat by **panting**. This cools blood flowing through the tongue and mouth.

Shivering

The repeated contraction of muscles to produce heat

Mammals produce most body heat by muscle ■ contraction. If a mammal becomes cold, its muscles tense up and eventually begin to shiver. This produces metabolic heat, which is carried around the body by the blood.

Vasodilation

A widening of blood vessels

Many mammals have a network of tiny blood capillaries beneath the skin. When a mammal gets too hot, the blood capillaries widen. This increases the blood flow to the skin, and allows heat in the blood to escape from the body. **Vasoconstriction** happens when an animal is cold and produces the opposite effect. Blood vessels narrow and decrease blood flow to the skin, reducing heat loss.

Muscle — *Layer of blubber*

Spinal cord

Seal
A seal's body is kept warm by a thick layer of fat called blubber.

Insulation

A body layer that slows down the passage of heat.

Many endothermic animals conserve their body heat by insulation. For example, most mammals have fur or thick layers of fat beneath the skin, and birds have feathers. Fur and feathers both trap an insulating layer of air next to the skin. If an animal raises its fur or feathers, the insulating layer becomes thicker, and less heat is lost.

See also

Hormones

A hormone is a chemical messenger that carries instructions from one set of cells in an animal's body to another. Together with the nervous system, hormones help the body function in a controlled way.

Hormone

A chemical messenger

Hormones are a form of chemical communication. In animals, they usually travel through the body in the blood until they reach their target cells ■ or tissues ■. Vertebrates ■ have at least 50 different hormones, which are released by particular groups of cells. Plants ■ also have hormones, which mainly affect growth.

Hypothalamus
Pituitary gland
Pineal gland
Thyroid gland
Adrenal glands
Pancreas
Ovaries

Endocrine system

Gland

A group of cells that produce and release chemicals

An animal's body has many different glands, but they fall into two distinct groups. Some, such as sweat glands, release substances through ducts onto body surfaces; they are called **exocrine glands**. Others, called the **endocrine glands**, make hormones that are released directly into the bloodstream. Endocrine glands include the **pituitary gland**, which is beneath the brain, the **thyroid gland**, the **adrenal glands**, and the **gonads**, which are the ovaries ■ in females and the testes ■ in males. Together, these glands form the body's **endocrine system**.

Target cell

A cell that is activated by a hormone

When a hormone reaches its target cells or **target tissues**, it attaches to a **receptor site**. This is a specific site on a cell's plasma membrane ■. The hormone then triggers a specific action. For example, some hormones make particular muscles contract, and others make their target cells grow more quickly. A hormone that targets an endocrine gland can trigger the production of another hormone.

Invertebrate hormone

A hormone produced by an invertebrate

Invertebrates ■ often use hormones in growth and development. A hormone called **ecdysone** makes insects molt, or shed their outer body case.

See also

Jokichi Takamine

Japanese-American biochemist
1854–1922

Jokichi Takamine was born in Japan, but spent much of his adult life in the United States. In 1901, he became the first person to isolate a hormone, when he prepared crystals of adrenalin, a hormone that increases the body's metabolic rate. The word hormone was first used in 1905, after the discovery of secretin, which stimulates the release of bile. "Hormone" is from a Greek word meaning "to stimulate."

Pheromone

A chemical released by one animal that has an effect on another

Pheromones work like hormones, but target other members of a species, instead of cells within the body. They are either released into the surroundings in sweat or urine, or passed directly from one animal to another, often through glands in the skin. Insects use pheromones for many different functions, including marking trails, signaling alarm, or attracting members of the opposite sex.

Trail marked by pheromones

Following a trail
Many female moths attract mates by leaving a pheromone trail or by releasing pheromones into the air.

Adrenalin

A hormone that prepares an animal's body for danger

When an animal faces danger, an **alarm reaction** is triggered in its body. This stimulates the adrenal glands to release the hormone adrenalin, which prepares the animal for "fight or flight." Unlike most hormones, adrenalin works rapidly. It increases blood pressure and heartbeat rate, accelerates the rate of respiration ■, and slows down digestion. Together, these changes give an animal a better chance of survival.

Female sex hormone

A hormone that prepares the female body for reproduction

Sex hormones trigger the development of secondary sexual characteristics ■ and prepare the body for reproduction. In women, sex hormones regulate ovulation and control pregnancy. They are produced by the pituitary gland and the ovaries, and include **estrogens**. Estrogens trigger female secondary sexual characteristics, such as breasts. These changes become apparent during a burst of development, called **puberty**.

Male sex hormone

A hormone that prepares the male body for reproduction

Male sex hormones produce male secondary sexual characteristics, such as facial hair, and regulate the production of sperm ■. The main male sex hormone is **testosterone**, which is produced by the testes. The production of sperm is triggered by the **follicle-stimulating hormone**, which is produced by the pituitary gland. This same hormone triggers the production of ova ■ in women. After puberty male sex hormones are produced throughout life.

MAJOR HUMAN HORMONES

Gland	Hormone	Effects
Pineal	Melatonin	Acts as a "biological clock" that helps to regulate the rhythms of the body
Hypothalamus	Releasing and inhibiting factors	Hypothalamus factors supervise the release of hormones from anterior pituitary gland
Anterior pituitary	Adrenocorticotrophic hormone	Stimulates secretion of corticosteroid hormones by adrenal cortex
	Growth hormone	Stimulates rate of growth, increases level of glucose in the blood
	Thyrotropin	Stimulates production of hormones by thyroid gland
	Follicle-stimulating hormone	Promotes production of sex cells in males and maturation of sex cells in females
	Luteinizing hormone	Stimulates production of sex hormones in males and females, stimulates ovulation in females
	Prolactin	Makes the female body ready to produce milk
Posterior pituitary	Oxytocin	Produces contractions of the uterus during birth, promotes production of milk when a baby feeds
	Vasopressin (Antidiuretic hormone)	Increases amount of water returned to blood by kidneys, raises blood pressure by making arterioles constrict
Thyroid	Calcitonin	Lowers the concentration of calcium in blood by building it into bones
	Thyroxin	Stimulates growth, increases the body's metabolic rate
Parathyroid	Parathyroid hormone	Increases concentration of calcium in blood by removing it from bones
Adrenal medulla	Adrenalin, or epinephrine	Prepares the body for stress by narrowing blood vessels, increasing heart rate, and increasing the amount of glucose in the blood
Adrenal cortex	Corticosteroids	Increase metabolism of fats, carbohydrates, and proteins
Stomach	Gastrin	Stimulates secretion of hydrochloric acid by cells lining the stomach
Pancreas	Glucagon	Raises blood glucose level by stimulating liver to convert stored glycogen into glucose
	Insulin	Decreases blood glucose level by stimulating liver to convert stored glucose into glycogen, increases amount of glucose absorbed by cells
Small intestine	Secretin	Stimulates pancreas to release bile and pancreatic juice to the intestine
Ovary	Estrogens	Promote development of secondary sexual characteristics in females
Corpus luteum	Progesterone	Prepares body to produce milk, and maintains the lining of the uterus
Testis	Testosterone	Promotes development of secondary sexual characteristics in males

Skeletons

All animals need some form of support to maintain their body shape and to allow them to move. In vertebrates, the body is supported by a bony framework called a skeleton. A skeleton protects the internal organs, and provides something for the muscles to pull against.

Apertures connecting the chambers

A nautilus shell
A nautilus seals off the shell behind it as it grows, creating a spiral of chambers.

Skeleton

A framework that supports an animal's body

A skeleton supports an animal's body and provides an anchor for its muscles ■. This enables the animal to move. Most skeletons are made of a hard material, such as bone, but some, such as that of the sea anemone, are made of outer body layers that are tough but flexible. A skeleton can also have other uses besides support. For example, a tortoise's shell may protect it from its enemies, and an insect's skeleton helps to prevent it drying out.

Head

Thorax

Wing case

Abdomen

Exoskeleton of a jewel beetle

Hydrostatic skeleton

A kind of skeleton that is held in shape by the pressure of fluid

A soft-bodied animal, such as an earthworm ■, maintains its shape because it is filled with fluid. An earthworm's body is divided into separate compartments. In each compartment, fluid in a cavity called the **coelom** presses against the worm's muscular body wall. Like air inside a tire, the fluid makes the worm's body firm. Starfish ■ keep their tube feet firm in this way.

Exoskeleton

A hard skeleton that surrounds an animal's body

An exoskeleton covers all or part of an animal's body and supports it from the outside. Muscles are attached to the inside of the exoskeleton, and pull against it to create movement ■. A **body case** is a kind of exoskeleton that is found in arthropods ■. It covers the whole of the body, including the antennae ■ and the eyes ■, and is made of plates that meet at flexible joints. A body case cannot expand, and must be shed, or molted, as the animal grows. A new, larger case develops after each molt.

Chitin

A substance found in the exoskeletons of arthropods

Chitin is a light, strong substance that is found in many exoskeletons. It contains hydrogen, carbon, oxygen, and nitrogen, and forms long molecules, like those of cellulose ■. The chitin molecules are laid down in crisscross layers, which help to strengthen the exoskeleton. Chitin also reinforces the cell walls ■ of fungi ■.

Shell

A hard, inflexible exoskeleton

A shell is a kind of exoskeleton that covers either the whole animal, or just part of it. Shells cannot change shape, although some, such as those formed by oysters, have a single hinge that allows them to open or close. A shell grows along its open edges. Unlike a body case, it does not have to be molted because the space inside the shell gets bigger as the animal grows.

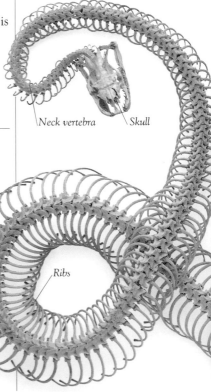

Neck vertebra   *Skull*

Ribs

Endoskeleton

A hard skeleton inside an animal's body

An endoskeleton is an internal framework that supports an animal's body. It is usually made of cartilage and bone, and has flexible joints that allow the body to move. Unlike most exoskeletons, an endoskeleton grows in step with the rest of the body. This means that the same skeleton lasts for the whole of an animal's life. All vertebrates ■ have endoskeletons. Turtles ■ and tortoises also have an external shell, which consists of scales made from the structural protein ■ keratin.

Snake skeleton

A snake's body is supported by an internal skeleton. Most of the skeleton is made up of a very flexible backbone, which has many pairs of ribs. Muscles bend the backbone to allow the snake to move.

Trunk vertebra

Tail vertebra

Bone

A hard material in the skeletons of vertebrates

Bone is a living substance. It supports a vertebrate's body, and forms a protective casing around delicate organs such as the brain ■. Bone is made of cells surrounded by layers of hard mineral ■ salts, such as calcium phosphate. It also contains the protein ■ collagen, which makes it slightly flexible. **Compact bone** is the dense outer layer of a bone. **Spongy bone** is the lighter, softer layer inside. Some bones are filled with **marrow**, which makes blood ■ cells.

Ball of hip joint

Spongy bone contains marrow

Outer layer of compact bone provides strength

Bone

A human femur, or thigh bone, is like a very strong tube. The inside of the tube contains spongy bone with spaces that are filled by marrow.

Cartilage

A tough, slippery substance in a vertebrate's skeleton

Cartilage, or "gristle," consists of cells set in fibers of collagen. It is strong, flexible, and slightly slippery. Cartilage allows bones to slide over each other at joints. The skeletons of cartilaginous fish, such as sharks and rays, are made up entirely of cartilage.

Ossification

The conversion of cartilage into bone

When a vertebrate's skeleton first forms, it consists entirely of cartilage. During the process of ossification, most of the cartilage becomes **calcified**. This means that it gradually hardens into bone. The skeleton of a newborn human baby is partly ossified, but still contains a large amount of cartilage. Ossification continues into adulthood. Eventually only small regions of cartilage are left in areas such as the nose and the joints.

Joint

A region where two bones meet

There are two main kinds of joint in a vertebrate's skeleton. **Fused joints**, such as those between the skull bones, keep bones locked together. **Synovial joints**, such as the elbow and hip, allow bones to slide over each other, so that an animal can move. The bones in a synovial joint are tipped with cartilage. The entire joint is enclosed by a **synovial membrane** and oiled by **synovial fluid**. The elbow is an example of a **hinge joint**, which can move in only one direction. The hip is an example of a **ball-and-socket joint**. It can move in several directions.

See also

Continued over page ➤

Axial skeleton

The central part of a vertebrate's skeleton

The axial skeleton contains the bones that lie on or near the axis, or midline, of a vertebrate's ■ body. It includes the bones of the skull ■, the backbone, and the ribcage. The number of bones in the axial skeleton varies greatly between animal groups. The human axial skeleton contains 80 bones, including the bones in the ear ■. A snake's axial skeleton can contain five times this number.

Backbone

A flexible chain of bones

The backbone is also known as the **vertebral column** or **spine**. It is made of short, separate bones called vertebrae. The joints between neighboring vertebrae allow only a small amount of movement. Over the whole spine, these joints make the backbone very flexible.

Vertebra

One of the bones that makes up the backbone

A vertebra (plural **vertebrae**) is a short, pillarlike bone with a ring-shaped arch attached to it. Together, the vertebrae form a hollow rod that contains and protects the spinal cord ■. Humans usually have 33 vertebrae. Some frogs have fewer than a dozen vertebrae, while snakes can have over 400.

Ribcage

A bony cage that allows breathing and protects internal organs

The ribcage is made up of curved bones called **ribs**, which are connected by muscles ■. During breathing ■, one set of muscles contracts to make the ribs swing upward and outward. This increases the volume of the chest and draws air into the lungs ■.

Appendicular skeleton

The bones of the girdles and limbs

The appendicular skeleton contains the bones that an animal uses for locomotion ■. It includes the upper and lower limbs and the girdles – the bones that attach the limbs to the axial skeleton. During evolution ■, vertebrates such as whales and snakes have lost some or all of their appendicular skeletons.

Limb

An appendage used in movement

Arms, legs, flippers, and wings are all limbs. Animals use their limbs mainly for locomotion. The limbs of reptiles, birds, mammals, and amphibians have the same bone arrangement. They are called **pentadactyl limbs**, because they usually have five fingers or toes.

Sea lion flipper

Porpoise flipper

Girdle

A ring of bones that anchors the limbs

Vertebrate skeletons usually have two girdles – the **pelvic** or **hip girdle** and the **pectoral** or **shoulder girdle**. Fish do not have girdles. Some whales and snakes have the remains of a pelvic girdle, but with no limbs attached to it.

Hindlimb

A limb near the back of the body

A vertebrate's hindlimbs usually have three main bones – the **femur**, or thighbone, in the upper hindlimb, and the **tibia** and the **fibula** in the lower hindlimb. The bones of the upper and lower hindlimb meet each other at the knee joint.

Forelimb

A limb near the front of the body

A typical vertebrate has three long bones in its forelimbs – the **humerus** in the upper forelimb, and the **radius** and the **ulna** in the lower forelimb. The upper and lower forelimb bones meet each other at the elbow joint.

Hand

A part of a limb that is used for gripping

A hand is similar to a foot, but more flexible. Only primates ■ have true hands, and they use them to grip things. Hands have three sets of bones – the **carpals**, the **metacarpals**, and the **phalanges**.

Foot

A part of a limb that is used for movement

A typical foot has five toes, or **digits**, and three sets of bones – the **tarsals**, the **metatarsals**, and the phalanges. Feet and hands often end in hard parts made from the structural protein ■ keratin. These include hooves, claws, or nails.

◄ *Continued from previous page*

HUMAN SKELETON

Pectoral girdle
The bones that anchor the forelimbs to the body

Clavicle
A bone that helps to anchor the humerus. Also known as the collarbone

Scapula
A bone that helps to anchor the humerus. Also known as the shoulderblade

Rib
One of a set of bones that curve around and forward from the backbone

Sacrum
A bone near the base of the spine that is formed from five fused vertebrae

Coccyx
A bone at the base of the spine that is formed from four fused vertebrae

Vertebra
A bone that forms part of the backbone

Intervertebral disk
A pad of cartilage that acts as a shock absorber between vertebrae and allows the backbone to bend without being damaged

Pelvic girdle
The bones that anchor the hindlimbs to the body

Skull
A bony case that forms the head and jaws

Sternum
The bone to which most of the ribs are attached. Also known as the breastbone

Humerus
The bone in the forelimb that is nearest the body

Radius and ulna
The two lower bones in the forelimb that meet the humerus at the elbow joint

Carpal
A wrist bone

Metacarpal
A hand bone

Phalanx (plural phalanges)
A finger or toe bone

Femur
The bone in the hindlimb that is nearest the body

Patella
A small buttonlike bone that protects the knee. Also known as the kneecap

Tibia and fibula
The two lower bones in the hindlimb that meet the femur at the kneecap

Tarsal
An ankle bone

Metatarsal
A foot bone

Skull
Clavicle
Sternum
Pectoral girdle
Scapula
Rib
Intervertebral disk
Vertebra
Radius
Humerus
Ulna
Pelvic girdle
Carpal
Sacrum
Metacarpal
Coccyx
Phalanges
Femur
Patella
Tibia
Fibula
Tarsal
Metatarsal
Phalanges

Skulls

A skull is a complex collection of interlocking bones. It protects a vertebrate's brain and sense organs, particularly the eyes and inner ears, and also enables the animal to feed.

See also

Bird 110 • Birth 163 • Bone 137
Cartilage 137 • Ear 154 • Jaw 119
Joint 137 • Membrane 18
Ossification 137 • Structural protein 30
Vertebrate 104

Skull

A bony case around a vertebrate's head

The bones on the outside of an animal's skull are dense and hard. They lock together tightly to form a solid case that allows the brain to withstand hard knocks without being damaged. The bones ■ inside the skull are much more delicate. They support the membranes ■ lining the nasal passages. A human skull contains 22 bones, excluding the ear ■ ossicles. With the exception of the lower jaw ■, the skull bones meet at fixed joints ■. This means they cannot move.

Human skull

Suture
Dome of cranium
Eye socket
Ear hole
Temporomandibular joint
Lower jaw or mandible

Cranium

A bony box that protects the brain

The cranium is a very tough box that surrounds the brain. It is made of several separate bones, locked together by jigsawlike fixed joints called **sutures**. In some animals, such as dogs, the cranium has a bony ridge on top that anchors the jaw muscles. The human cranium has eight bones, two of which are fused together to form an extra-strong bone across the forehead. A baby's cranium is slightly elastic, which allows it to pass through the pelvic girdle during birth ■.

Facial bone

One of the bones of the face

Facial bones make up the front of the skull. They house the eyes and the ears, and include the jaw. Some of the facial bones contain internal spaces called **sinuses** which help to lighten the skull. In large land animals, such as elephants, the skull is honeycombed with these weight-saving holes.

Fontanelle

A gap between the bones in the cranium

When a young vertebrate ■ first develops, its skeleton is made of cartilage ■. The cartilage slowly turns to bone in a process called ossification ■. In humans, this process is not completed until several months after birth. Until then, a baby has soft gaps, or fontanelles, in parts of its cranium.

Antler

A bony projection from the skull

Antlers look quite like horns, but they are made of solid bone, instead of the structural protein ■ keratin. They are also attached directly to the skull. Deer grow antlers. They usually shed their antlers every year, and grow a new pair. New antlers are covered with skin.

Beak

A pair of long jaws without teeth

Birds ■ use their beaks to collect and eat their food, and also to preen and build nests. A bird's beak consists of two bony jaws covered by a layer of the structural protein keratin.

Gannet skull

Large, forward-pointing eyes to spot fish
Beak
Streamlined point for diving

Skin

In most vertebrates, the skin is the largest organ in the body. It forms a tough, waterproof barrier that protects against harmful bacteria, injury, and the damaging rays of the Sun.

Skin

The outer body covering in vertebrates

Skin is a type of **integument**, or body covering. It protects an animal's internal organs, and helps to prevent its body from drying out. Skin also prevents microorganisms ▪ from getting into the body. In endothermic ▪ animals, skin plays an important part in thermoregulation ▪, or body temperature control.

Dermis

The inner part of the skin

The dermis lies below the epidermis and is much thicker. It contains a dense network of blood capillaries ▪, and tiny nerve endings that sense pressure or temperature. The dermis also contains hair follicles, sweat glands, and collagen fibers. Collagen is a structural protein ▪ that makes the skin elastic.

Marcello Malpighi

Italian biologist
1628–94

Malpighi was one of the earliest scientists to look at the detailed structure of animals through a microscope. He was the first person to see capillaries, and investigated many other tissues ▪, such as nerves ▪ and the skin. Many body features are named after him, including **Malpighian bodies**, which form part of the kidney's nephrons ▪ and the Malpighian layer in the skin.

Nail

A hard flap that protects parts of the skin

A nail is an outgrowth of the epidermis. Like hair, it is made of keratin, and grows constantly. Nails protect the tips of fingers and toes, and enable fingers to pick up small objects. **Hooves**, **claws**, and **horns** are also made of keratin and grow constantly.

Scale

A small plate that protects the skin

Many animals have scales, including fish, reptiles, and some mammals. Scales are plates made of either keratin or a bony substance. They overlap to protect the soft skin underneath, rather like the tiles on a roof.

Pangolin scales

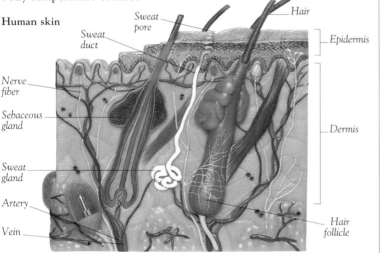

Human skin

- Sweat pore
- Sweat duct
- Hair
- Epidermis
- Nerve fiber
- Sebaceous gland
- Dermis
- Sweat gland
- Artery
- Vein
- Hair follicle

Epidermis

The outer part of the skin

In most mammals, the epidermis has three layers. The lowest is the **Malpighian layer**. This thin band contains living cells that divide constantly to replace the cells shed from the skin's surface. Cells from the Malpighian layer push up through the **granular layer** toward the skin's surface. Here, dead cells make up the skin's surface, or **cornified layer**.

Hair

A protective outgrowth from a mammal's skin

A hair contains cells packed with the structural protein keratin. Each hair grows from a pit in the dermis called a **hair follicle**. The pit has a small **sebaceous gland** attached to it that coats the hair with an oily substance called **sebum**. In most mammals, hair, **wool**, or **fur** helps keep the body warm.

See also

Muscles

Animals use muscles to move around. Muscles are also important for other processes. Without muscles, the heart would not beat, blood would not flow around the body, and food would not pass through the digestive system.

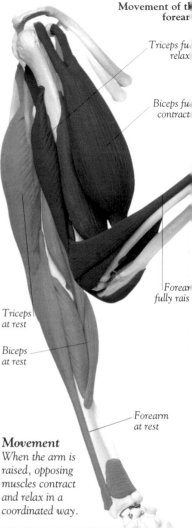

Triceps fu relax

Biceps fu contract

Forear fully rais

Triceps at rest

Biceps at rest

Forearm at rest

Movement
When the arm is raised, opposing muscles contract and relax in a coordinated way.

Muscle

A tissue that contracts to produce movement

Muscles are made of cylindrical cells called **muscle fibers**. These cells can be several centimeters long, and they can shorten, or contract. An individual muscle often contains thousands or millions of fibers, and their combined force gives the muscle its strength. Muscle fibers obtain the energy they need to contract from respiration ▪. Most muscle fibers contract when they are triggered by nerves ▪.

Involuntary muscle

A muscle that is not under conscious control

Involuntary muscles, also called **smooth muscles**, are not under an animal's direct control. They are **unstriated**, which means they do not look striped when seen under a microscope. Involuntary muscles contract automatically when triggered by the autonomic nervous system ▪, or by chemicals such as hormones ▪. These muscles are usually connected to soft parts of the body, and change the shape of an organ ▪ or other body part when they contract. Involuntary muscles are important in homeostasis ▪. They adjust conditions inside the body and move food along the alimentary canal. Many involuntary muscles contract and relax rhythmically, and exert a steady but gentle pull.

Cardiac muscle

The muscular tissue of the heart

Cardiac muscle is a kind of involuntary muscle found only in the heart. It contracts and relaxes automatically and has an inbuilt rhythm. This rhythm can be altered by nerves and by hormones such as adrenalin ▪.

Voluntary muscle

A muscle that is under conscious control

Voluntary muscles, also called **skeletal muscles**, can be consciously controlled by an animal. They are **striated**, which means that they appear striped under a microscope. Voluntary muscles are the largest muscles in a vertebrate's body and are connected to bones either by sheets of tissue ▪ or by tough cords called **tendons**. When a voluntary muscle contracts, it makes part of the skeleton ▪ move. The human body contains over 600 different skeletal muscles, which make up two-fifths of its total weight.

Voluntary muscle
When magnified, voluntary muscle has light and dark stripes.

Antagonistic pair

A pair of muscles that work against each other

Muscles can pull, but they cannot push. They are therefore often arranged in pairs or groups, so that when one muscle contracts, the other relaxes. For example, in humans, the arm is raised by the **biceps** and **brachialis** muscles, and lowered by the **triceps** muscle. In soft-bodied animals such as earthworms ▪, **circular muscles** contract to make the body longer, and **longitudinal muscles** contract to make it shorter.

Muscle contraction

The shortening of a muscle

A muscle contracts when its fibers shorten, and it relaxes when they return to their original length. During an **isotonic** contraction, a muscle exerts a steady pull and gets noticeably shorter. This kind of muscle contraction creates the pull that is needed to make part of the body move. During an **isometric** contraction, a muscle exerts a strong pulling force, or **tension**, but shortens by just a small amount. An isotonic contraction is used to lift a weight, while an isometric contraction holds the weight in position.

Muscle tone

The continuous partial contraction of a muscle

A muscle's fibers are often partially contracted even when the muscle seems to be at rest. This partial contraction tones the muscle, which means that it makes it firm. Muscle tone is important for maintaining the shape of an animal's body. It is particularly important in land animals, including humans. Without muscle tone, our bodies would fold up under the effect of gravity.

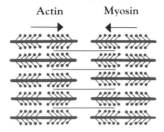

1 Muscle relaxed
In a relaxed muscle, the filaments of actin and myosin only partly overlap.

Actin   Myosin

2 Muscle contracted
During contraction, a chemical change makes the myosin filaments slide past those of the actin.

Sliding filament theory

A theory that suggests how muscles contract

Muscles contain two proteins ■, **actin** and **myosin**. Their molecules form long threads, or **filaments**, which are arranged in parallel stacks, like overlapping decks of cards. According to the sliding filament theory, muscles contract because the actin and myosin filaments slide past each other. The more they overlap, the shorter the muscle becomes. When the filaments slide back again, the muscle relaxes.

Cramp

The involuntary contraction of a voluntary muscle

Cramp is a sudden and unwanted contraction in a muscle. It makes many of the muscle's fibers contract at the same time. This creates a powerful pull, or **spasm**. In an ordinary muscle contraction, only a limited number of muscle fibers contract at once.

Muscle fatigue

A gradual weakening in the pull of a muscle

When the same muscles are used for a long period of time, lactic acid builds up inside the muscle, preventing it from working efficiently. This is called muscle fatigue. Lactic acid is made when the muscle becomes short of oxygen. It is formed by anaerobic respiration ■, and can only be broken down when oxygen is available once more. Until this oxygen debt ■ has been "repaid," the muscles cannot work at full efficiency. Cardiac muscle has a very good oxygen supply, and never becomes fatigued.

Catch muscle

A muscle that can contract and then lock

To avoid drying out at low tide, many mollusks ■ use catch muscle to keep their shells tightly closed for hours. Catch muscle is a special kind of muscle tissue that uses energy to contract, but requires little extra energy to remain contracted.

Luigi Galvani

Italian anatomist
1737–98

Luigi Galvani made an important discovery about muscle contraction. When he pegged the legs of a dead frog to an iron frame using brass pins, he noticed the legs began to twitch. Galvani realized that electricity was involved, but thought that it came from the frog's muscles. In fact, he had accidentally created an electric circuit involving two metals: it was the electric current that made the muscles contract.

Animal movement

In the animal world, movement is a sign of life. Many animals move around to find their food and to escape from predators. Some also move to seek out partners and to bring up their young.

Movement

The motion of all or part of an animal's body

Movement is a characteristic of all animals. Vertebrates ■ are very **mobile** animals, which means that they spend a lot of time moving around. Some invertebrates ■ are sessile, which means that they spend all or part of their lives in one place.

Locomotion

The movement of an animal's body from place to place

During locomotion an animal moves its entire body from one place to another. Very simple organisms often move by beating cilia ■ or flagella ■, or by amoeboid movement ■. Larger animals use their muscles ■ to travel. All forms of locomotion require coordination, so that an animal moves in the right direction and avoids danger.

Ciliary movement

A form of locomotion powered by beating cilia

The surface of many single-celled organisms is covered with tiny hairs, or cilia. The cilia beat in a coordinated way to make the cell move through water, or over moist surfaces. Some flatworms have cilia on their undersides. They use these cilia together with muscles to glide over surfaces.

Flagellar movement

A form of locomotion powered by beating flagella

A flagellum is a whiplike thread that beats from side to side to produce movement. Many single-celled organisms use flagella to move. They include plantlike dinoflagellates ■, and single-celled parasites ■ that swim through blood.

A dogfish swims by sending a wave of movement down its body

Horizontal fins keep the dogfish's body level in the water

Longitudinal movement

A form of locomotion powered by waves of muscular contraction

Many soft-bodied animals move by muscular waves that travel from one end of their bodies to the other. In a snail, for example, waves of contraction move forward along the snail's foot, and the snail is carried in the same direction. Earthworms ■ also lengthen and shorten their body segments by muscular waves.

Swimming

A form of locomotion in which the body is propelled through water

Living things swim in different ways. The smallest organisms beat tiny cilia or flagella, while large animals use fins or flippers. A cartilaginous fish ■, such as a shark, bends its body into curves. Its body and fins push the surrounding water sideways and backward, and this propels the fish forward. Most bony fish keep their bodies straight. They push themselves forward by beating their tail fin from side to side. A whale swims in the same way, but beats its tail flaps, called flukes, up and down.

At the end of each wave, the dogfish's tail flicks backward against the water

Jet propulsion

A form of locomotion used by some mollusks

When an octopus wants to move quickly, it contracts a water-filled chamber called a **mantle cavity**. This forces a stream of water out of its body through a nozzle called a siphon ■ and pushes the animal in the opposite direction. An octopus can swivel its siphon to alter the direction in which it moves.

Tentacles trailing behind head

Jetting away
An octopus swims backward with its tentacles trailing behind it. This streamlined shape allows it to slip easily through the water.

Serpentine movement

A form of locomotion in which the body snakes from side to side

In serpentine movement, an animal's body curves from side to side. The curves push backward, and the animal moves forward. This kind of locomotion works in water, on solid surfaces, and on loose ground such as sand. Most snakes move by serpentine movement. Some annelid worms also use it to swim.

Jumping ahead
A sidewinder throws its body over sandy ground, leaving a trail of parallel lines behind it.

Jumping

A form of locomotion in which the body is propelled through the air

Many animals, including fleas, frogs, and kangaroos, move by jumping. Small animals are able to jump farthest in relation to their body length because they produce more power in relation to their weight. A frog jumps using powerful muscles that extend its back legs. A flea jumps in a different way – by squeezing pads of a rubbery material called **resilin**. When the resilin is released, it makes the flea's hindlegs flick out, and the flea is flung backward into the air. During its jump, the flea experiences the most rapid acceleration of any animal.

Making a leap
A frog's hind legs produce enough leverage to propel its body a long way through the air.

Digitigrade mammal

A mammal that walks on its toes

A digitigrade mammal walks on its toes, or digits. Many predators ■, such as cats and dogs, move this way. It enables them to move quickly because they have a small area in contact with the ground.

The head turns right at the beginning of the next wave

Swimming dogfish
This sequence of photographs shows the S-shaped wave of movement that passes through the dogfish's body as it swims.

The dogfish's body swivels around a point just behind its head

The dogfish's head points left at the end of one body wave

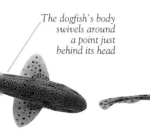

Walking

A form of locomotion in which the body is raised and moved by legs

An animal walks by pushing backward on the ground with its legs. This moves it forward. The precise way in which an animal walks is known as its **gait**. An animal's gait often varies according to its speed. For example, when a horse walks, it always has three feet in contact with the ground. When it breaks into a gallop, all four feet can be in the air at once.

Plantigrade mammal

A mammal that walks with its feet flat on the ground

Most amphibians and reptiles walk with their feet flat on the ground. The first mammals also walked in this way, and some of today's mammals, including bears and humans, still do. However, this way of walking slows an animal down, because a large surface area comes into contact with the ground. Many other mammals have evolved different ways of walking, with a much smaller part of their feet touching the ground. This allows the animal to move more quickly.

Unguligrade mammal

A mammal that walks on tiptoe

Unguligrade mammals walk with just their hooves touching the ground. The surface area of a hoof is small, so the animal can move quickly and efficiently. Unguligrade mammals include horses, antelope, cattle, and other ungulates ■.

See also

Continued over page ➤

Beetle flight
A cockchafer's flat hindwings provide the driving force for flight, while its curved forewings provide lift.

Flight

A kind of movement that is supported by air

Many animals can travel through the air for short distances, but only insects ■, birds ■, and bats ■ are capable of **powered flight**. In powered flight, these animals use energy to flap their wings. Their wings counteract the downward pull of gravity, and this allows the animal to stay airborne.

Wings sweep upward and almost touch

Wingbeat

An up-and-down wing movement

Animals flap their wings to move through the air, or to hover. A bird beats its wings using powerful **pectoral muscles** that connect its wing bones with its chest and with part of its breastbone, called the **keel**. Small insects, such as mosquitoes, do not power their wings directly. Instead, they have muscles that change the shape of the thorax, and this makes their wings click up and down.

Feathers fan out to form a large surface

Pectoral muscles pull wings down

Flying squirrel
When it launches itself from a high branch, a flying squirrel can glide nearly 330 feet (100 meters).

Gliding

Unpowered flight on a downward gradient

Gliding is a form of unpowered flight, in which an animal gradually falls to the ground. However, winglike flaps slow its fall, so that the animal moves forward at the same time. Flying squirrels glide through the air on flaps of stretchy skin between their legs. Flying fish glide above the water with large fins that open out like fans.

Wings begin to rise again

Feathers flick forward for next wingbeat

Bird flight
The broad, streamlined surface of a pigeon's wings produce lift. Wings also push the bird forward through the air.

Wing

A surface that provides lift

Wings work in different ways. A bird's wings have a special shape, called an **airfoil**, that is curved from front to back. When air flows over a bird's wings, it produces an upward force, called **lift**. Insect wings are often much flatter and work like paddles. When they push downward against the air, the animal's body is pushed upward.

Soaring

Gliding in rising air

Air rises when it heats up, or when it blows against obstacles such as cliffs or mountains. Some animals travel long distances by riding on columns of warm rising air, called **thermals**. Birds of prey ■ are experts at soaring upward in one thermal, and then gliding down to the bottom of the next. Migrating insects, such as butterflies and aphids, are also carried upward in rising air.

Hovering

Flying over a fixed spot

Hovering is a very strenuous form of flight, and uses a great deal of energy. Many insects are good at hovering because they have light bodies. Most birds cannot hover without a breeze to help them stay up, although hummingbirds ■ hover while they are feeding.

See also

Bat 112 • Bird 110 • Bird of prey 111
Hummingbird 111 • Insect 102

◄ Continued from previous page

Nerves

Nerve cells work like telegraph wires. They flash messages from one part of an animal's body to another. This allows the animal to coordinate its actions.

See also

Active transport 22 • Cell 18
Ion 24 • Nervous system 148
Plasma membrane 18

Nerve

A bundle of cells that carries signals

Nerves help an animal's body to work as a single unit. They carry messages from one part of the body to another.

Neuron

An individual nerve cell

A neuron is a cell ▩ that can transmit electrical signals, or nerve impulses. Neurons are the longest cells in an animal's body, and they are often bundled together to form nerves. Neurons make up the nervous system ▩. Unlike most cells, they do not normally divide once they have been formed.

Axon

A long filament in a neuron

An axon is a threadlike part of a neuron. It can be over 3 feet (1 meter) long, and conducts nerve impulses. The impulses always travel along the axon in the same direction.

Myelin

A substance that insulates neurons

The axons of vertebrate nerve cells are often enclosed by other cells. These cells wind around the nerve cells like a sheath, and are rich in a fatty substance called myelin. Myelin works like plastic around an electrical wire, and helps to speed up the transmission of nerve impulses.

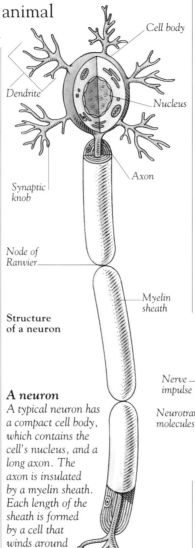

Cell body

Dendrite

Nucleus

Axon

Synaptic knob

Node of Ranvier

Myelin sheath

Structure of a neuron

A neuron
A typical neuron has a compact cell body, which contains the cell's nucleus, and a long axon. The axon is insulated by a myelin sheath. Each length of the sheath is formed by a cell that winds around the neuron.

Dendrite

A finely branched thread from the cell body of a neuron

Dendrites are like axons, but are much shorter and have many branches. Dendrites allow a neuron to receive signals from its neighbors, through synapses.

Nerve impulse

A signal that passes down a neuron

Positive sodium ions ▩ constantly pass out of a neuron by active transport ▩. This creates a tiny negative electrical charge across the plasma membrane ▩ of the neuron. When the cell receives a signal, or stimulus, from another nerve cell for example, sodium ions flood back into it, reversing the charge. This creates an **action potential**, or nerve impulse, which flashes along the cell's axon. Nerve impulses can travel at 330 feet (100 meters) per second in vertebrates. They are usually much slower in invertebrates.

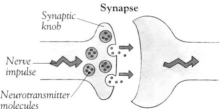

Synapse

Synaptic knob

Nerve impulse

Neurotransmitter molecules

A synapse
Chemicals called neurotransmitters travel from one nerve cell to another.

Synapse

A junction between two neurons

A synapse is a junction that allows one neuron to pass signals to another. It consists of a tiny knoblike swelling that is very close to a neighboring neuron. When a nerve impulse arrives at the synapse, the swelling releases a **transmitter** substance. This triggers an impulse in the neighboring cell. Some neurons have over 10,000 synapses with the cells around them. In each synapse, signals can travel only in a single direction.

Nervous systems

An animal's nervous system enables it to react quickly to its surroundings. It collects and processes information so that the animal can respond. In large animals, the nervous system can contain billions of interconnected cells.

Nervous system

A network of nerve cells

Very simple animals, such as sponges ■, do not have nervous systems. Some invertebrates ■ have elementary nervous systems, called **nerve nets**, others have a more elaborate nervous system. In vertebrates ■, the nervous system is divided into two parts – the central nervous system and the peripheral nervous system.

Clusters of nerve cells

Nerve network

Jellyfish
Jellyfish have a simple nervous system, made up of a small number of similar nerve cells.

Receptor

A cell or nerve ending that reacts to something inside or outside the body

Receptors provide an animal with information about its body and its surroundings. Each receptor reacts to a particular **stimulus**, such as pressure, light, or sound, and converts it into a nerve impulse ■. Some receptors are scattered throughout the body. Others are clustered in special **sense organs**, such as the eyes ■ or the ears ■.

Effector

Any cell or organ that is triggered by a nerve

Effectors allow an animal's body to **respond** to a stimulus from a nervous impulse. In vertebrates, the most important effectors are muscles ■.

Central nervous system

The brain and spinal cord

A vertebrate's central nervous system, or **CNS**, consists of the brain ■ and the spinal cord. It sorts incoming nerve impulses, and controls the impulses that are sent out to muscles and other effectors. The central nervous system also stores information, so that an animal can learn from its past experiences.

Spinal cord

A column of nervous tissue that runs through the backbone

The spinal cord is a tube of soft tissue that is protected by the vertebrae ■. It carries messages to the brain, and is also involved in many reflexes. The spinal cord is made up of neurons ■. A narrow cavity filled with **cerebrospinal fluid** runs down the center of the cord. This fluid circulates around the spinal cord and brain, and acts as a liquid shock absorber.

Peripheral nervous system

The nerves connecting the brain and spinal cord with the rest of the body

The peripheral nervous system runs throughout the body. It contains two kinds of neuron. Sensory neurons collect information from receptors, and carry it to the central nervous system. Motor neurons carry instructions to effectors.

Food receptors

Simple brain

Nerve cord

Flatworm nervous system containing brain

Sensory neuron

A neuron that carries signals to the central nervous system

Sensory neurons are also called **afferent neurons**. They carry nerve impulses from receptors to the spinal cord and brain. Some have sensitive nerve endings. Others are connected to receptors that can detect stimuli such as light or chemicals.

Motor neuron

A neuron that stimulates an effector

Motor neurons are also called **efferent neurons**. They carry nerve impulses away from the central nervous system to an effector, such as a gland ■ or a muscle. When nerve impulses arrive at a muscle, they make the muscle contract.

Central nervous system

The central nervous system processes information. It is made up of two parts – the brain and the spinal cord.

Association neuron

A neuron that passes signals from one nerve cell to another

Association neurons are found only in the brain and spinal cord. They link sensory neurons and motor neurons, so that nerve impulses can be passed on and coordinated. In the brain, association neurons are the cells that are used to think and to remember. They often have many synapses ■ with neighboring cells.

Autonomic nervous system

The part of the nervous system that controls involuntary actions

An animal's autonomic nervous system helps to keep its body running smoothly. Autonomic nerves control the involuntary muscles ■ of the body, and many glands. The autonomic system is divided into two parts, the **sympathetic system** and the **parasympathetic system**. These have opposite effects. For example, the sympathetic system speeds up the heartbeat ■, while the parasympathetic system slows it down.

Peripheral nervous system

The peripheral nervous system consists of a branching network of nerves that spread throughout the whole body.

Human central and peripheral nervous systems

Brain

Cranial nerves

Spinal cord

Spinal nerves

Rita Levi-Montalcini

Italian neurophysiologist born 1909

A scientist who studies the way in which nerves work is called a **neurophysiologist**. Rita Levi-Montalcini researched the way that nerves develop during an animal's early life. She found that animal embryos have more nerve cells than they actually need, but that many die as the nervous system develops. She also discovered that a hormone ■ called **nerve growth factor** stimulates the growth of nerve cells. This means an animal's body maintains a large enough number of nerves for it to function properly.

Reflex

A rapid response to a stimulus

When a bird pecks at an earthworm, the worm will immediately pull its body away. This lifesaving response is an example of a reflex. A simple reflex like this is automatically built into the nervous system and does not have to be learned. A conditioned reflex is different, because an animal learns it during its lifetime. Most animals show a mixture of both reflexes.

See also

The brain

An animal's brain is the control center of its nervous system. It receives and analyzes information from the rest of the body, and sends out messages that control the body's behavior.

See also

Association neuron 149 • Axon 147
Balance 155 • Breathing 124
Heartbeat 125 • Hormone 134
Myelin 147 • Nervous system 148
Neuron 147 • Spinal cord 148
Vision 152 • Voluntary muscle 142

Brain

An organ that processes information

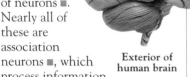

Exterior of human brain

A brain is a large mass of neurons ■. Nearly all of these are association neurons ■, which process information and control the body's activities. Invertebrates usually have simple brains, while vertebrates have complicated brains with distinct regions. The human brain weighs about 3 pounds (1.3 kilograms) and contains about a trillion neurons.

Cerebrum

The part of the brain involved in voluntary actions

In mammals, the cerebrum is a folded mass of nerve cells that sits over the rest of the brain. It is divided into two parts, called **cerebral hemispheres**. Each hemisphere controls actions on the opposite side of the body from which it is situated: for example, the right hemisphere controls the left side of the body, and vice versa. The cerebrum coordinates voluntary movements, such as running or jumping, and is also involved in memory, learning, and sensing things. In humans, the cerebrum is bigger than all the other parts of the brain put together. Simpler vertebrates, such as fish, have a much smaller cerebrum that is not folded.

White matter

A tissue consisting mainly of axons

The inner part of the cerebrum is made up mainly of axons ■ surrounded by layers of myelin ■. The myelin gives this part of the brain a white color. White matter is also found in the outer layer of the spinal cord ■.

Gray matter

A tissue consisting mainly of neuron cell bodies

The outer layer of the cerebrum is called the **cerebral cortex**. It is made up mainly of neuron cell bodies. These give the cortex a gray color. Gray matter is also found inside the spinal cord.

Sensory area

A region of the cerebrum that analyzes information from the senses

Sensory areas receive signals from all parts of the body. A separate region deals with signals from each different body part. Together, sensory areas enable an animal to pinpoint sensations, and to react to them.

Motor area

A region of the cerebrum that controls voluntary movement

Motor areas control voluntary muscles ■. Each area sends out nerve impulses to the muscles that move a different part of the body. For example, one motor area controls muscles that move the fingers, another controls the muscles that move the eyes.

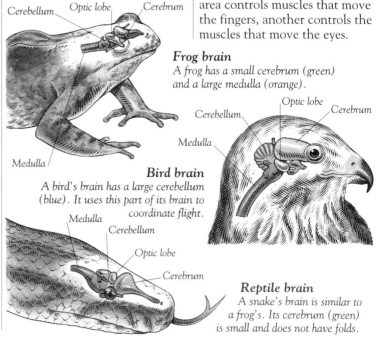

Cerebellum   Optic lobe   Cerebrum

Medulla

Frog brain
A frog has a small cerebrum (green) and a large medulla (orange).

Cerebellum   Optic lobe   Cerebrum

Medulla

Bird brain
A bird's brain has a large cerebellum (blue). It uses this part of its brain to coordinate flight.

Medulla
Cerebellum
Optic lobe
Cerebrum

Reptile brain
A snake's brain is similar to a frog's. Its cerebrum (green) is small and does not have folds.

Brainwave

An electrical wave created by nerve cells

The human brain contains over a trillion neurons. As they work, they create a changing **electric field**. This field can be measured using an instrument called an **electroencephalogram**, or **EEG**. An EEG shows the changing strength of the brain's electric field.

Section through a human brain

Hypothalamus

Pituitary gland

Brain power
The human brain is dominated by the highly folded cerebrum.

Optic lobe

A part of the brain that analyzes signals from the eyes

Vision ■ requires a lot of neurons, and many animals have special brain lobes that deal with signals from their eyes. In mammals, these signals are dealt with by the optic lobe, which is part of the cerebrum.

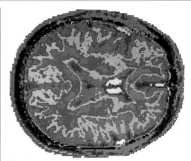

Brain scan
This Magnetic Resonance Image (MRI) shows a transverse section of a human brain.

Thalamus

Cerebrum

Cerebellum

Hypothalamus

A region of the brain that monitors the state of the body

The hypothalamus is a small area near the base of the brain. It constantly monitors factors such as the body's temperature, water content, and food supply, and issues instructions to correct any imbalances that occur. Some of these instructions are carried by the nervous system ■. Others are carried in the form of hormones ■, which stimulate the nearby pituitary gland. Directly linked to the hypothalamus is the **thalamus**. The thalamus sends sensory signals from the spinal cord to the cerebrum, and motor signals in the opposite direction.

Midbrain

Medulla

Spinal cord

Medulla

The part of the brain that controls involuntary processes

The medulla, or **medulla oblongata**, is an extension of the spinal cord. It controls the processes that are essential for life, such as breathing ■ and the rate of heartbeat ■. In simple vertebrates, such as frogs, the medulla makes up a large part of the brain. In more advanced vertebrates, such as mammals, the medulla is much smaller than the parts of the brain that deal with voluntary movements.

Cerebellum

The part of the brain that coordinates subconscious movements

When you move, many of your muscles have to work together. Each one has to contract at exactly the right time with just the right strength. In humans and other vertebrates, the muscles are coordinated by the cerebellum. The cerebellum constantly receives information from the muscles, joints, and organs of balance ■. It sends out signals to coordinate movement, and maintain the body's **posture**. Posture is the relative positioning of the body's moveable parts.

Vision

All animals rely on their senses to find out about the world around them. Animals use their sense of vision to see the outside world, and for many mammals it is the most important sense of all.

Vision

A sense that detects light

A **sense** is something that allows an animal to find out about its environment. Vision, or **sight**, is one of the most important animal senses. Most animals can tell the difference between light ■ and dark. Animals with more advanced vision can build up an accurate picture, or **image**, of the world around them.

Eye

A sense organ that detects light

An eye is an organ ■ that detects the light reflected from, or given off by, an object. Eyes respond to light using special cells called **photoreceptors**. In vertebrate ■ eyes, photoreceptors are packed together in a membrane called a retina. Light is focused onto the retina by a **lens**, and the signals from the photoreceptors are carried to the brain ■ by the **optic nerves**. The brain then processes the signals to perceive an image. Some vertebrates have muscles ■ that swivel their eyes. However, many other animals have eyes that cannot move. To change their **field of view**, they have to move their heads.

See also

Eyeball

A spherical eye that swivels in a socket

The human eyeball consists of three layers – a tough outer coat, the **sclera**, a pigmented middle, the **choroid**, and an inner layer, the retina. The front of the eye is covered by a transparent layer called the **conjunctiva**, which lies over the **cornea**. Most of the eye contains a clear, jellylike substance called the **vitreous humor**. Between the lens and cornea is a more watery fluid, called the **aqueous humor**. The entire eyeball sits in a bony socket called the **orbit**, and is washed by **tears**. Tears lubricate the eye, and help kill bacteria ■.

Retina

A membrane containing cells that detect light

A retina is a curved light-sensitive surface. It can contain over 100 million photoreceptors, packed closely together. In mammals ■, the nerve cells that connect with the photoreceptors lie over the surface of the retina. Light therefore has to pass through the nerves before it can be sensed. Many other animals have nerve cells behind the retina's surface. A mammal's retina has an area called the **blind spot** where the optic nerve leaves the retina, and a central region called the **fovea**.

Iris

A mechanism that controls the amount of light entering the eye

An iris contains two opposing sets of muscles. These can alter the size of the hole, or **pupil**, that lets light into the eye. When a cat hunts at night, its pupils open wide. This allows its eyes to take in as much light as possible. In bright daylight, its pupils become narrow slits. These changes happen automatically, and are examples of a reflex ■.

Human eye
A human eye has a single lens. The lens is flexible and changes shape to focus light onto the retina. In bright light, muscles in the iris narrow the pupil to reduce the amount of light striking the retina. In dim conditions, the opposite happens.

Iris

Conjunctiva

Aqueous humor

Cornea

Pupil

Involuntary muscles of iris

Lens

Visual pigment

A chemical in eyes that absorbs light

When light strikes a photoreceptor, it is absorbed by molecules ■ of a pigment. Light temporarily changes the shape of the pigment molecule, and if enough molecules are affected, a nerve impulse ■ is triggered. In humans and many animals, the visual pigment is a protein ■ called **rhodopsin**.

Compound eye

Facet

Conical lens

Optic nerve fibers

Single ommatidium

Vitreous humor

Optic nerve

Retina

Choroid

Sclera

Compound eye

An eye that is made of many separate compartments, each with its own lens

A compound eye is split into many separate compartments, called **ommatidia** (singular **ommatidium**). Each ommatidium receives light from a narrow part of an animal's field of view. The animal's brain puts together the images from all the ommatidia to create a complete picture. Most crustaceans ■ and insects ■ have compound eyes. Vertebrates have **simple eyes**, which have a large single lens.

Compound eye
Each compound eye of the common darter dragonfly contains up to 5,000 ommatidia.

Color vision

The ability to distinguish different wavelengths of light

An animal needs to be able to sense different wavelengths of light in order to see colors. The human eye uses photoreceptors called **cones** to see colors. Cones have three slightly different types of rhodopsin, and they respond to either red, green, or blue wavelengths. The brain then combines their signals to perceive a color image. **Rods** respond to dim light but cannot distinguish between wavelengths.

Ludwig van Helmholtz

German physicist, physiologist, and mathematician 1821–94

Ludwig van Helmholtz made important breakthroughs in many fields of science. He was particularly interested in the way the eyes detect color. He was one of the inventors of the **ophthalmoscope**, a device that shines a beam of light into the eye, so that the retina can be seen. Oculists still use ophthalmoscopes today.

Binocular vision

A kind of vision that uses two eyes

In binocular vision, each eye sees an object from a slightly different position. The brain compares the signals from both eyes, and uses this information to work out how far away the object is. Binocular vision is common in both predatory and tree-dwelling animals.

Defect of vision

A characteristic that prevents the eye from forming a sharp image

To bring an object into focus, the lens in the eye changes shape. This is called **accommodation**. If a lens cannot focus the light in exactly the right place, the image the eye sees will be blurred. In **short sight**, or **myopia**, the lens bends the light too much, so that it is focused before it reaches the retina. In **long sight**, or **presbyopia**, the light is not bent enough, so it reaches the retina before it is focused. Both defects of vision can be corrected by lenses fitted in front of the eye.

Hearing

Hearing enables animals to perceive sounds, to communicate, and to detect danger. Most animals pick up sounds through their ears.

Hearing

A sense that detects sound

Sound is formed by waves of pressure, or vibrations, that travel through fluid and solids. The loudness of a sound depends on the strength of the waves. The **pitch** of a sound depends on how close together the waves are, or their **frequency**. The highest sound humans can hear has a frequency of 20,000 Hz (waves per second). Bats ■ can hear sounds at up to 100,000 Hz.

Outer ear

The external part of a mammal's ear

The outer ear is a collecting device. In humans and other land mammals, it has a flap called a **pinna**, which is made of cartilage ■. Sound waves funnel through the pinna into a tube called the **auditory canal** inside the skull. Here, they meet a taut membrane called the **eardrum**. The sound waves make the eardrum vibrate.

Middle ear

An air-filled space in the skull that contains the ear bones

A mammal's middle ear contains three tiny bones, called **ear ossicles**. These are the **malleus** or **hammer**, the **incus** or **anvil**, and the **stapes** or **stirrup**. They work like a system of levers to carry vibrations from the eardrum to the **oval window** of the inner ear. The **Eustachian tube** joins the middle ear to the throat.

Inner ear

A system of chambers containing sensory cells

The inner ear, or **labyrinth**, is made up of the **cochlea**, a coiled tube filled with fluid, and the **organs of balance**. These are the **vestibule** and the semicircular canals. Vibrations from the middle ear pass into the cochlea, and travel along a membrane. These vibrations are detected by receptors called **hair cells**. Each cell responds to vibrations of a particular frequency. They send signals to the brain along the **auditory nerve**, and the brain perceives the signals as sound.

Echolocation

A way of sensing surroundings using high-frequency sound

Animals that use high-frequency sound to build up a picture of their surroundings include bats, dolphins, and some whales. They send out high-pitched squeaks that bounce off anything in their path and return to the animal as echoes. The animal's brain then analyzes the echo pattern to form an image.

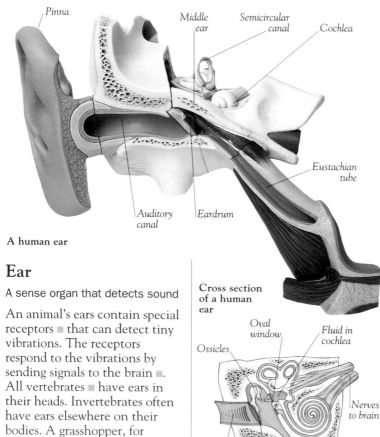

Pinna

Middle ear

Semicircular canal

Cochlea

Eustachian tube

Auditory canal

Eardrum

A human ear

Ear

A sense organ that detects sound

An animal's ears contain special receptors ■ that can detect tiny vibrations. The receptors respond to the vibrations by sending signals to the brain ■. All vertebrates ■ have ears in their heads. Invertebrates often have ears elsewhere on their bodies. A grasshopper, for example, can have ears on the sides of its thorax or on its legs.

Cross section of a human ear

Oval window

Ossicles

Fluid in cochlea

Nerves to brain

Sound waves

Eardrum

Eustachian tube

See also

Bat 112 • Brain 150 • Cartilage 137
Receptor 148 • Vertebrate 104

Touch & balance

Touch and balance tell an animal about its immediate surroundings and about the movement and position of its body.

Labyrinth of a human ear

Utricle
Saccule
Vestibular nerve
Ampulla
Cochlea
Oval window
Semicircular canal

Touch

A sense that detects pressure

An animal uses touch to sense things that are in direct contact with its body. Touch is detected by **mechanoreceptors** and bare nerve ■ endings in the skin. The nerve endings usually detect light touch on the surface of the body. Some receptors, such as Pacinian corpuscles, detect firmer pressure.

Pacinian corpuscle

An oval pressure receptor deep in the skin

Pacinian corpuscles look like tiny onions. Each one is made up of a nerve ending, wrapped in layers of other cells. Pacinian corpuscles are found in the dermis ■ and detect firm pressure.

Balance

A sense that detects gravity and movement

An animal's sense of balance tells it which way up it is and whether or not its body is moving. In mammals, the organs of balance are located in the labyrinth, or inner ear.

Balancing act
A tightrope walker must have a very good sense of balance.

Organs of balance
The three semicircular canals form part of the inner ear, or labyrinth. They are surrounded by bone.

Semicircular canal

An organ in mammals that detects changes in motion

In mammals, the semicircular canals form part of the inner ear. Each ear has a set of three canals. These are filled with fluid and lined with hair cells. When an animal moves its head, the fluid is set in motion. This bends the hair cells, and produces nerve signals that tell the brain ■ about the direction of movement. The semicircular canals can detect acceleration and deceleration but not steady movement.

Saccule

An organ in mammals that detects the pull of gravity

The saccule is a small part of a mammal's inner ear. It forms part of the vestibule, and contains hair cells that detect the position of mineral crystals. These tell the brain about changes in the position of the head. Next to the saccule is the **utricle**, which works in the same way.

Statocyst

An organ in invertebrates that detects the pull of gravity

A statocyst is a small, round chamber lined with sensory hairs. It contains a stony ball called an **otolith**, which is free to move. Gravity pulls the ball downward, and makes it press against a lining of the chamber. The animal can tell which way is up by sensing which of the hairs are being pressed.

Lateral line

A sensory system that detects pressure waves in water

A lateral line is a row of receptors along the side of an animal's body. The receptors detect changes in water pressure, and the animal uses this to sense any movement nearby. Most fish have lateral lines, and so do many amphibians during the early part of their lives. Reptiles, birds, and mammals do not have lateral lines.

See also

Brain 150 • Dermis 141 • Nerve 147

Taste & smell

Taste and smell are senses that detect chemicals. They enable animals to communicate and find food, and to avoid things that are harmful.

Taste

A sense that detects dissolved chemicals

An animal's sense of taste enables it to tell the difference between things that are good to eat and things that may be dangerous. When an animal tastes something, cells ■ called **chemoreceptors** respond to dissolved chemicals. Mammals taste with chemoreceptors on their tongues. Some animals have chemoreceptors on their feet or antennas, or all over their bodies.

Taste bud

A small organ that detects dissolved chemicals

A taste bud is a small sense organ ■, usually on the **tongue**. Each taste bud contains a cluster of chemoreceptors, together with other cells. Substances dissolved in saliva enter the taste bud by a small opening, called a **taste pore**. The substances stimulate the chemoreceptors inside the taste bud, which send signals to the brain ■. The human tongue has about 2,000 taste buds. They are sensitive to only four tastes – sweet, sour, salt, and bitter. The **flavor** of a food is produced by the senses of taste and smell working together.

Smell

A sense that detects airborne chemicals

Most organic compounds ■ are volatile, which means they constantly give off airborne molecules ■. Animals that live on land use their sense of smell, or **olfactory sense**, to detect these molecules. The sense of smell has a much lower **threshold** than taste, which means that it is triggered more easily. It can also distinguish a far greater range of substances.

Olfactory membrane

A sheet of cells used to detect airborne chemicals

When a dog sniffs the air, it draws air through its **nostrils** and into the **nasal cavity**. Here, airborne chemicals flow over a thin, moist lining called the olfactory membrane. This contains densely packed chemoreceptors that end in **olfactory hairs**. The hairs detect different chemicals in the air and then send signals to the dog's brain, where the smell is identified. The human sense of smell also works this way.

Puff adder

Smelling the air
A snake's forked tongue gathers airborne molecules and presses them against an organ in its mouth. This tells the snake if food is nearby.

Jacobson's organ

A special sense organ that snakes use to detect smells

A snake ■ has a very good sense of smell. It smells by using its nose, and by flicking its tongue in and out. The tongue collects airborne chemicals, which are then transferred to sensory cells in the roof of the mouth, called the Jacobson's organ. This organ smells or tastes the chemicals collected by the tongue.

Antenna

A sensory feeler

An antenna (plural **antennas**) is a sensory structure on an arthropod's head. It can detect air movements, vibrations, and smells, and send information to the brain to be processed. Male moths often have feathery antennas covered in tiny sensory hairs. These detect airborne chemicals called pheromones ■.

Sensory antennas
A male cockchafer beetle's antennas have a row of flat blades. These fold up like a fan when not in use.

Antenna fan blades

Eye

Communication

Animals use communication to keep in touch with other members of their species, and to warn rivals or enemies to stay away.

Communication

The exchange of information

Animals often need to exchange information. Sometimes the information contains a simple message, such as "feed me" or "keep away." Other messages are more complicated. For example, the **dance** of a foraging **honeybee** (*Apis mellifera*) shows other bees where food can be found, and how far away it is.

Tactile communication

A form of communication that uses touch

Touch is the simplest form of communication. Many parent animals communicate with their young by touch, and adult animals often use touch to communicate during courtship ▪. Tactile communication is important for animals that live underground, such as **prairie dogs** (*Cynomys ludovicianus*), and for social animals ▪, such as termites ▪.

Friendly touch
Kittens greet each other by rubbing together.

See also

Chemical communication

A form of communication that uses chemicals

Some animals can communicate with others over a great distance by releasing chemicals into the air or water. Many female moths release chemicals called pheromones ▪ to attract males. Social insects use pheromones to signal danger, and to mark trails. Many mammals ▪ recognize each other by their **scents**; they also use these personal chemical markers to show their territories ▪. A chemical message can last for a long time.

Sound communication

A form of communication that uses sounds

Many animals communicate by making sounds. Grasshoppers ▪ produce chirruping noises by rubbing parts of their bodies together, or **stridulating**. Birds ▪ make sounds with a chamber called a **syrinx** near the base of the trachea ▪. Mammals have **vocal cords** near the top of the trachea. Vocal cords vibrate when air flows past them and can be stretched by muscles to produce different sounds.

Song thrush

Language

A complex communication system

Humans communicate by speaking. We use our vocal cords to formulate different words, which convey information. Words vary from one language to another, but all languages work in a similar way. Most forms of animal communication can pass only on a single message at a time, but human language can communicate complex sequences of information.

Visual communication

A form of communication that uses shapes, colors, or movements

Animals with good eyesight can communicate visually. Male animals often use bright colors and patterns to attract a mate. However, some animals, such as wasps ▪, use bright colors as warning coloration ▪ to deter predators. Many mammals, such as primates ▪, communicate with facial expressions and body posture. This is called **body language**, and it is important for mammals that live in groups.

Warning song
A male thrush sings to tell other males to keep out of his territory.

Behavior

An animal's behavior consists of the things that it does, and the way that it does them. Different patterns of behavior help animals to survive and to reproduce. Some kinds of behavior are learned, others are inherited.

Behavior

A pattern of responses to the outside world

All living things respond to the world around them. For example, sea anemones ■ will stretch out their tentacles if they sense food, and **hedgehogs** (*Erinaceus*) will curl into a ball if they sense danger. Responses such as these enable an animal to survive and to reproduce. Together, they make up its behavior. Some kinds of behavior are inbuilt, while other kinds are learned during an animal's life.

Instinctive behavior

A pattern of behavior that is inherited

When a spider ■ spins a web, it knows instinctively where to position the web and what shape it should be. The spider's web-building is an example of instinctive, or **innate**, behavior. This kind of behavior is built into an animal's nervous system ■, and is handed on genetically ■ from one generation to another.

Aggressive behavior
When the Australian frilled lizard is faced with danger, it erects the large frill of skin around its neck in an impressive threat display.

The wider the lizard opens its mouth, the more erect its frill becomes

Tail lashes back and forth

Flexible feet and extended claws for balance

Learned behavior

Behavior that is the result of experience

Unlike instinctive behavior, learned behavior is not inherited. It is acquired during an animal's lifetime, in response to its environment. Learned behavior is more flexible than instinctive behavior, and allows an animal to adapt ■ to changing circumstances.

Imprinted behavior

A form of learned behavior that takes place in young animals

Some young animals memorize the shape, sound, or smell of their parents, or their birthplace. This special kind of learning is called **imprinting**; it can occur only during a brief period in an animal's early life.

Circadian rhythm

A cycle that is about 24 hours long

The behavior of many animals follows a 24-hour cycle called a circadian rhythm. For example, a **diurnal** animal is active during the day and inactive at night, while a **nocturnal** animal is active at night and inactive during the day. Circadian rhythms are influenced by hours of daylight, and also by an internal **biological clock**. The clock is triggered by chemical reactions ■ that have an inbuilt rhythm.

See also

Adaptation 46 • Arachnid 101
Arthropod 100 • Bird 110
Chemical reaction 25 • Fish 104
Gene 36 • Insect 102
Mammal 112 • Metabolic rate 32
Nervous system 148 • Reflex 149
Sea anemone 96 • Spider 101
Termite 102 • Wasp 103

Ivan Pavlov

Russian physiologist
1849–1936

Many features of behavior are based on inbuilt reflexes ■. Ivan Pavlov found that reflexes can also be modified by learning. He noted that dogs produce a lot of saliva when they are given food. Before serving food to his dogs, he rang a bell. The dogs learned to associate the sound of the bell with food. Eventually, they developed a **conditioned reflex**, and would salivate when Pavlov rang the bell, even if no food appeared.

Hibernation

A winter sleeplike state

Many small animals, such as the **fat dormouse** (*Glis glis*), and some bears, survive the winter months by hibernating. An animal's body enters a state of **torpor** during hibernation. In this state, its body temperature drops and its metabolic rate ■ slows down. In the spring, the animal becomes active again. In places with hot, dry summers, some animals enter a summer sleep called **aestivation**.

Migration

A seasonal movement to a more favorable environment

Changing seasons create a changing supply of food. Many animals travel, or migrate, with the seasons to more favorable conditions. They raise their young in places where food is abundant, but spend the rest of the year elsewhere. Many birds ■, mammals ■, fish ■, and insects ■ make long migratory journeys. Every year, the **Arctic tern** (*Sterna paradisaea*) migrates over 25,000 miles (40,000 kilometers).

Territory

An area claimed by an animal

Animals often have to compete for food, a mate, or somewhere to raise their young. Many animals do this by claiming a territory, which they defend against rivals. If a rival tries to enter the territory, the owner responds with an aggressive **threat display**, and a fight may break out. Sizes of territory vary – the territory of a **tiger** (*Panthera tigris*) covers many square miles, but the territory of a nesting **gannet** (*Sula bassana*) covers only the area around its nest.

Courtship

Behavior that forms a bond between a male and a female

Before they breed, many animals carry out set patterns of behavior called **courtship rituals**. These often involve special signals or complicated dances. During courtship, the two partners get used to each other and make sure they have chosen a suitable mate. In some animals, such as the **orb web spider** (*Araneus diadematus*), the male and female are different sizes. In these cases, courtship rituals ensure that one partner does not attack or eat the other.

Spider courtship
By giving the correct courtship signals, a male spider prevents the female from attacking him.

Careful parents
A female emperor penguin lays a single egg. The male incubates the egg through the long Antarctic winter. The female spends the winter at sea and returns with food soon after the egg hatches.

— *Father's body heat keeps chick warm*

Parental care

The care of young by parents

Some animals produce large numbers of young, but do not help them to survive. Others produce fewer young, but feed and protect their offspring. As a result, relatively more of these offspring survive. Most birds and mammals look after their young. Birds usually have an **incubation** period during which they sit on their eggs to keep them warm. Some invertebrates, such as arachnids ■, also show parental care.

Social animal

An animal that lives in a group

Social animals live in a group and work together to find food, to fend off enemies, and to raise their young. Social behavior has evolved in many animals, including arthropods ■, fish, birds, and mammals. The most complex groups, or **societies**, have evolved in **social insects**, such as wasps ■ and termites ■.

Animal reproduction

Animals have developed a remarkable variety of ways to reproduce, but all follow two basic plans. Some animals can produce offspring without having to mate, but in most animals, two parents come together to produce a fertilized egg.

See also

Bird 110 • Cartilaginous fish 104
Cell 18 • Chromosome 38
Cnidarian 96 • Diploid cell 39
Embryo 164 • Gene 36 • Genotype 37
Insect 102 • Mammal 112
Monotreme 112 • Nucleus 19
Ovary 162 • Penis 162 • Placenta 163
Reptile 108 • Sex cell 41 • Species 48
Testis 162 • Variation 42

Reproduction

The production of offspring

Every living thing has a limited life span. Thus living things need to reproduce to ensure the continued existence of their species ■. All living things have the potential to increase their numbers, but factors such as food shortages and predators usually keep their numbers in check.

Egg

Head of caterpillar appears

Hatching caterpillar egg

Asexual reproduction

Reproduction involving a single parent

Many simple animals reproduce without mating. Some cnidarians ■ do this by budding off small parts of themselves, while some other animals develop from unfertilized eggs. These are both examples of asexual reproduction. Asexual reproduction is often simple and rapid, but it usually produces offspring with exactly the same genetic blueprint, or genotype ■, as the parent. Together, the offspring form a **clone**, which is a group of cells ■ or organisms with exactly the same genes ■.

Parthenogenesis

Reproduction from unfertilized female sex cells

Parthenogenesis is a form of asexual reproduction that is common in insects ■. During parthenogenesis, female sex cells are produced, but they develop without being fertilized. Aphids often reproduce in this way. They use parthenogenesis to produce lots of young when food is abundant. Later, when food is scarce, they reproduce sexually.

Caterpillar waves its body around to help it struggle free

Head

Sexual reproduction

Reproduction involving two parents

In sexual reproduction, there are always two parents. Each parent produces sex cells ■, or gametes, which are formed by sex organs called **gonads**. When a male sex cell and a female sex cell come together, they form a fertilized egg cell called a **zygote**. The zygote then develops into a new individual. Offspring produced by sexual reproduction each have a unique collection of genes. This variation ■ means that some offspring will be better equipped.

Sperm

A male sex cell

A **spermatozoon** (plural **spermatozoa**), or sperm, is a male sex cell. It is produced in an organ called a testis ■ by a process called **spermatogenesis**. A sperm has a head, and one or more tails that lash from side to side to push the cell along. Sperm swim to an ovum in order to bring about fertilization. In many animals, millions of sperm are produced, but only one sperm fertilizes a single ovum.

Whole caterpillar emerges from the egg

Ovum

A female sex cell

An ovum (plural **ova**) is an **egg cell** or female sex cell. It is formed in an ovary ■ by a process called **oogenesis**, and is usually larger than a male sex cell. An ovum consists of a nucleus ■ and a substance called **yolk**, which is a food store. In mammals ■, the egg is small and contains only a little yolk, but in birds ■ and reptiles ■ it is much larger. The ova of mammals are formed before birth and released at a steady rate during adult life.

Cross section of a bird's egg

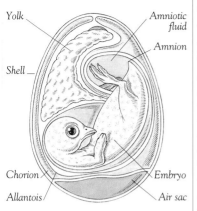

Yolk

Shell

Chorion

Allantois

Amniotic fluid

Amnion

Embryo

Air sac

Egg

The fertilized ovum

An egg is a cell that develops to produce a new animal. Some eggs develop inside the body of the mother, but others are passed out of the body, or laid. The eggs of reptiles, birds, and mammals develop three different internal layers called **egg membranes**. An inner membrane called the **amnion** surrounds the embryo ■. It is filled with fluid and prevents the embryo from drying out. It also acts as a shock absorber. A membrane called the **allantois** forms a bag that collects waste, and a tough outer membrane, the **chorion** surrounds the whole egg. This is enclosed by a shell in birds, reptiles, and monotremes ■.

Mating

The coming together of a male and a female to bring about fertilization

In sexual reproduction, male and female sex cells have to be brought together so that fertilization can take place. In most land-dwelling animals, the male injects sperm into the female's reproductive tract with his penis ■. A male octopus uses a special arm to transfer his sperm, and male sharks use organs called **claspers**, which funnel sperm into the female.

Fertilization

The union of a male sex cell and a female sex cell

During fertilization, a sperm binds to the outer surface of an ovum, and the membranes around the sperm and ovum join together. The sperm's nucleus then enters the ovum and fuses with the ovum's nucleus. This forms a fertilized cell, or zygote. The zygote is diploid ■, which means that it contains a set of chromosomes ■ from each parent. A **fertilization membrane** forms around the zygote to prevent other sperms from getting in. Animals that live on land usually carry out **internal fertilization**, which takes place inside the female's body. Most aquatic animals carry out **external fertilization**, which takes place outside their bodies.

Viviparity

Reproduction by giving birth to live young

A **viviparous** animal keeps its eggs inside its body. As the offspring develop, they are often nourished by the mother through a placenta ■. This form of development occurs in most mammals, and also in some reptiles and cartilaginous fish ■.

Oviparity

Reproduction by laying eggs

An **oviparous** animal lays or spawns eggs, which then develop and hatch outside its body. The eggs are fertilized either before they leave the female's body or once they have been laid. In an **ovoviviparous** animal, the eggs develop and hatch inside the female's body but do not receive nourishment from her. Many reptiles develop in this way.

Female frog

Male frog

Eggs

Mating frogs
Common frogs carry out external fertilization. The male frog clasps the female as she lays her eggs and fertilizes them by spraying them with his sperm.

Human reproduction

Unlike many animals, humans reproduce very slowly. A baby develops for nine months before it is ready for birth, and it takes many years before it can have children of its own.

Conception

The fertilization of an ovum

Like all mammals, humans reproduce by sexual reproduction ■. This process begins with conception, which is the fertilization ■ of a female egg, or ovum ■, by a male sperm ■. Once conception has taken place, a woman becomes **pregnant**. This means that a baby begins to develop inside her uterus. The time taken for the the baby to develop is called the **gestation period**. In humans, the gestation period is about 280 days.

Testis

An organ in males that produces sperm

A testis (plural **testes**) is one of two small oval organs that make the male sex cells ■, or sperm. The sperm are made inside tiny tubes called **seminiferous tubules**. They then move into an organ called the **epididymis** (plural **epididymides**) where they mature. Together, the testes can produce over 250 million sperm a day. They also make the male sex hormone ■ testosterone.

See also

Cell 18 • Estrogen 135
Fertilization 161
Male sex hormone 135 • Ovum 160
Oxytocin 135 • Progesterone 135
Sex cell 41 • Sexual reproduction 160
Sperm 160 • Tissue 23

Penis

The organ in males that transfers sperm into the female's body

Humans reproduce by internal fertilization, which takes place inside the woman's body. The penis is the male organ used to transfer sperm into the female reproductive tract, or vagina. This takes place during **sexual intercourse**. Before intercourse, the spongy tissue ■ of the penis fills with blood. This causes the penis to stiffen, enabling it to be inserted in the vagina. During sexual intercourse, muscles pump sperm from the epididymides along a tube or **sperm duct** called the **vas deferens**. The sperm are mixed with a liquid that nourishes them and helps them to move along. This **seminal fluid** is ejaculated from the penis into the woman's body.

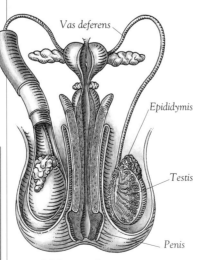

Male reproductive organs

Vagina

The female reproductive tract

The vagina is a muscular tube that leads to the uterus. During sexual intercourse, sperm enters the woman's body through the vagina, and when a baby is born, the baby passes out of the uterus along the vagina.

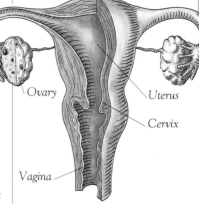

Female reproductive organs

Uterus

The organ in females in which a baby develops

The uterus, or **womb**, is the muscular chamber in which a baby develops. At its base, there is an opening called the **cervix**, which leads into the vagina. At the top of the uterus, there are two **Fallopian tubes** or **oviducts** which lead to the ovaries.

Ovary

An organ in females that produces ova

An ovary is one of two organs inside a woman's body that contains eggs, or ova. Ovaries contain a lifetime's supply of ova from the moment of birth. From puberty onward, the ova are released at the rate of about one per month. This process is called ovulation. The ovaries also produce the female sex hormones estrogen ■ and progesterone ■.

Ovulation

The release of an ovum from an ovary

During ovulation, an ovum is released from an ovary, and the body is prepared for pregnancy. Ovulation occurs in a cycle called the **ovarian** or **menstrual cycle**, which lasts about 28 days. The cycle begins when the uterus lining thickens in readiness to receive a fertilized ovum. At the same time, a ball-shaped **Graafian follicle** develops inside an ovary. This contains an ovum. During ovulation, the Graafian follicle bursts, and the ovum travels along the Fallopian tube toward the uterus. If the ovum is fertilized, it implants itself in the uterus lining. If the ovum is not fertilized, the lining of the uterus is shed during a process called **menstruation**, and the cycle begins again.

Amniotic fluid

Fetus

Uterus wall

Corpus luteum

A gland formed in an ovary after an ovum has been expelled

After a Graafian follicle has shed its ovum, it forms a corpus luteum, or **yellow body**. This secretes hormones, including progesterone, which prepare the uterus for a fertilized ovum. If fertilization does not occur, the corpus luteum breaks down.

Implantation

Attachment of a blastocyst to the lining of the uterus

An ovum is a single cell ■. After it has been fertilized, it begins to divide until it forms a tiny ball of cells called a blastocyst. The blastocyst then implants itself into the lining of the uterus. The uterus lining has a rich supply of blood, and it forms a surface on which the blastocyst can develop. During implantation, the blastocyst breaks down some of the tissue that forms the uterus lining and becomes surrounded by a thin layer of the lining's cells. From this moment on, it is supplied with oxygen and food from the mother.

Nine-month-old fetus in uterus just before birth

Spine

Bladder, squashed by enlarged uterus

Cervix and vagina

Rectum

Placenta

An organ that allows substances to pass between the bloodstream of a baby and that of the mother

The placenta is a spongy mass of tissue that attaches the developing embryo, or fetus, to the uterine wall. In the placenta, the blood systems of the baby and the mother come close together but do not join. This allows oxygen, carbon dioxide, and dissolved food substances to pass between mother and baby. The baby's blood reaches the placenta through the **umbilical cord**.

Birth

The expulsion of a baby from the uterus

Before a baby is born, it turns around in the uterus so that its head points down toward the cervix. At the onset of birth, a hormone called oxytocin ■ triggers the muscles in the uterus wall to produce powerful **contractions**. During **labor**, the contractions gradually become stronger. Eventually, the amnion surrounding the baby breaks and releases the fluid that supported the baby. Muscles then push the baby through the cervix and vagina, and out of the mother's body. Once the baby has emerged, it takes its first breath, and blood immediately begins to circulate through its lungs. Soon afterward, the placenta is expelled from the uterus. This is called the **afterbirth**.

Development

Every animal that is produced by sexual reproduction starts life as a single fertilized cell. Through a series of extraordinary changes, this cell develops into a complete animal.

Development

An increase in complexity

When a living thing develops, it changes in a way that makes it more complex. This process usually happens at the same time as growth ■, but it can also occur without any growth being involved. During growth, cells ■ normally make identical copies of themselves. During development, cells become differentiated ■, which means that they change to become suited for a specific task. The cells may also change position.

Development of a frog

A frog's eggs are fertilized as they are laid. Each one consists of a single cell surrounded by a layer of jelly.

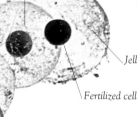

Jelly

Fertilized cell

Morphogenesis

The development of form in a living thing

Morphogenesis is the process that produces an adult form in a living thing. In animals, it involves a combination of cell division ■, differentiation, and the movement, or migration, of groups of cells. These are programmed by the cells' genes ■.

Embryo

A living thing at an early stage of development

A living thing is known as an embryo from the moment the fertilized ovum ■ begins to divide, until birth ■ or hatching. In most animals, an embryo is contained inside an egg ■, or in the case of mammals, inside the uterus ■. In humans, the word embryo refers to the first two months of development. After two months, a human embryo is called a **fetus**.

During cleavage, the single fertilized cell begins to divide. This cell has divided twice to form four new cells.

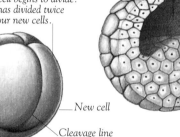

New cell

Cleavage line

Cleavage

The division of a fertilized egg into many cells

Cleavage is the first stage of development, and it usually happens soon after fertilization ■. The single cell of a fertilized ovum divides in two again and again until a ball-shaped cluster of cells is produced. This stage is called a **morula**. In some animals, the cells in the morula are all the same size, but in other animals, the cells are different sizes. This is an early sign of differentiation.

Blastula

A hollow ball of cells

A blastula is a hollow ball that develops from a morula. It contains a fluid-filled cavity called the **blastocoel**. The formation of a blastocoel depends on the amount of yolk in an egg, or ovum. Birds' eggs contain so much yolk that they cannot form a hollow ball of cells. Instead, the dividing cells form a tiny round patch, called a **blastodisc**, which sits on the yolk's upper surface. In mammals, a blastocoel is called a **blastocyst**, and is the stage at which implantation ■ into the uterus occurs.

The ball folds in on itself to form a gastrula.

Blastocoel

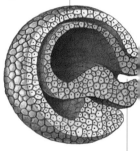

Lip of gastrula

The single cell becomes a hollow, fluid-filled ball, or blastula. It now contains hundreds or thousands of cells.

Gastrulation

The infolding of a gastrula to form different layers

During gastrulation, the blastula folds inward. This creates a **gastrula** with layers of cells that eventually develop into an animal's organs. In vertebrates ■, the outer layer, the **ectoderm**, produces the skin and nerves. The inner layer, the **endoderm**, produces the cells that line the alimentary canal, the lungs, and other organs. A middle layer, the **mesoderm**, forms bones, muscles, and blood, as well as the organs that produce sex cells ■.

Regeneration

The replacement of a missing part

If a starfish loses an arm, a new arm slowly grows in its place. The cells that remain divide and differentiate to reproduce the lost part. Not all animals can regenerate such large parts of themselves. In mammals, skin cells regenerate to heal a cut, and bone cells can regenerate to mend a fracture, but a missing limb cannot be regenerated.

Row of tiny teeth

Tail is longer than body

Coiled gut

Within about two weeks of fertilization, the tadpole's body is fully formed. Its first meal is the jelly that surrounds the egg.

Spine forming within body

Head

Eyes

The gastrula grows longer, and develops the beginnings of a spine. A head and eyes start to form.

Embryology

The study of early development in living things

Embryologists investigate the processes that result in development. In some simple animals, they can trace the origin of every cell as the body takes shape. Experiments by embryologists have shown that the way a cell develops is usually influenced by its neighbors. This is called **induction**, because a cell's neighbors cause, or "induce," it to develop.

Ontogeny

The development of an individual

A living thing goes through characteristic changes in body form as it develops. For example, a human embryo has gill pouches and a tail during its early stages, and for a while looks quite like an adult fish. At one time, biologists thought that each step in development mirrored a step in an organism's evolutionary history, or phylogeny ■. This theory is called the **principle of recapitulation**. Today, embryologists know this is not true. Different living things often have the same early steps in development, but each one has added steps of its own, as a result of evolution ■.

Sexual characteristic

A characteristic found only in one sex

In animals that have separate sexes, males and females develop in different ways. The most important differences are in their **primary sexual characteristics**. A female has organs that produce ova, and a male has organs that produce sperm ■. **Secondary sexual characteristics** are those in other parts of the body. For example, most male deer have antlers, but females do not. In humans, secondary sexual characteristics include facial hair in men and breasts in women.

Male

Female

Colorful characteristics
Secondary sexual characteristics are usually easy to see in birds. Males are often brightly colored. This helps them to attract a mate.

Aging

A gradual loss of function in cells and whole organisms

As an animal gets older, the cells in its body gradually deteriorate. Some cells, particularly those of the nervous system ■, die and are not replaced. Over a period of time, these changes affect the whole body and produce aging, or **senescence**. Most animals in the wild die before they become very old but, because humans are not exposed to many natural threats, aging can last a long time. Scientists do not know exactly why aging occurs. It may be caused by a buildup of poisonous waste products from the metabolism ■, or it may be programmed by genes.

A pair of pintailed whydah

Metamorphosis

A young ladybug looks quite unlike its parents, yet both are different stages in the same life cycle. The young ladybug is transformed into an adult by a series of dramatic changes in body shape. This process is called metamorphosis.

Metamorphosis

A change in body shape

All animals change shape as they mature into adults. For example, a day-old chick has long legs, but an adult chicken has very short legs in relation to the rest of its body. Some animals, particularly invertebrates ■ and amphibians ■, undergo much greater changes as they grow up. These changes are known as metamorphosis.

Nymph

A young insect that develops by incomplete metamorphosis

A nymph looks similar to its parents, but it is smaller, has no wings, and cannot reproduce. Nymphs usually live in the same habitat ■ as their parents and eat the same food. Dragonflies are an exception. The nymphs live in water and feed on aquatic animals, while the adults catch insects in midair. Nymphs become adults by incomplete metamorphosis.

Incomplete metamorphosis

A gradual change in body shape

Many insects ■, including bugs, dragonflies, termites, and grasshoppers, undergo gradual body changes called incomplete metamorphosis. When a grasshopper nymph hatches from an egg, it looks like a miniature adult. However, its wings are just tiny buds, and it has no working reproductive organs. As it gets older, the nymph periodically sheds its outer skin, or **molts**. The stages between molts are called **instars**. With every molt, the nymph's wings become larger and its internal organs become more developed. When it sheds its skin for the fifth and final time, the grasshopper emerges as an adult. Animals that undergo incomplete metamorphosis are said to be **hemimetabolous**.

Deadly larvae
The larvae of the great diving beetle are voracious carnivores that can attack tadpoles and even small fish.

Larva

A young animal that develops by complete metamorphosis

A larva (plural **larvae**) looks quite unlike its parents. It often lives in a different habitat and eats different food. Larvae can look after themselves. Some have feathery legs for filtering food from water, and others have powerful jaws for chewing leaves. Sedentary animals like corals ■ often have larvae that move about. This allows the species ■ to disperse. The term **grub** refers to many insect larvae, especially those of beetles, wasps, and bees. A larva becomes an adult by complete metamorphosis.

Protective warning coloration

Mature larva

Larva hatching from egg

Pupa forming

Larva attaching itself to a leaf

Ladybug eggs

Ladybug metamorphosis
Adult ladybugs and their larvae both feed on aphids. The larvae are slow-moving, but the adults have wings and can fly quickly from one plant to another. They can travel long distances to find new sources of food and suitable places to lay eggs.

Complete metamorphosis
A total change in body shape

Most invertebrates, as well as many fish ■ and amphibians, start life as free-living larvae, and then change into adults with a different body form. In fish and amphibians, the change is usually gradual, but in many insects, it happens very suddenly. Cells ■ in the larva's body are broken down by lysosomes ■, and new cells develop to form the body of an adult. Animals that undergo complete metamorphosis are known as **holometabolous**.

Tadpole
The larva of a frog or toad

A tadpole lives entirely in water and breathes through gills ■. It has a long tail instead of legs and feeds on plants. As the tadpole grows, its gills shrink and become covered by flaps of skin. It slowly adopts a carnivorous ■ diet and develops lungs ■, which allow it to breathe air. At about this time, tiny legs start to appear. As the tadpole undergoes the last stage of metamorphosis into an adult frog or toad, its legs and lungs grow quickly and its tail vanishes. It is now ready for life on land.

Caterpillar
The larva of a butterfly or moth

A caterpillar is the wingless larva of a butterfly ■ or moth. It has a long body and three pairs of true legs, and four pairs of stumplike **prolegs** toward the back of its body. A caterpillar has a large head with tough jaws. Most caterpillars feed on plants or dead material such as wool. Many are **camouflaged**, which means they blend in with their surroundings, while others are protected by bright warning coloration ■, or by irritating hairs.

Pupa
The resting stage of some insects during which they change shape

Insects that undergo complete metamorphosis **pupate**, which means that they form a pupa. A pupa is the stage in the insect's life cycle during which it changes shape. It is often protected by a tough case. When a caterpillar is ready to pupate, it stops feeding and often fastens itself to a solid object. It then sheds its skin and a soft new skin forms beneath it. This often becomes hard and shiny, forming a **chrysalis**. During pupation, most of the caterpillar's cells are broken down. Small pockets of cells remain alive, and begin to divide and develop, eventually forming the adult body, or **imago**.

See also

Amphibian 106 • Butterfly 103
Carnivorous 116 • Cell 18
Coral 96 • Crustacean 100 • Fish 104
Gill 122 • Gland 134 • Habitat 168
Insect 102 • Invertebrate 96
Lung 124 • Lysosome 19
Parasite 175 • Plankton 64
Species 48 • Warning coloration 47

Cocoon
A protecting case made of silk

Many pupating insects protect themselves from danger by spinning cocoons out of silk, which they secrete from special glands ■. The **silk moth** (*Bombyx mori*) makes large cocoons that can be unwound and made into silk cloth. Ants make tiny cocoons, which are often mistakenly called "ants' eggs."

Hypermetamorphosis
A change in body shape that involves more than one larval form

Some animals have more than one kind of larva during their life cycles. This is common in parasitic ■ insects, and also in animals that grow up as a part of plankton ■. For example, a barnacle is a crustacean ■ that hatches into a **nauplius** larva. This has one eye, three pairs of legs, and forms part of plankton. The nauplius then changes into a rounded **cyprid** larva before becoming an adult barnacle, which has a hard case and lives attached to a rock.

Soft yellow wing cases will gradually harden and turn red as they dry

Ladybug hatching from pupa

Pupa

Red wing cases

Adult ladybug

Ecology

The living world is built on complex relationships between plants, animals, and the places they inhabit. Ecology is the study of these relationships. It helps us to understand how living things depend on each other for survival.

Ecology

The study of the relationships between living things and their environments

The term "ecology" comes from the Greek words *oikos*, meaning "house," and *logos*, meaning "the study of." Ecology is the study of a living thing's home, or its place in the natural world. Scientists who study ecology are called **ecologists**. In recent years, ecologists have shown the harmful effects of pollution ■ and the need for conservation ■ to preserve the natural world.

Environment

The surroundings in which a living thing exists

A living thing's environment is everything in its surroundings. Part of its environment is made up of nonliving matter, such as air, water, or other chemicals. Another part is made up of other living things, such as its prey or predators ■. The term environment is also used in a wider sense, to mean all or part of the entire living world. A living thing's internal environment is the environment inside its body, or inside its cells.

See also

Conservation 176 • Darwin 45
Food web 172 • Metamorphosis 166
Nutrient cycle 170 • Pollution 176
Predator 174 • Species 48

Biosphere

All the parts of the Earth that make up the living world

The biosphere includes every region of the Earth inhabited by living things, from the depths of the sea to the lower part of the atmosphere. All parts of the biosphere are linked by nutrient cycles ■.

Ecosystem

A community and its environment

Ecologists often divide the biosphere into units called ecosystems to make it easier to study. An ecosystem can be anything from a small piece of rotting wood to a vast lake. Each ecosystem is made up of a community of living things, together with their surroundings.

Community

A collection of living things that are found in the same area

A community is a collection of plants, animals, and microorganisms that live together in the same area or habitat. In a simple community there may be just a small number of species, but in a complex community there can be many hundreds. The different species ■ are linked by a food web ■, and each species often depends on many others for its survival. Together, the individuals from each species make up separate **populations**.

Habitat

The living place of a species

A habitat is somewhere that has a characteristic range of conditions, such as temperature or rainfall. Some species are found in a variety of habitats, although usually there is one habitat that suits them best. Other species are more specialized, which means that they can survive in only one habitat. Animals that develop by metamorphosis ■ often occupy different habitats at different stages of their lives.

A shrinking habitat
Wild giant pandas live in the bamboo forests of central China. They can live only in this one habitat and have become endangered because large areas of bamboo forest have been cut down.

Niche

A living thing's role in its environment

A niche is a place that something can fit into. An ecological niche means the precise way in which a living thing fits into its environment. A living thing's niche is defined by factors such as its habitat, the food it lives on, its predators, and its tolerance to temperature. Although two species may share the same habitat, they never share the same niche.

Ernst Haeckel

German zoologist
1834–1919

Ernst Haeckel
invented the
term ecology.
He was a keen naturalist and
was fascinated by the world of
undersea life. At a time when
most zoologists studied single
species in isolation, Haeckel
realized the importance of
looking at the links between
living things. He was a great
admirer of Charles Darwin ■,
but unlike Darwin, he was
sure that evolution always
produced living things that
were bigger and better. He
believed that humans were
the final "goal" of evolution.

Succession

An orderly change of species in
a community

If a patch of ground is cleared of
vegetation, it does not stay bare
for long. Soon, plants and then
animals move in to make use of
it. As time goes by, the species
in this new community change.
The first arrivals are gradually
replaced as different species
establish themselves. This is
called succession. Finally,
succession stops and a
stable community, called
a **climax community**,
develops.

Opportunist species

A species that is quick to make
use of new opportunities

Opportunist species are usually
small and have short life cycles.
These characteristics enable
them to spread quickly, so that
they can make use of new
environments before other
species arrive. However,
when other species
establish
themselves,
opportunist species
are often squeezed
out. They are also
known as **fugitive
species**, because they
are always "on the run"
from one place to
another.

Succession in action

*The diagram below shows three stages
in ecological succession. In this
example, succession eventually
produces deciduous forests.*

Sparrowhawk

Mature
oak tree

Woodpecker

Squirrel

Swallow

Deer

Cow parsley Hogweed

Bracken

Oak sapling

Grass

Rabbit

Butterfly

Shepherd's
purse

Dandelion

Spider

Poppy

Grass

Pioneer stage
*During the pioneer stage,
opportunist plants and animals
move into an area of bare ground.*

Climax community
*When succession is complete,
the result is a climax community, in this
case, woodland. The trees shade out the
light, and prevent other plants from gaining a
foothold. Climax communities are not always
woodlands – they vary from one ecosystem to another.*

Nutrient cycles

Living things constantly exchange chemical substances with the world around them. These substances move in continuous cycles between the living and the nonliving worlds.

Nutrient

Any material taken in by a living thing to sustain life

A nutrient is any material taken in by a living thing. It may be a mineral 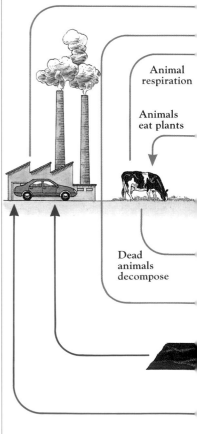, such as phosphorus, or an organic compound , such as a carbohydrate .

Nutrients for life
Plants obtain nutrients from the soil and from the air around them. They pass these on to animals.

Nutrient cycle

The circulation of a chemical element between the environment and living things

The organic compounds in living things are built up from about 25 different chemical elements . Living things constantly replenish these vital elements by taking in nutrients. The elements are later returned to the environment. Each element follows a different pathway, called a nutrient cycle or **mineral cycle**. Some parts of a cycle happen quickly, but others can last for thousands of years.

See also

Bacteria 60 • Carbohydrate 26
Carbon 24 • Chemical compound 24
Chemical reaction 25 • Element 24
Fossil 44 • Mineral 29 • Nucleic acid 34
Organic compound 24 • Pea family 74
Photosynthesis 84 • Protein 30
Respiration 32 • Water 25

Carbon cycle

A cycle involving carbon

All living things contain the element carbon . Carbon also forms carbon dioxide gas in the atmosphere. Plants and bacteria remove carbon dioxide from the atmosphere by photosynthesis . They use it to make organic compounds, such as carbohydrates, which become part of their tissues. When plants are eaten by animals, their carbon is passed on. Animals use the carbohydrates from plants during respiration . Respiration, in turn, releases carbon dioxide back into the atmosphere. This process forms a rapid part of the carbon cycle.

Carbon sink

A carbon store

A large amount of carbon is locked in stores called carbon sinks. Some carbon is held in the sea, because carbon dioxide dissolves in water; some is locked up in rocks as calcium carbonate, and some is stored in fossil fuels.

Fossil fuel

A fuel formed by the remains of living things

Coal, oil, and natural gas are all fossil fuels. They contain carbon which was once part of living things. Over millions of years, the remains of living things become transformed into carbon-rich fossils . When a fossil fuel is burned, the carbon is released into the atmosphere.

Nitrogen cycle

A cycle involving nitrogen

Living things cannot exist without nitrogen, which forms proteins and nucleic acids . The atmosphere is about 80 percent nitrogen gas, but only bacteria can use nitrogen in this form. All other living things have to use compounds of nitrogen, such as **nitrates**. Most nitrates are produced by bacteria in the soil. Nitrogen reaches other living things through plants, which absorb these nitrates through their roots. Animals obtain nitrogen either by eating plants, or other animals that eat plants. When living things die, their nitrogen is returned to the atmosphere by denitrification.

Fossil fuels burned in factories and cars

Animal respiration

Animals eat plants

Dead animals decompose

Nitrogen fixation

The conversion of nitrogen gas into a chemical compound

When an element is fixed, it is combined with another element to form a chemical compound ■. Nitrogen is fixed when it is combined with oxygen to form nitrates. In the natural world, nitrogen fixation happens in two ways. Some nitrates are formed when lightning flashes through the atmosphere and triggers chemical reactions ■. Far more nitrates are formed by bacteria, which live either in the soil or in close contact with plants. Some of these bacteria form special swellings, called **nodules**, on the roots of plants, particularly those of the pea family ■.

Denitrification

A process that returns nitrogen to the atmosphere

Denitrifying bacteria complete the nitrogen cycle. They break down nitrates and other compounds to release nitrogen gas back into the atmosphere.

Phosphorus cycle

A cycle involving phosphorus

Living things use phosphorus to make many compounds. Plants absorb phosphorus compounds, called **phosphates**, from the soil and then pass on phosphorus to other living things. Phosphates are eventually washed into water, and pile up in sediment. After millions of years, this forms rock.

Justus von Liebig

German chemist
1803–73

Liebig was an organic chemist who developed an accurate method of analyzing organic compounds. He also examined how animals obtain energy. Liebig founded the science of agricultural chemistry, which studies the role of minerals in plant growth. He showed that adding elements such as potassium and phosphorus to the soil can greatly increase crop yields.

Water cycle

A cycle involving water

All living things depend on water ■. Many of the substances inside living things are dissolved in a watery mixture, and water is vital for chemical reactions such as photosynthesis. Respiration creates water as a by-product. Water circulates between the sea, the atmosphere, and the land in a continuous cycle called the water cycle, or **hydrological cycle**. During this process, some of the water passes through living things.

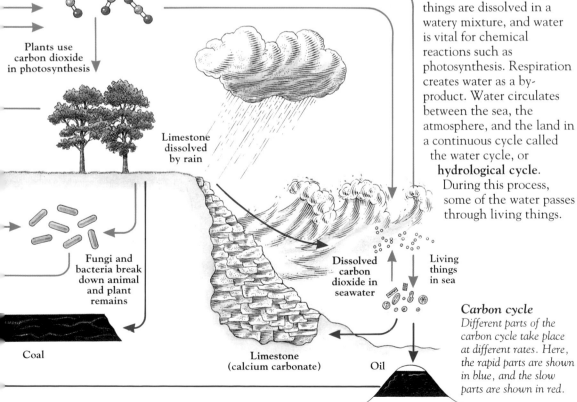

THE CARBON CYCLE

Carbon dioxide in atmosphere

Plants use carbon dioxide in photosynthesis

Limestone dissolved by rain

Fungi and bacteria break down animal and plant remains

Coal

Limestone (calcium carbonate)

Dissolved carbon dioxide in seawater

Living things in sea

Oil

Carbon cycle
Different parts of the carbon cycle take place at different rates. Here, the rapid parts are shown in blue, and the slow parts are shown in red.

Food chains & webs

In the living world, every form of life is food for another. Food chains and webs show how food and energy are passed between species.

Food chain

A food pathway that connects one species with another

A food chain is a food pathway that links different species ■ in a community ■. In a food chain, energy and nutrients ■ are passed from one organism to another. Food chains rarely contain more than six species because the amount of energy passed on diminishes at each stage, or trophic level. The longest chains usually involve aquatic animals.

Food web

A collection of food chains

A community of living things may contain hundreds or even thousands of different species. Each species is usually involved in several different food chains. Therefore different food chains often interconnect to form a large network, called a food web. Even in a small ecosystem ■, such as a pond, food webs can be extremely complicated.

Trophic level

The position of a species in a food chain

In a food chain, each species occupies a certain position in the chain. This position is called a trophic level. For example, owls eat mice, so if a food chain contains an owl and a mouse, the owl will be at a higher level. The number of trophic levels is the same as the number of species in the food chain. The same species may occupy different trophic levels in different food chains.

Producer

A living thing that uses energy to turn simple substances into food

A producer is an autotroph ■, which means that it can make its own food. Producers form the first trophic level of a food chain, because they make the food that supports the other species in the chain. Green plants ■, and some kinds of bacteria ■, are the most important producers. They harness the Sun's energy to make food by photosynthesis ■. A few species of bacteria make food by **chemosynthesis**, which uses the energy in chemicals.

Consumer

Something that takes in food

Consumers are heterotrophs ■, or living things that cannot make food for themselves. They survive by taking in food that has been made by other living things. A food chain contains several kinds of consumer, each of which occupies a different trophic level. A **primary consumer** eats producers, a **secondary consumer** eats primary consumers, and a **tertiary consumer** eats secondary consumers, and so on.

See also

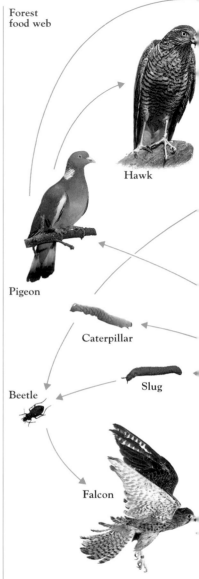

Forest food web

Hawk

Pigeon

Caterpillar

Slug

Beetle

Falcon

Decomposer

A living thing that breaks down the remains of other living things

Decomposers, or saprotrophs ■, are a vital part of food webs. During the process of **decay**, they break down the organic compounds ■ in dead remains and release their raw materials, such as carbon dioxide, back into the environment. Bacteria and fungi ■ are the most important decomposers. Nutrients are also released by detritivores ■.

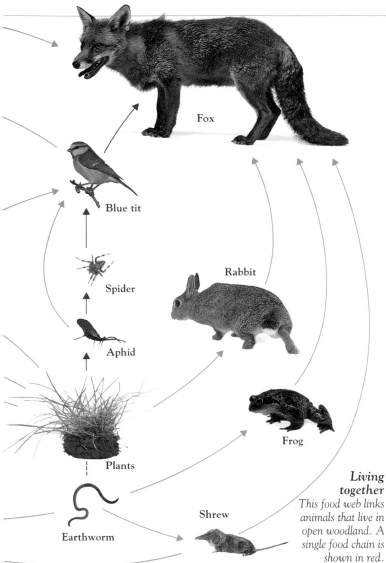

Fox

Blue tit

Spider

Rabbit

Aphid

Frog

Plants

Earthworm

Shrew

Living together
This food web links animals that live in open woodland. A single food chain is shown in red.

Biomass

The combined mass of living matter in a particular area

Biomass is the total mass, or amount of living matter in an area. The world's total biomass is unevenly spread. Very little of it is made up of life in open oceans or deserts, but a great deal is made up of living things near shores and in forests. In a pyramid of numbers, the biomass usually decreases sharply at each trophic level.

Productivity

The rate at which living things produce organic matter

Primary productivity is a measure of how quickly producers make new biomass. It varies greatly from one kind of community to another. It depends on the amount of energy received in the form of sunlight, but it is also affected by other limiting factors such as rainfall. **Secondary productivity** is a measure of how rapidly the consumers make organic matter. It is always less than the primary productivity, because consumers convert only a small amount of their food into organic matter.

Limiting factor

Something that limits productivity

If an area of desert is supplied with water, or **irrigated**, its productivity quickly increases. If the irrigation is stopped, the productivity drops back to its earlier level. This shows that, in deserts, water is a limiting factor, because it holds back productivity when it is in short supply. In different kinds of habitat, other limiting factors can include the amount of energy received from sunlight, temperature, and the supply of mineral nutrients in the soil.

Pyramid of numbers

A diagram that shows the relative numbers of species at different trophic levels

In a food chain, an animal passes on only about 10 percent of the energy it receives. The rest is used up in maintaining its body or in movement ■, or it escapes as heat. The amount of available energy decreases at every trophic level, and each level supports fewer individuals than the one before. This results in a pyramid of numbers with many organisms at the bottom and few at the top.

Pyramid of numbers
This pyramid shows that the number of animals decreases sharply at each level. There are many primary consumers, compared with far fewer large predators, such as birds of prey.

How species interact

Most living things depend on other species for their survival. One species usually exploits another, but two species can sometimes join forces in the struggle to survive.

Predator

A living thing that kills and eats others

A predator is carnivorous ■. This means that it lives by eating other animals, which are known as its **prey**. The term predator usually refers to animals that catch and kill other animals. Most predators are larger than their prey; they have special adaptations ■ to help them find and catch their food. These include good vision ■, a keen sense of smell ■, or strong legs for rapid movement ■.

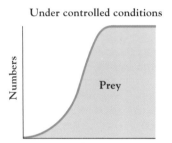

Under controlled conditions

Living alone
In the absence of predators, a species quickly increases in numbers. Eventually, a shortage of resources forces the population to level out.

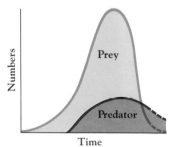

Living together
If a predator is introduced, the numbers of its prey fall. Both populations soon decrease, but in nature, the prey rarely dies out altogether.

Symbiosis

A relationship between two different species

Many living things spend all or part of their lives in close partnerships with members of different species. For example, lichens ■ are formed by a **symbiotic relationship** between a fungus ■ and an alga ■. In lichens, both partners probably benefit, but in many other partnerships, one species gains much more than the other. The term symbiosis correctly refers to any kind of partnership, but is sometimes used to mean only those relationships in which both species benefit.

Commensalism

A symbiotic relationship in which one species benefits, but the other neither benefits nor suffers harm

The **clownfish** (*Amphiprion species*) is an example of a **commensal** animal. This small fish ■ lives among the tentacles of sea anemones ■, but it is not affected by their stinging threads. The clownfish feeds on the anemone's leftover food, but the anemone probably receives nothing in return.

A living home
Clownfish use sea anemones as a source of food and as a place of safety. Commensal partnerships like this one are difficult to identify in nature. This is because it is hard to prove that a host animal is neither gaining nor being harmed.

Mutualism

A symbiotic relationship in which both partners benefit

The living world is full of species that benefit by living together. Sometimes the partnership is a loose one, and both species can survive without each other if they have to. However, often the the partnership is **obligatory**, which means that neither species can survive without the other. For example, the **wild fig** (*Ficus carica*) depends on a particular species of wasp ■ to pollinate its flowers, and the wasp depends on the fig for food.

Sea anemone

Parasite

A species that benefits at the expense of its host

A parasite lives in or on another species and exists at the expense of that species. Nearly all animals and plants are home to parasites of some kind. A parasite is usually smaller than its host, and may have special adaptations to meet the needs of its way of life. An **ectoparasite** lives on the surface of its host, while an **endoparasite** lives inside it. A **hyperparasite** lives on another parasite. A **flea** is an ectoparasite. It is adapted to live in the fur or feathers of animals. It does not have wings, and its body is laterally flattened to help it slip through feathers or fur. It also has hindlegs adapted for leaping from host to host.

Host

An organism that provides food for a parasite

A host organism provides a parasite with food and somewhere to live. Most parasites are **host-specific**, which means they can use only certain hosts. However, a single parasite species may have two or more hosts, and these parasites usually alternate between one host and the other during their life cycles. For example, the adult **beef tapeworm** (*Taenia saginata*) lives in the large intestine of humans, but its larval ▪ stage develops in cattle, while the parasite *Plasmodium* ▪, which causes malaria, alternates between humans and mosquitoes.

Stranger in the nest
As soon as it hatches, a young cuckoo heaves all the other eggs out of the nest. It can then eat all the food provided by its foster parents.

Brood parasite

An animal that uses the parents of another species to raise its young

Raising young takes a great deal of time and energy. A brood parasite is an animal that uses the parent of another species, called a foster parent, to do this work. The foster parent does not realize that it has been tricked, and raises the parasite's young as its own. The **common cuckoo** (*Cuculus canorus*) is a widespread brood parasite. Cuckoos parasitize small birds ▪ such as warblers, and their eggs often match those of their hosts.

Vector

A living thing that carries a parasite or pathogen from one host to another

A vector is something that helps parasites or disease-carrying organisms, called pathogens ▪, to spread. It often transfers the parasite or pathogen by biting a new host. This allows the parasite or pathogen to enter the host's tissues. Common vectors include insects such as biting flies ▪.

Clownfish

Conservation

Humans use up a large share of the Earth's resources and create vast quantities of harmful waste and pollution. By practicing conservation, we can make our way of life less damaging to the other living things that share our planet.

Conservation

The management of resources to protect the natural world

Many human activities damage other forms of life. Farming and fishing often interfere with natural food chains ■, and building roads and houses destroys natural habitats ■. Conservation involves careful planning and use of resources to make sure that we harm the natural world as little as possible.

The aerial garbage dump
During the 20th century, many different polluting chemicals have been dumped into the air we breathe.

Pollution

The disruption of the natural world by the release of chemicals or other agents

Pollution alters the chemical balance of the natural world. Humans produce an enormous variety of **pollutants**, such as domestic trash, sewage, harmful chemicals, and other waste. Some pollutants enter the atmosphere, some are dumped on land, and some flow into rivers. The long-term damage caused by wastes is often unknown.

Biodiversity

The variety of species in an area

Biodiversity varies between habitats. A tropical rain forest has a huge variety of species ■ but, in comparison, an area of desert has very few. The growing human population is having a serious effect on biodiversity. As a result of human activities, it is estimated that 20 percent of all species will have become extinct ■ by the end of the 20th century.

Acid rain

Rain that has been made strongly acidic by atmospheric pollutants

Rainwater dissolves gases in the atmosphere. If the atmosphere contains pollutant gases, such as sulfur oxides from power stations, and nitrogen oxides from cars, the rain becomes highly acid. In some parts of Europe and America, acid rain has killed large areas of forest.

Ozone depletion

The thinning of the Earth's ozone layer

The ozone layer is a band of ozone gas about 25 miles (40 kilometers) above ground level. It shields the Earth from some of the harmful ultraviolet radiation in sunlight ■. In recent years, synthetic gases, such as **chlorofluorocarbons**, or **CFCs**, have built up in the atmosphere. These gases react with ozone, making parts of the ozone layer thinner. Ozone depletion allows more ultraviolet radiation to reach the Earth. This is dangerous for living things, because ultraviolet radiation can disrupt nucleic acids ■, causing genetic errors and cancer.

Conservation of Antarctica
The Antarctic is the largest area of true wilderness left on Earth. Without strict conservation, even this remote continent could be threatened by the search for oil and minerals.

Deforestation

The permanent removal of forests

Many parts of the world have been completely cleared of trees to make space for farming. This deforestation often leads to **desertification**. During this process, mineral nutrients in the soil are washed away from the bare earth, turning fertile land into semidesert.

Greenhouse effect

The trapping of heat by the Earth's atmosphere

When sunlight reaches the Earth, some of its energy is reflected back into the sky. Not all of this energy escapes because gases in the atmosphere, such as carbon dioxide, trap some of it. These gases keep the Earth warm enough to support life, like the glass in a greenhouse. During the 20th century, the amount of carbon dioxide in the atmosphere has increased rapidly, due to deforestation and the burning of fossil fuels ■. The result has been an increase in the Earth's average temperature, or **global warming**. If this continues, it may damage the Earth's ecosystems ■.

Eutrophication

The introduction of nutrients to water-based ecosystems

Many of the waste substances produced by human activities contain mineral nutrients, such as nitrates and phosphates. If these are washed into water, they act as a fertilizer and may cause algal blooms ■. The algae ■ makes the level of oxygen in the water drop sharply, which kills fish and other forms of life.

Biocide

A chemical that kills living things

There are two main kinds of biocide. A **herbicide** kills **weeds**, or unwanted plants, and a **pesticide** kills **pests**, or animals that interfere with farming practices. Biocides are effective, but many often harm other species as well as the ones they are designed to kill. A safer alternative involves natural pest control methods called **biological controls**. These make use of the natural predators ■ or parasites ■ of a pest species, which attack the pest without harming other species or leaving dangerous chemicals in the environment.

Rachel Carson

American biologist and author
1907–64

Rachel Carson wrote *Silent Spring*, one of the most important books in the history of ecology. Published in 1962, it explains how synthetic chemicals could poison the environment. The book's title was intended as a warning, suggesting that pesticides may eventually kill so many birds that none will be left to herald the arrival of spring. *Silent Spring* made many people aware of environmental damage for the first time and marked the birth of the modern environmental movement.

Biodegradable

A substance that can be broken down by natural processes

Biodegradable substances, such as paper, will eventually be broken down by decomposers ■ if they are thrown away. Many plastics are **nonbiodegradable**, which means that they cannot be broken down by decomposers.

Pioneers of biology

Addison, Thomas
British doctor (1793–1860)
Investigated the adrenal glands, and helped to found the science of endocrinology.

an-Nafis, Ibn (*See page 127*)

Anning, Mary
British fossil collector (1799–1847)
Discovered a fossilized ichthyosaur, and the first known fossils of a plesiosaur and pterodactyl.

Aristotle (*See page 14*)

Avery, Oswald
American bacteriologist (1877–1955)
Showed that one form of bacteria could be altered or "transformed" by exposing it to DNA from another – an indication that DNA carries genetic instructions.

Avicenna, Ibn Sina
Arab doctor (980–1037)
Wrote a medical compendium that remained in use in Europe until the 17th century.

Bacon, Francis
British philosopher and writer (1561–1626)
Investigated scientific method, and emphasized the importance of collecting data.

Baer, Karl von
Estonian embryologist (1792–1876)
Founder of modern embryology. Discovered that a Graafian follicle contains an ovum, and investigated the development of animal form.

Banks, Sir Joseph
British naturalist (1734–1820)
Traveled extensively in the southern hemisphere, and introduced many exotic plants to Europe.

Banting, Sir Frederick
Canadian physiologist (1891–1941)
Devised a way of obtaining insulin from the pancreas, providing a way to control the effects of diabetes.

Bary, Anton de (*See page 77*)

Bates, Henry
British naturalist (1825–92)
Proposed the idea that some harmless animals imitate harmful ones – now called Batesian mimicry.

Bateson, William
British geneticist (1861–1926)
Proposed that living things evolve in jumps, interspersed with periods of little change.

Benenden, Edouard van
Belgian cytologist (1846–1910)
Discovered that every species has a characteristic number of chromosomes in its cells.

Bernard, Claude
French physiologist (1813–78)
Investigated the ways by which the body maintains a stable state; put forward the idea of homeostasis.

Bichat, Marie François
(*See page 23*)

Blackman, Frederick
English physiologist (1866–1947)
Showed that plants exchange gases through stomata.

Boussingault, Jean-Baptiste
French chemist (1802–87)
Showed that plants in the pea family can fix nitrogen directly from the air.

Boveri, Theodor
German cell biologist (1862–1915)
Showed that normal development occurs only if a cell contains a full set of chromosomes.

Broca, Paul
French surgeon (1824–80)
First person to show that particular regions of the brain control specific functions of the body.

Brown, Robert
British botanist (1773–1858)
Discovered the random movement caused by molecules (Brownian motion); the first person to observe nuclei in living cells.

Buchner, Eduard
German chemist (1860–1917)
Showed that fermentation could occur outside living cells, leading to the understanding of enzymes.

Buffon, Count Georges-Louis
French naturalist (1707–88)
Speculated about the possibility of evolution, and published a 44-volume encyclopedia of the natural world.

Calvin, Melvin
American biochemist (born 1911)
Discovered the pathways followed by carbon atoms during photosynthesis.

Camerarius, Rudolf
German botanist (1665–1721)
Produced experimental evidence to show that flowering plants reproduce sexually.

Candolle, Augustin de
Swiss botanist (1778–1841)
Investigated relationships between plants based on similarities in form.

Carson, Rachel
(*See page 177*)

Chain, Sir Ernst
German–British biochemist (1906–79)
Helped to isolate penicillin so that it could be used as a drug.

Chargaff, Erwin
American biochemist (born 1905)
Showed how the four different bases pair up in a DNA molecule.

Colombo, Matteo
Italian anatomist (1516–59)
Demonstrated that blood flows from the heart to the lungs, and then back again.

Crick, Francis
(*See page 35*)

Cuvier, Baron Georges
French biologist (1769–1832)
Pioneered the reconstruction of extinct animals from incomplete fossils, and carried out important work in animal classification.

Darwin, Charles (*See page 45*)

De Vries, Hugo
Dutch botanist (1848–1935)
Investigated genetics, and helped to advance the largely overlooked work of Gregor Mendel.

Doisy, Edward
American biochemist (1893–1986)
Isolated vitamin K, which plays a part in the clotting of blood.

Dubois, Marie Eugene
Dutch paleoanthroplogist
(1858–1941)
Discovered fossilized bones of Java Man, a form of *Homo erectus*.

Dutrochet, Henri
French physiologist (1776–1847)
Discovered stomata on plant leaves, and showed that only green parts of plants absorb carbon dioxide.

Duve, Christian de
Belgian biochemist (born 1917)
Discovered lysosomes, and investigated their effects.

Ehrlich, Paul
German biochemist (1854–1915)
Identified substances that can be used as drugs to target and destroy bacteria in the body.

Eijkman, Christiaan
Dutch doctor (1858–1930)
Discovered that the deficiency disease **beriberi** can be cured by a change in diet.

Enders, John
American virologist (1897–1985)
Developed ways of culturing viruses in the laboratory.

Fabre, Jean-Henri
French entomologist (1823–1915)
Popularized the study of insects through his writings.

Fallopio, Gabriello (Fallopius)
Italian anatomist (1523–62)
Discoverer of the tubes that conduct ova to the uterus (Fallopian tubes).

Fisher, Ronald
British geneticist (1890–1962)
Used statistical analysis to investigate the effects of sexual selection.

Fleming, Sir Alexander
British microbiologist (1881–1955)
Discovered pencillin, the first antibiotic.

Flemming, Walther
German cell biologist (1843–1905)
Discovered chromatin, and was the first person to observe mitosis.

Florey, Sir Howard
Australian pathologist (1898–1968)
Helped to isolate penicillin so that it could be used as a drug.

Franklin, Rosalind
(*See page 35*)

Frisch, Karl von
Austrian ethologist (1886–1982)
Investigated the function of food-dances in bees.

Galen, Claudius (Galenus)
Roman anatomist (AD 129–199)
Investigated the structure and function of the human body; his teachings stayed in use for many centuries.

Galvani, Luigi (*See page 143*)

Golgi, Camillo
Italian histologist (1844–1926)
Developed a method for staining nerves, and discovered the Golgi body.

Goodall, Jane
English biologist (1934–93)
Studied the behavior of wild chimpanzees, and promoted their conservation.

Gould, Stephen Jay
(*See page 49*)

Gowland Hopkins, Frederick
British biochemist (1861–1947)
Carried out wide-ranging experiments into the effects of vitamins.

Gram, Hans
Danish bacteriologist (1853–1938)
Developed the Gram stain, which divides bacteria into two overall groups.

Haeckel, Ernst (*See page 169*)

Haldane, John
British biologist (1892–1964)
Investigated many aspects of physiology and biochemistry, and speculated about the origins of life.

Hales, Stephen
British chemist (1677–1761)
Published *Vegetable Staticks*, a book describing detailed experiments on plant growth and transpiration.

Harden, Arthur
British biochemist (1865–1940)
Investigated the function of enzymes in fermentation.

Harvey, William
British doctor (1578–1657)
Published the first full account of how blood circulates round the body.

Helmholtz, Ludwig van
(*See page 153*)

Helmont, Jan Baptista van
Belgian chemist (1579–1644)
Carried out early experiments on plant growth.

Hershey, Alfred
American biochemist (born 1908)
Showed that the DNA of bacteriophages carries genetic information.

Hippocrates
Greek doctor (c.460–377 BC)
Founded the science of medicine, which relies on informed diagnosis rather than myth and magic.

Hodgkin, Dorothy
British biochemist (born 1910)
Used X-ray crystallography to analyze the structure of penicillin and other important biochemicals.

Hofmeister, Wilhelm
German botanist (1824–77)
Discovered alternation of generations in plants.

Holmes, Arthur
British geologist (1890–1965)
Developed a system of geological time-scales.

Hooke, Robert (*See page 21*)

Hooker, Joseph
British botanist (1817–1911)
Traveled widely and brought plants from all over the world to Europe.

Huxley, Hugh
British physiologist (born 1924)
Helped to devise the sliding filament theory of muscle contraction.

Huxley, Thomas
British biologist (1825–95)
Influential advocate of Darwin's ideas on evolution.

Ingenhousz, Jan (*See page 85*)

Jenner, Edward
British doctor (1749–1823)
Pioneered the use of vaccination to combat the disease smallpox.

Continued over page ➤

Kekulé, Friedrich
(*See page 25*)

Kettlewell, Henry
British geneticist (1907–79)
Demonstrated industrial melanism
in the peppered moth.

Khorana, Har Gobind
(*See page 37*)

Kitasato, Shibasaburo
Japanese bacteriologist (1852–1931)
One of the discoverers of the
plague bacterium, which causes
a deadly disease.

Koch, Robert (*See page 61*)

Krebs, Hans (*See page 33*)

Kühne, Wilhelm
German physiologist (1837–1900)
Investigated chemical changes in
the light-sensitive pigments of
the eye.

Lamarck, Jean
French naturalist (1744–1829)
Pioneered evolutionary theory; the
originator of Lamarckism, which
suggests that living things pass on
characteristics acquired during
their lifetime.

Landsteiner, Karl
Austrian immunologist (1868–1943)
Discovered human blood groups.

Lavoisier, Antoine
French chemist (1743–94)
Pioneer of modern chemistry;
deduced that living things oxidize
food during respiration.

Leakey, Louis, Mary and Richard
(*See page 55*)

Leeuwenhoek, Antony van
Dutch microscopist (1632–1723)
Developed the single-lens
microscope, and observed bacteria
and other microorganisms.

Levi-Montalcini, Rita
(*See page 149*)

Liebig, Justus von (*See page 171*)

Lind, James
British doctor (1716–94)
Found that citrus fruit prevents
scurvy, a disease caused by
vitamin C deficiency.

Linnaeus, Carolus (Carl Linné)
(*See page 59*)

Lorenz, Konrad
Austrian ethologist (1903–89)
Pioneer of ethology – the study
of behavior.

Ludwig, Karl
German physiologist (1816–95)
Pioneered techniques for
investigating how the body works.

Lyell, Charles
British geologist (1797–1875)
Advocated the principle of
uniformitarianism – the idea that
rock formations are slowly built up
and worn away. This idea provided
Darwin with important evidence
for evolution.

Lysenko, Trofim
Russian geneticist (1898–1976)
Instigated crop-breeding
techniques based on the erroneous
ideas of Lamarck; his prominence
led to the persecution of Mendelian
geneticists during the Communist
regime in the former Soviet Union.

Malpighi, Marcello (*See page 141*)

Malthus, Rev. Thomas
British cleric (1766–1834)
Wrote an *Essay on the Principle of
Population*, which later prompted
Darwin to understand the struggle
for survival in nature.

Mantell, Gideon
British geologist (1790–1852)
Discovered the first fossil dinosaurs
known to western science.

McClintock, Barbara
American geneticist (born 1902)
Discovered that some genes can move
about on or between chromosomes.

Mead, Margaret
American anthropologist (1901–78)
Carried out detailed studies of
human behavior in a number
of different societies.

Mendel, Gregor Johann
(*See page 43*)

Meyerhof, Otto
German-American biochemist
(1884–1951)
Discovered how lactic acid is
formed in muscles.

Miller, Stanley (*See page 52*)

Monod, Jacques
French biochemist (1910–76)
Discovered a mechanism that
controls the way genes are turned
on and off.

Morgan, Thomas
American geneticist (1866–1945)
Developed the theory that
chromosomes carry genetic
information.

Müller, Johannes
German physiologist (1801–58)
Pioneer physiologist; investigated
the circulation, senses, and
nervous system.

Müller, Paul
Swiss chemist (1899–1965)
Developed DDT, a powerful but
persistent insecticide.

Nägeli, Karl
Swiss botanist (1817–91)
Made important observations on
plant growth and cell division.

Nicolle, Charles
French microbiologist (1866–1936)
Showed that lice transmit the
disease typhus.

Oparin, Alexandr
Russian biochemist (1894–1980)
Advocated the idea that life could
have arisen on Earth by chemical
processes.

Palade, George
Romanian-American cell biologist
(born 1912)
Discovered ribosomes, and
investigated the function of
mitochondria in cells.

Pasteur, Louis
French microbiologist (1822–95)
Pioneered the science of
microbiology; investigated
fermentation and infectious diseases,
and helped to refute the idea of
spontaneous generation.

Pauling, Linus
American biochemist (born 1901)
Investigated protein structure, and
helped to shape ideas about the
structure of DNA.

Pavlov, Ivan
(*See page 159*)

◄ *Continued from previous page*

Payen, Anselme (*See page 31*)

Perutz, Max
Austrian biochemist (born 1914)
Discovered the structure
of hemoglobin.

Pliny (Gaius Plinius)
Roman naturalist (c.AD 23–79)
Wrote *Historia Naturalis*, an early
encyclopedia of nature; died from
suffocation while observing the
eruption of Vesuvius.

Priestley, Joseph
British-American chemist
(1733–1804)
Discovered oxygen, and showed
that it is produced by plants and
used by animals.

Pringsheim, Nathanael
(*See page 69*)

Purkinje, Johannes
Czech cell biologist (1787–1869)
Made detailed observations of
cells, and discovered highly
branching neurons in the brain
(Purkinje cells).

Ramón y Cajal, Santiago
Spanish physiologist
(1852–1934)
Pioneer of the study of nerves, and
of nerve staining techniques.

Ray, John
British naturalist (1627–1705)
Pioneer of plant classification.

Réaumur, René Antoine
French naturalist and physicist
(1683–1757)
Carried out detailed investigations
of invertebrates, particularly insects.

Redi, Francesco
Italian doctor (1626–97)
Carried out early experiments
in order to test the idea of
spontaneous generation.

Ross, Ronald
British medical scientist
(1857–1932)
Unravelled the life cycle of the
parasite that causes malaria.

Roux, Pierre
French bacteriologist (1853–1933)
Discovered that bacteria release
powerful poisons (toxins) that
produce the symptoms of some diseases.

Sachs, Julius von
German botanist (1832–97)
Showed that photosynthesis
takes place in chloroplasts; he also
investigated the way plants take
up minerals.

Sanctorius (Santorio Santorio)
Italian doctor (1561–1636)
Carried out investigations into the
way the body functions; studied
metabolism by living in a giant
weighing machine for days at
a time.

Sanger, Frederick
British biochemist (born 1918)
Developed techniques for
establishing the sequence of
base pairs in DNA molecules.

Schleiden, Jakob
(*See page 21*)

Schwann, Theodor
German physiologist (1810–82)
Helped to devise the ideas of cell
theory, and tested the theory of
spontaneous generation.

Snow, John
British doctor (1813–58)
Discovered the role of contaminated
water in the spread of cholera, a
disease caused by bacteria.

Spallanzani, Lazzaro
(*See page 53*)

Stanley, Wendell
American biochemist (1904–71)
Showed that purified viruses could
be crystallized.

Starling, Ernest
British physiologist (1866–1927)
Introduced the term "hormone"
and laid the foundations for the
study of glands, or endocrinology.

Sturtevant, Alfred
American geneticist
(1891–1970)
Developed techniques for
mapping chromosomes, by
identifying genes that are
usually inherited together.

Szent-Györgyi, Albert von
Hungarian biochemist
(1863–1986)
Investigated muscle contraction,
and observed muscle proteins
contracting outside living tissue.

Takamine, Jokichi
(*See page 134*)

Theophrastus
Greek naturalist (c.372–286 BC)
Wrote a series of books on plants,
laying the foundations for the science
of botany.

Tinbergen, Nikolaas
Dutch ethologist (1907–88)
Carried out a famous series of studies
of animal behavior, using simple but
revealing experiments.

Twort, Frederick
British microbiologist (1877–1950)
Discovered bacteriophages – viruses
that replicate by attacking bacteria.

Urey, Harold
(*See page 52*)

Vavilov, Nikolai
Russian botanist (1887–1942)
Devised a range of breeding techniques
for improving crop yields; died in a
prison camp after opposing the views
of Lysenko.

Vesalius, Andreas
Belgian anatomist (1514–64)
Published the first accurate account
of the structure of the human body.

Virchow, Rudolf
German cell biologist (1821–1902)
Helped to establish cell theory,
and laid the foundations for
modern pathology.

Wallace, Alfred Russel
(*See page 45*)

Watson, James
(*See page 35*)

White, Rev. Gilbert
British naturalist (1720–93)
Wrote *The Natural History of
Selborne*, a classic description of
animal and plant life.

Wilson, Edward
American biologist (born 1929)
Researched animal societies;
founded the science of
sociobiology.

Wöhler, Friedrich
German chemist (1800–82)
Showed that urea, an organic
compound, could be made from
inorganic raw materials.

Index

The index gives the page number of every entry and subentry in this book. For a subentry, the main entry under which it appears is given in parentheses. Tables and table entries are shown by the italic word *table*.

Acknowledgements

Dorling Kindersley would like to thank:
Esther Labi: editorial assistance, index;
Lucy Pringle: picture library; Miriam
Farbey: database. Photography: Dennis
Avon, Peter Anderson, Steve Bartholomew,
Geoff Brightling, David Burnie, Jane
Burton, Peter Chadwick, Geoff Dann,
Richard Davies, Philip Dowell, Andreas
Einsiedel, Neil Fletcher, Yaël Freudmann,
Frank Greenaway, Steve Gorton, Stephen
Hayward, Colin Keates, Dave King, Cyril
Laubscher, Michael Leach, Mike Linley,
Andrew McRobb, Roger Phillips,
Susannah Price, Tim Ridley, Karl Shone,
Kim Taylor, Spike Walker, Matthew
Ward, Andrew Webb, Jerry Young.

PICTURE CREDITS t = top
b = bottom c = centre l = left r = right
**Archiv für Kunst und Geschichte,
Berlin** 35cr, 77tr. **Biophoto Associates**
27br. **British Antarctic Survey** 177b.
Bruce Coleman 49c Jen & Des Bartlett
25br; Jane Burton 53tc, 53c, 117bc; Eric
Crichton 78tr; Adrian P. Davies 78c; Jeff
Foott 71c; CB & DW Frith 168cr; David

Hughes 145cl; Felix Labhardt 30tc; Dieter
& Mary Plage 44tl; Leonard Lee Rue III
173cb; Frieder Sauer 77bl; Nancy Sefton
99br; Kim Taylor 79cl, 96bc, 100tc, 117tl,
157br; Gunter Ziesler 99tr. **David Burnie**
75tc, 87bc. **Camera Press** 49tr /Grazia neri
149tr. **Mary Evans Picture Library** 14tr,
141tr, 143br, 153tr, 171tr, 159tl. **Derek
Hall** 74bl, 75cr. **Robert Harding Picture
Library** 48c, 53br. **Hulton Deutsch
Collection** 21tr, 23tr, 33tr, 35tr, 37tr, 45tr,
55tr, 169tl, 177tr. **Mansell Collection** 43tr,
53tr. **Nature Photographers** /Nicholas
Brown 173cl. **NHPA** /Berthoule 104bc;
Stephen Dalton 93cl; Scott Johnson 97cl;
John Shaw 83bl, 83cl. **Oxford Scientific
Films** 26h, 86bc /Doug Allan 159tr;
G.I. Bernard 123cr; Mike Birkhead 175tr;
P. Breck 47tc; Michael Leach 172tr; Photo
Researchers Inc. /Nick Bergkessel 146tr;
David Thompson 159bc. **Performing Arts
Library** /Laurie Lewis 155bl. **Planet Earth
Picture Library** /K. Ammann 115tr;
Geoff du Feu 48tr; Chris Howes 176cl;
Doug Perrine 98tr. **Harry Smith
Collection** 172cb. **Science Photo Library**
25tr, 35tc, 59tr, 151tr /Biocosmos /Francis
Leroy 129c; Biology Media 131cl, 142c;

Biophoto Associates 38c; Martin Bond
10cl; Dr Jeremy Burgess 7bl, 20bl, 45tc,
79cb, 92tl, 93bc; John Burbridge 23cl; Dr
R. Clark & M.R. Goff 133cl; CNRI 38tr,
39c, 39cr, 128c, 128bc, 131cr; John
Durham 79br; Manfred Kage 23b, 63c,
64cr; Omi Kron 61c; Prof. P. Motta 19cr,
127cl; NASA /Dr Gene Feldmann /GSFC
64b; Division of Computer Research &
Technology /National Institute of Health
130bc; National Library of Medicine 61tr;
NIBSC 18bl; Claude Nuridsany & Marie
Perennou 63bl; David Parker 11b; John
Reader 54cl; Roger Ressmeyer 52br; J.C.
Revy 135b; Andrew Syred 10cr.

ARTWORK CREDITS
John Woodcock 6, 64, 65bl, 67, 68, 84tc,
93, 96, 122r, 123, 124, 125, 133, 150, 154,
161, 171. **Janos Marffy** 5c, 34, 35, 36, 37,
38, 40, 41c, 58, 65tc, 85t, 127r, 130, 131,
132, 134c. **Andrew Green** 5c, 22, 34, 35,
36, 37, 40, 41c, 65tc, 143. **Sandra Pond /
Will Giles** 59, 62, 63, 83, 91, 97, 122bl,
134br, 148, 169, 173. **Peter Visscher** 42,
117. **Sean Milne** 164, 165. **Nick Hall**
153. **Yaël Freudmann** 31, 41r. **Simone
Ward** 126, 127bl, 162.